Troubleshooting & Supporting Networks

This training manual may be used:

- for the Troubleshooting & Supporting Network course.

- as a study guide for Novell course 801, NetWare Service & Support, test # 50-602

- as a NetWare reference manual.

© 1993 - 96 · PC Age, Inc. All Rights Reserved · 20 Audrey Place · Fairfield, NJ 07004 · U.S.A. · Tel: 201-882-5370

Copyright © 1993-95 by PC Age, Inc. All rights reserved. No part of this work may be reproduced or transmitted in any form or by any means, electronic or mechanical, including photocopying or recording, or by any information storage or retrieval system without the prior written permission of PC Age, Inc., unless such copying is expressly permitted by federal copyright law. Address inquiries to PC Age, Inc., 20 Audrey Place; Fairfield, NJ 07004.

This book is sold as is, without warranty of any kind, either express or implied, respecting the contents of this book, including but not limited to implied warranties for the book's quality, performance, merchantability, or fitness for any particular purpose. Neither PC Age, Inc., nor its resellers shall be liable to the purchaser or any other person or entity with respect to any liability, loss, or damage caused or alleged to be caused directly or indirectly by this book. Further, PC Age, Inc. reserves the right to make changes to any and all parts of this manual at any time, without obligation to notify any person or entity of such changes.

ISBN 1-57739-006-7

PC Age guarantees that if the Novell certification test based on this manual changes within 6 weeks from the purchased date of the course manual, PC Age will replace the manual with the updated one free of charge. Please arrange to take the Novell test within the six week period. In the United States and Canada, call 1-800-RED-EXAM (1-800-733-3926) to arrange the Novell test.

Contents

CHAPTER 1: TROUBLESHOOTING A SYSTEM

PREVENTION TECHNIQUES 1-1
   PHYSICAL ENVIRONMENT FOR COMPUTERS 1-2
TROUBLESHOOTING PROCEDURES 1-8
   1. COMPLETE PRE-SITE PLANNING 1-9
   2. CHECK ERROR LOG 1-9
   3. OBTAIN PHYSICAL LAYOUT 1-10
   4. ISOLATE THE PROBLEM 1-10
   5. DIVIDE COMPONENT INTO SUBUNITS 1-11
   6. TEST EACH SUBUNIT 1-11
   7. TAKE CORRECTIVE ACTION 1-11
DOCUMENTING THE NETWORK 1-13

CHAPTER 2: TROUBLESHOOTING TOOLS

CHECK✓IT PRO 2-1
   SYSINFO 2-1
   TEST & TOOLS 2-2
WINCHECKIT 2-3
NSEPRO 2-4
   INSTALLING NSEPRO 2-4
   NSEPRO (WINDOWS VERSION) 2-5
   NETWORK SYSTEMS SUPPORT 2-7
   CONTENTS OF SERVICE & SUPPORT VOLUME 2-8
NETWIRE 2-10
   NETWIRE FORUMS 2-10
   THE NETWIRE LIBRARIES 2-11
   USING NETWIRE 2-13
   USING WINCIM 2-13
   USING NOVCIM 2-16
NOVELL ON THE INTERNET 2-17
NAVIGATING NOVELL INTERNET SERVICES 2-18

© 1993 - 96 · PC Age, Inc. All Rights Reserved · 20 Audrey Place · Fairfield, NJ 07004 · U.S.A. · Tel: 201-882-5370

WORLD WIDE WEB (WWW) 2-18
FILE TRANSFER PROTOCOL (FTP) 2-18
GOPHER 2-19
THE MICRO HOUSE TECHNICAL LIBRARY 2-20
SEARCHING THE MTL 2-22
HANDS-ON EXERCISES 2-23
HOW TO USE NSEPRO (WINDOWS VERSION) 2-23
NSEPRO EXERCISE 1 2-35
NSEPRO EXERCISE 2 2-36
NSEPRO EXERCISE 3 2-37
NSEPRO EXERCISE 4 2-38
NSEPRO EXERCISE 5 2-39
NSEPRO EXERCISE 6 2-40
HOW TO USE THE MICRO HOUSE TECHNICAL LIBRARY (MTL) 2-42
USING THE MTL ENCYCLOPEDIA OF MAIN BOARDS 2-43
USING THE MTL NETWARE INTERFACE TECHNICAL GUIDE 2-44
USING NETWIRE 2-46

CHAPTER 3: NETWORK BOARDS AND CABLING

CONFIGURING ELEMENTS 3-1
JUMPERS 3-1
DIP SWITCHES 3-1
MOST POPULAR NETWORK BOARDS 3-3
ETHERNET 3-3
DIFFERENT TYPES OF ETHERNET 3-4
THICK-ETHERNET CABLING 3-5
10BASE2 (THIN-ETHERNET) 3-7
10BASE2 CABLING 3-7
10BASET (TWISTED PAIR ETHERNET) 3-9
10BASET CABLING 3-10
SETTING ETHERNET BOARDS 3-10
ETHERNET FRAME TYPES 3-12
SETTING UP A 3.12 SERVER FOR MULTIPLE FRAME TYPES 3-13
TROUBLESHOOTING AN ETHERNET NETWORK 3-14
TOKEN RING 3-16
TOKEN RING ADVANTAGES 3-18
TOKEN RING DISADVANTAGES 3-19
TOKEN RING OPERATION 3-19
TOKEN RING OVER UNSHIELDED TWISTED PAIR 3-21
TOKEN RING CABLE TYPES 3-22
BEACONING 3-23

Troubleshooting Tips 3-25
ARCnet 3-26
    ARCnet Network Features 3-27
    Disadvantages 3-27
    ARCnet frame types 3-28
    ARCnet Cabling (Coax cable) 3-30
    Fiber Optic ARCnet 3-31
    ARCnet Bus with UTP 3-31
    Setting ARCnet Boards 3-32
    Troubleshooting Tips 3-34
ARCnet Plus 3-35
Thomas Conrad Network System (TCNS) 3-35
FDDI 3-36
    FDDI Characteristics 3-37
    Advantages of FDDI 3-39
    Disadvantages of FDDI 3-39
    FDDI Token-Passing Process 3-39
    Management Features 3-40
    Troubleshooting Tips 3-40
ATM 3-41
    Computer Bus Architecture and Card Compatibility 3-43
    Exercise 3-1 3-46
    Exercise 3-2 3-49
    Troubleshooting Exercises 3-50

CHAPTER 4: WORKING WITH STORAGE DEVICES

Hard Drives 4-1
    ST-506 4-1
IDE - Integrated Drive Electronics 4-2
ESDI - Enhanced Small Drive Interface 4-2
    SCSI - Small Computer Systems Interface 4-2
SCSI II 4-2
Setting Up Hard Drives 4-4
    1. Configuring the drive 4-4
    2. Physical Installation 4-6
    3. Hard Drive Cabling 4-9
    4. Setting The Drive Type in CMOS 4-10
    5. Preparing the Disk for Use: Formatting and Partitioning 4-11
Hard Drives Tips 4-15
Mirroring and Duplexing 4-15
    Mirroring and Duplexing Troubleshooting Tips 4-16

OTHER NETWORK STORAGE DEVICES 4-18
 RAID 4-18
CD-ROM (COMPACT DISK-READ ONLY MEMORY) 4-22
 CD-ROM TIPS 4-22
NETWARE CD-ROM SUPPORT 4-24
 CD-ROM TROUBLESHOOTING TIPS: 4-26
 MAGNETO-OPTICAL (M-O) DRIVES 4-28
EXERCISE: MIRRORING AND SPANNING 4-29
 PROCEDURE: 4-29

CHAPTER 5: TROUBLESHOOTING THE WORKSTATION

CONNECTING WORKSTATIONS 5-1
WORKING WITH IPX AND NETx 5-1
 IPX.COM (INTERNETWORK PACKET EXCHANGE) 5-2
 NETx 5-2
 HOW IPX AND NETx WORK 5-3
OPEN DATA-LINK INTERFACE 5-4
NETWARE DOS REQUESTER 5-7
DOS REQUESTER INSTALLATION 5-10
 NETWARE 3.12 WORKSTATION SOFTWARE INSTALLATION 5-10
NETWARE 4.1 WORKSTATION SOFTWARE INSTALLATION 5-12
NET.CFG FILE 5-14
 CONVENTIONS 5-14
 LINK DRIVER SECTION 5-14
 LINK SUPPORT SECTION 5-15
 NETWARE DOS REQUESTER SECTION 5-15
 PROTOCOL SECTION 5-15
 A SAMPLE NET.CFG FILE 5-16
WORKSTATION TROUBLESHOOTING TECHNIQUES 5-17
 GENERAL TROUBLESHOOTING TIPS 5-17
 TROUBLESHOOTING TIPS WHEN USING IPX/NETx 5-19
 TROUBLESHOOTING TIPS WHEN USING ODI FILES/VLM 5-20
WORKING WITH DISKLESS WORKSTATION 5-21
 STEPS TO USE DOSGEN UTILITY 5-22
 TRACK ON COMMAND 5-25
TROUBLESHOOTING WORKSTATION CONFLICTS 5-28
 INTERRUPT REQUESTS (IRQ) 5-28
 DIRECT MEMORY ACCESS (DMA) 5-30
 I/O ADDRESS (INPUT/OUTPUT ADDRESS) 5-31
 BASE MEMORY ADDRESSES 5-32
WORKSTATION SETUP 5-34

Contents

CMOS Setup 5-34
Automatic Setup Routine 5-34
IBM Reference Diskette 5-35
EISA Configuration Program 5-35
PC - Modes of Operation 5-36
Memory Types 5-37
Conventional Memory 5-37
Extended Memory 5-38
Expanded Memory 5-39
Upper Memory 5-40
High Memory 5-40
Memory Optimization 5-40

CHAPTER 6: TROUBLESHOOTING AND OPTIMIZING THE SERVER

Server Abends and Lockups 6-1
Server Abends 6-1
Server Lockups 6-2
Troubleshooting Server Abends and Lockups 6-3
Using the Latest Patches, NLMs, and Utilities 6-4
General Optimization Points 6-6
Optimizing Using Hubs, Bridges, and Routers 6-10
Hubs 6-10
Bridges 6-10
Routers 6-11
Troubleshooting Tips for Hubs, Bridges, and Routers 6-11
Using a Protocol Analyzer (LANalyzer) 6-13
Using LZFW 6-13
Troubleshooting Using LZFW 6-17
Typical Ethernet Errors 6-18
Typical Token Ring Errors 6-21

CHAPTER 7: TROUBLESHOOTING NETWORK PRINTING

Physical Printer Problems 7-2
Laser Printer Tips 7-3
PostScript Printer Tips 7-3
Dot Matrix Tips 7-4
Problems in the Network Printing Setup 7-5
Problems with Queues 7-6

© 1993 - 96 · PC Age, Inc. All Rights Reserved · 20 Audrey Place · Fairfield, NJ 07004 · U.S.A. · Tel: 201-882-5370

    PROBLEMS WITH PRINT SERVERS... 7-7
    PROBLEMS WITH REMOTE PRINTERS 7-8
PROBLEMS WITH PRINTING UTILITIES 7-10
    PCONSOLE 7-10
    PRINTCON... 7-11
    PRINTDEF 7-11
    CAPTURE AND NPRINT 7-12
    COMMON PROBLEMS ASSOCIATED WITH NETWORK PRINTING 7-13

CHAPTER 8: DISASTER RECOVERY

    VREPAIR 8-1

CHAPTER 9: NETWORK MANAGEMENT

    NETWORK MANAGEMENT... 9-1
    INTRODUCTION TO MANAGEWISE 9-4

APPENDIX A
APPENDIX B
ANSWERS TO REVIEW QUESTIONS
MULTIPLE-CHOICE PRACTICE QUESTIONS
INDEX
TEST OBJECTIVES

Chapter 1   Troubleshooting a System

To maintain and troubleshoot a computer system, you need to learn how to prevent problems at the first place and how to troubleshoot a system.

Prevention Techniques

Long term prevention begins with careful installation of the physical components of the system, particularly protecting the power cables and data cables from physical damage and electromagnetic interference.

The site supervisor should be responsible for maintaining proper documentation to include: the manufacturers' manuals; the warranties of the original installation; and a log of all actions taken which affect the physical components or the software of the system.

The site supervisor should also perform periodic inspections of the system's physical components and should clean the hardware and perform other such tasks as needed.

The repair person should acquire suitable tools for physical repairs including cable, tools for connectors and meters. A basic software kit should also be maintained with diagnostics for printers and hard disks as well as proper bootable disks.

Let's discuss prevention for the physical environment of computers in detail.

Physical Environment for Computers

Microcomputers are not too sensitive to their physical environment. However, you should pay attention to the following factors to extend the life of your computer:

Temperature

A good temperature range for a computer is usually between 5°C to 40°C (41°F to 104°F). A very high or very low temperature can damage a computer's Integrated Circuits (ICs). It is also important to maintain a consistent temperature around computer components.

One important way to keep a consistent temperature around computer components is to avoid unnecessary ON/OFF cycling. Computers last longer if they are ON all the time. Turning them ON and OFF all the time can also shorten the hard disk life.

Air Quality

Dust, pencil erasure grit, smoke, and the like can damage computer components. Humidifiers can be used to reduce static electricity.

Magnetism

People are usually unaware of the effects of magnetism on computer data. It can corrupt computer data. Watch for magnetic note-posters, magnetic paper clip holders, telephones that ring, and stereo speakers. Avoid keeping floppy disks close to these items.

Electrical Environment

Most problems in a network are because of poor electrical conditions. There are four sources of problems related to electrical environment:

- **Transients (or Spikes)**
  High voltage and/or high current bursts of energy (spikes) can seriously damage computer components. Transients or spikes occur whenever another device on the same circuit suddenly needs a large amount of power, lightning, or because of a power station switching process.

  Computers should be on a separate circuit with a separate circuit breaker. Use three-prong plugs. Consider using transient suppressors besides Uninterruptable Power Supplies (UPSs) if severe transient conditions exist.

- **Noise**
  Noise is a low-voltage, low-current, high frequency signal that occurs in an observable pattern. Two common sources of noise are Electromagnetic Interference (EMI) and Radio Frequency Interference (RFI). Noise destroys computer signals and data. Common sources of EMI include fluorescent lights, large motors and power supplies, power tools, and appliances. Potential RFI sources include microwaves, furnaces, transmitters, cordless phones, and perhaps the computer equipment itself (an RFI problem may be created by putting computers very close to each other).

  To avoid noise problems, do not run cables near fluorescent lights, ground equipment properly, use shielding, and be aware of the proximity of possible EMI/RFI sources.

- **Cross-talk**
Cross-talk occurs when two wires in physical proximity interfere with each other's signals through magnetic fields. This is a common problem with Unshielded Twisted-Pair (UTP) cabling. This problem can be reduced by using a Shielded Twisted-Pair (STP) cable or by using the proper number of twists per foot on the cable. (Note: a minimum of two twists per foot is often recommended.)

- **Electro-Static Discharge (ESD)**
Electro-Static Discharge (ESD) is static electricity that damages computer components and data. We feel a static charge when ESD is approximately equal to 3000 volts, but computer components may be destroyed by as few as 20-30 volts. ESD can also cause computer components to degrade, thus failing faster.

To prevent static problems:
- Use a wrist strap and an anti-static mat in your working environment.
- Never touch components by their electrical leads.
- Avoid being touched you when you are working on Integrated Circuit (IC) boards.
- Be aware that non-conductors such as plastic and styrofoam are also sources of static; keep them away from an open computer.
- Do not place components on a conductive surface, like metal.

- Maintain proper humidity. Low humidity is also a cause of static problems.

EDP (Electronic Data Processing) Environmental Security

NetWare operating system comes with many security features, but to protect your data from destruction, corruption, and disclosure/eavesdropping, and your business operation from interruption, you should have proper plans for security of the entire EDP environment.

Following are some suggestion for EDP environmental security:

- Control access to computer facilities. Pay special attention to people who use your computer facilities on a "need-to-be-there" basis. It also includes vendor maintenance staff.

- NetWare comes with security features such as minimum password length, periodic password change, and time restriction; implement them as needed.

- If you have remote users, change phone numbers frequently, put proper security on dial-up phone lines, and consider using applications that use encryption schemes to transfer data over telephone lines.

- Arrange for off-site backup and plan to get services in case of big disasters such as fire or flood.

- NetWare system redundancy features such as mirroring/duplexing of server's hard disk and server duplexing (SFT III) are important and the extra cost is justifiable in some environments.

- Also consider using UPSs at least for servers. Make sure all your hardware error detection capabilities and other security plans are in proper working condition before any actual disaster.

Virus Protection

A virus is a computer program that makes undesirable changes to files and copies itself onto other disks or connected computers.

Viruses most often effect executable files such as .COM and .EXE files. Memory, file allocation tables, and disk boot sectors may also be affected.

NetWare's file tables, disk sectors, or other low-level structures are usually resistant to viruses, but viruses can damage files on the server.

The following virus protection techniques can be used:

- Educate users about viruses and virus protection.

- Control the use of modems and the installation of applications.

- Check even new application disks for viruses before installation.

- Use diskless workstations if possible.

- Download files first to floppies and check them for viruses before copying them to the hard disk.

- Use the latest versions of virus detection programs on regular basis.

- Flag all executable files as Read Only and Execute Only. When you set Read Only attribute, Delete Inhibit and Rename Inhibit attributes are set automatically.

  Note: Be aware that some executable files store configuration information internally; If you set Read Only attribute for these files, you will have difficulty using these files.

- Grant users only the necessary rights (usually Read and File Scan) to the PUBLIC, LOGIN, and application's directories.

- Require users to scan any floppies brought in from outside the network (for example, home, school, or other sources) for viruses.

- If a virus is detected, remove it immediately.

Troubleshooting Procedures

To troubleshoot a system, check for the simple things first. It includes eliminating user error. Sometimes the user himself is not doing it right or he is not realizing that it is working fine. Check for other simple things such as if all cables are connected, whether power is on, etc. Also check that monitor switch is on or brightness of the monitor is adjusted properly if user thinks computer is not working.

A quick solution may be turning every thing off and then on again.

You can also try to boot the computer with a bootable floppy disk with no AUTOEXEC.BAT and CONFIG.SYS. It will eliminate the possibility of loading any TSR (Terminate-and-stay-Resident) programs and other drivers that may have conflicts.

It is important to backup files and data if you are modifying files or working with disks for troubleshooting.

Once a problem is reported, the repair person should have a predetermined plan of action to follow.

The troubleshooting model recommended by Novell is explained below:

1. **Gather Basic Information**
   Get a complete description of the problem, including what is not working and whether only one user, a group of users, or all users are affected. Is there anything broken or is the network too slow and just saturated. Ask for recent changes to the system and for any error messages.

2. **Develop a Plan to Isolate the Problem**
   Based on the information gathered in step 1, decide whether the problem is related to hardware or software. Create 2 or 3 hypothesis to try. Prioritize your hypothesis based on your experience. You would like to try the hypothesis first that has better chances of fixing the problem. If a hypothesis is a quick check, you may want to try that first.

3. **Execute the Plan**
   Test out your hypothesis by changing only one thing at a time. For example, if only a workstation is not attaching to the server, check cable and NIC one at a time. If you change both and it works, you would not know if the problem was with the cable or NIC.

   Use good reliable tools only and get help from sources such as NSEPro, CompuServe, Internet, and friends.

4. **Document the Solution**
   Document your problem and solution for future references. Also take prevention steps to avoid the same problem in future.

Documenting the Network

A complete documentation of your network is a great help in troubleshooting the system. It should include a detailed graphic display of the network that identifies locations of components of the network and cabling, the network inventory, detailed record of each workstation including workstation configuration files, and record of all hardware and software changes in the network.

There are software packages available to help document the network, such as ManageWise from Novell and OpenView from Hewlett-Packard.
You should also keep all product documentation with phone numbers of technical support people in a handy place.

Review Questions

Q.1. If you do not have proper number of twists when using twisted pair cable, which problem will you most probably get?

    a. transient   b. noise
    c. crosstalk   d. ESD

Q.2. To protect your system from viruses, you shouldn't:

    a. Control the use of BBS
    b. Download BBS files to hard disks
    c. Control the installation of new applications
    d. Use virus scan software every day.

Q.3. If lightning is common in your area, what should you consider using?

    a. power monitor
    b. transient suppressor
    c. high quality cable
    d. proper FCC rating equipment

Q.4. If you have devices that draw a lot of power, on the same circuit with computers, which problem will you most probably get?

    a. transient   b. noise
    c. crosstalk   d. ESD

Q.5. If you are running cables close to fluorescent lights, which problem will you most probably get?

    a. transient   b. noise
    c. crosstalk   d. ESD

Q.6. Shielding can protect from _____ .

    a. transient   b. noise
    c. crosstalk   d. ESD

Q.7. You should use shielded twisted pair or fiber optic cable to _____ .

    a. avoid crosstalk
    b. get speed more than 10 Mbps
    c. avoid transient
    d. avoid ESD

Q.8. To feel an ESD, the charge should be equal to _____ volts, but computer components may be destroyed or degraded by discharges as low as _____ volts.

    a. 1000, 20 or 30   b. 3000, 30 or 40
    c. 5000, 10 or 20   d. 3000, 20 or 30

Q.9. It is difficult to trace intermittent problems caused by _____ .

    a. transient   b. noise
    c. crosstalk   d. ESD

Q.10. To prevent static you should _____ . (select the one that is not true)

    a. use a proper wrist strap and mat before working on printed circuits
    b. use a proper wrist strap before working on monitors.
    c. never touch computer components and ICs by their electrical leads
    d. not let any one touch you when working on ICs
    e. transport and store computer boards and ICs in static shielding bags

Q.11. To prevent static you should _____ . (select the one that is not true)

   a. transport and store computer boards and ICs in static shielding bags
   b. keep humidity low
   c. keep nonconductors, such as plastic and styrofoam away from components
   d. never place components on any conductive surface

Q.12. To ensure EDP (Electronic Data Processing) environmental security, you should _____ . (select the one that is not true)

   a. restrict access to computer facilities on a "need-to-be-there" basis
   b. put proper security on dial-up phone lines
   c. change phone number frequently
   d. not touch computer components and ICs by their electrical leads

Chapter 2   Troubleshooting Tools

Troubleshooting tools are used to diagnose and solve problems. In this chapter we will discuss four major tools to troubleshoot NetWare networks:

1. Check✓It Pro
2. NSEPro
3. NetWire
4. The Microhouse Technical Library

Check✓It Pro

Check✓It Pro is a diagnostic program that provides configuration information about computer hardware. It has two modules: SYSInfo and Test & Tools.

SYSInfo

This module is used to get system information such as the BIOS date, the type of processor, and the amount of memory installed in your computer. It performs benchmark readings on system performance. It can check on IRQ, I/O address, and memory address conflicts. A very good feature of Check✓It Pro is that it allows you to view, edit, and save CMOS (Complementary Metal Oxide Semiconductor) settings, to restore them to the same computer in case of battery loss, or to copy them to other computers.

Test & Tools

Test & Tools is a diagnostic tool that tests system boards, memory hard drives, floppy drives, video adapters, serial and parallel ports, keyboards, mouse devices, and printers. You can perform repetitive testing as a system burn-in procedure. Test & Tools also includes virus scan software and a universal Low-Level Formatter that works with all types of hard drives.

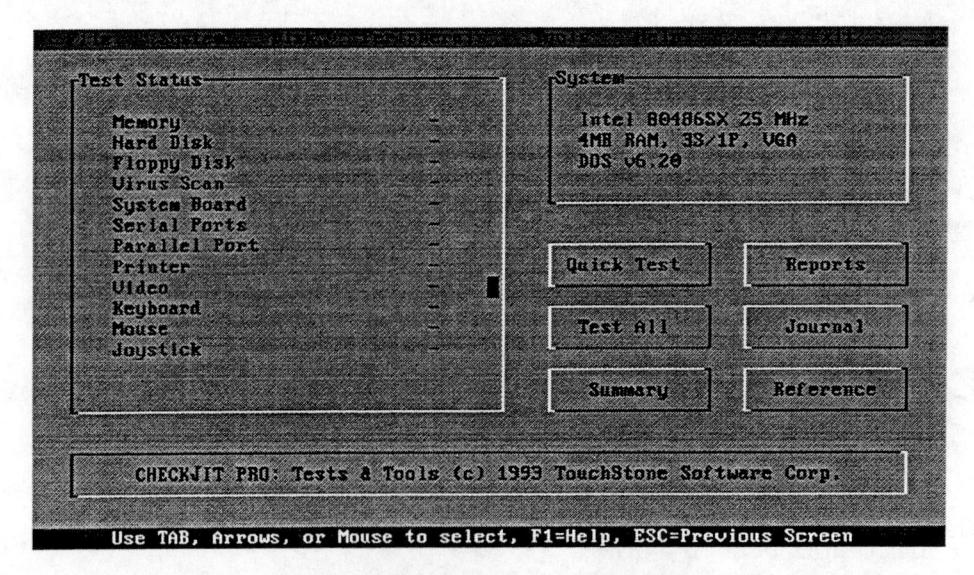

Figure 2-1: Check✓It Pro Tests & Tools Screen

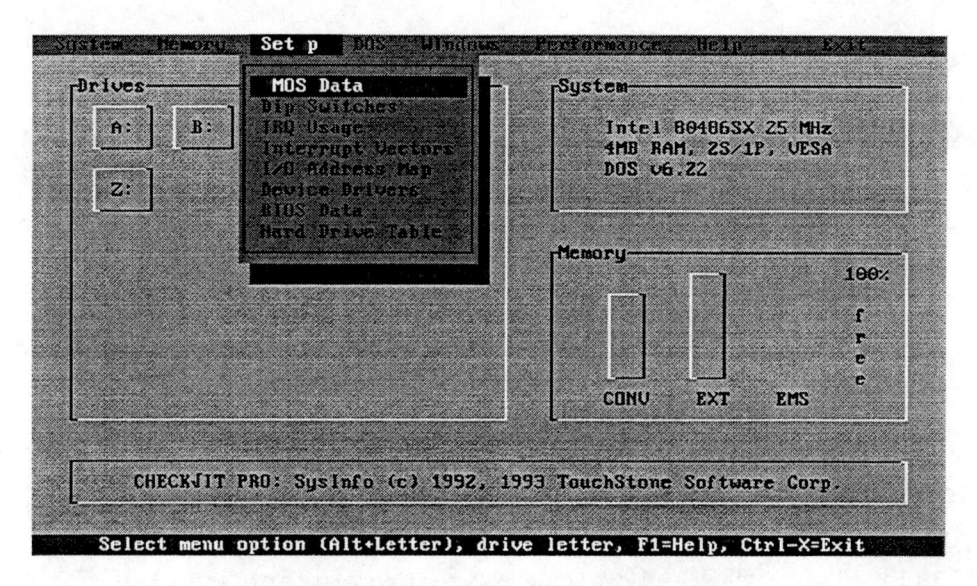

Figure 2-2: Check✓It Pro SysInfo Screen

WINCheckIt

WINCheckIt, the Windows 3.1 version, has the following additional capabilities:

- A clean-up utility to detect unneeded files, Windows 3.1 memory defragmentation utility (memory tune-up utility), and a utility to un-install Windows applications.

- The Setup Advisor can be used to find out compatibility problems between currently installed hardware and the software you want to install.

- The Software Shopper is used to find out about compatibility between software.

NSEPro

NSEPro (Network Support Encyclopedia Professional Volume) is a database of information distributed by Novell on CD-ROM. When you subscribe to NSEPro, you get an updated version every month.

NSEPro is built on a database search engine called Folio Pre Views (from the Folio Corporation). You can access its information directly from the CD-ROM or copy it to a network drive. Note that more than 650 MB of disk space is needed to copy the entire contents of NSEPro including downloadable files. You need about 380 MB to store NSEPro contents without downloadable files. (This disk storage requirement changes with each version of NSEPro.)

NSEPro provides information in two forms: records and views. A record is an article or information on a specific topic. A view is a collection of records. A view is created when you search the information base on a topic of interest.

Installing NSEPro

To install Windows version of NSEPro, insert the NSEPro CD-ROM, select **Run** from the Windows **File** menu, and type D:SETUP (where D is drive letter for the CD-ROM).

To install DOS version of NSEPro, insert the NSEPro CD-ROM and switch to the CD-ROM drive. Type **SETUP**. Follow the on-screen instructions to complete NSEPro installation.

You may need to create a search drive mapping or path statement for NSEPro files similar to the following.

MAP S16:=SYS:NSEPRO\PROGRAMS\WIN

OR

PATH=C:\PROGRAMS\WIN

To install UnixWare and Macintosh versions of NSEPro, refer to the README.UNX file and README.MAC file respectively at the root of the CD-ROM.

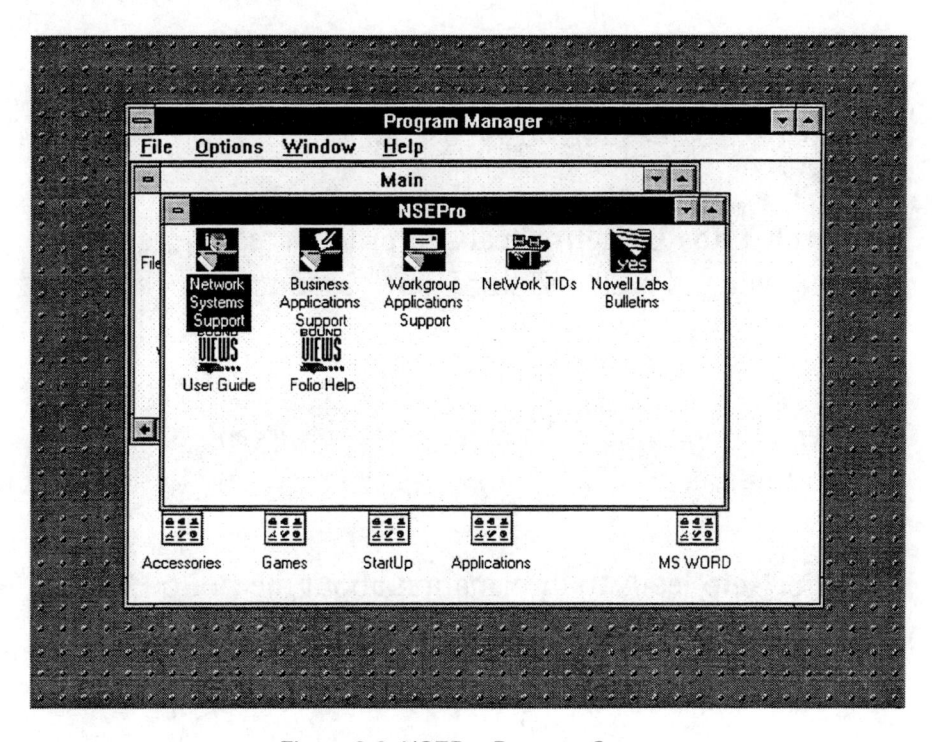

Figure 2-3: NSEPro Program Group

NSEPro (Windows Version)

A Windows 3.1 installation of NSEPro produces the following icons in the NSEPro group (see Figure 2-3).

1. **Network Systems Support** leads to information about NetWare, for example, versions 3.12 and 4.1.

2. **Business Applications Support** leads to information about Novell business applications software, for example, Word Perfect.

3. **Workgroup Applications Support** leads to information about Novell Workgroup Applications software, for example, GroupWise™.

4. **Network TIDs** leads to a collection of technical information documents (TIDs) produced by Novell in response to questions from users.

5. **Novell Labs Bulletins** leads to product testing reports concerning Novell and third party product compatibility with NetWare.

6. **User Guide** leads to NSEPro installation and use information.

7. **Folio Help** leads to information about the Folio Brand Viewers software that manages the NSEPro database.

Chapter 2: Troubleshooting Tools

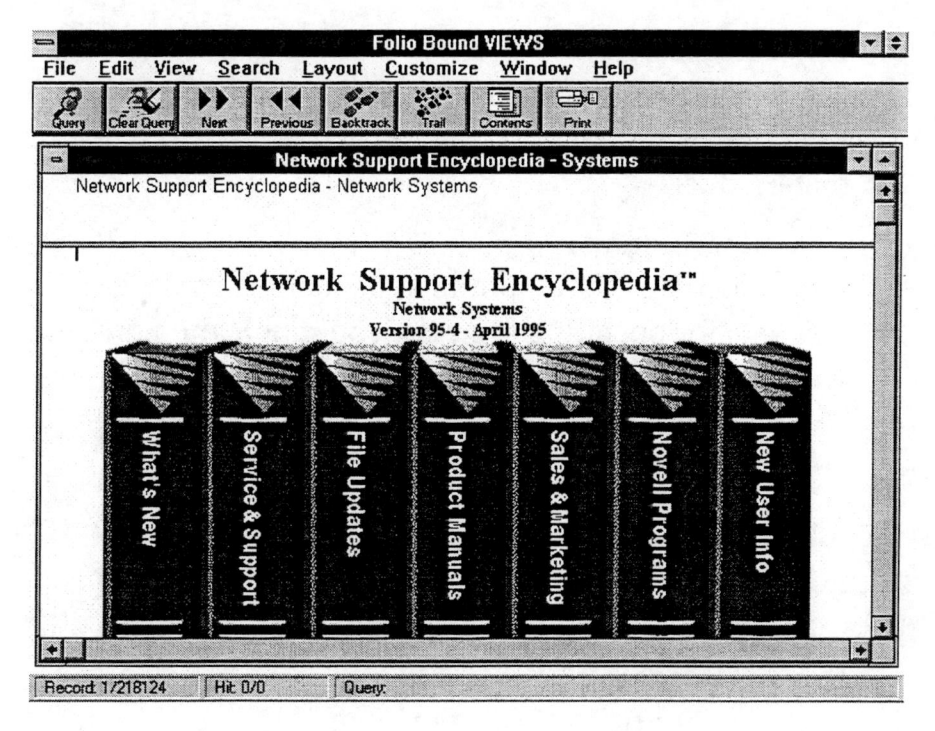

Figure 2-4: Network Support Encyclopedia

Network Systems Support

The following topics are available when you select the **Network Systems Support** icon. The network systems support main menu pictures each topic as a volume or book (see Figure 2-4).

1. **What's New:**
   This volume covers all the new items added to NSEPro since the last update. You can access all new items directly from this volume's contents.

2. **Service & Support:**
   This volume provides troubleshooting help. The volume's subdivisions are listed in the following sections of this manual.

3. **File Updates:**
   This volume is subdivided by product and each subdivision contains the patches and fixes available for that product.

4. **Product Manuals:**
   Here you have Novell product manuals. It includes manuals for operating systems, communication products, and other Novell products.

5. **Sales & Marketing:**
   This volume contains information about all of Novell's products and services.

6. **Novell Programs:**
   Here you can find information about Novell education programs like the CNE program. This section has information about the CNE Professional Association (CNEPA) and NetWare Users International (NUI).

7. **New User Info:**
   This volume has helpful hints for new users.

Contents of Service & Support Volume

1. **Technical Information Documents:** Include bulletins and FYIs (For Your Information) written by Novell engineers and technicians. Bulletins usually have more reliable information than FYIs.

2. **Files, Patches, and Drivers:** Lists all downloadable files from all NetWire libraries. This library listing for each downloaded file contains the file name, the upload date,

the location of the file, and a description. You can use this section to download files instead of downloading from NetWire that is expensive.

3. **Third Party Files:** An alphabetical listing of files supplied by third parties. You can download these files from this section.

4. **Novell Application Notes:** Contain all AppNotes. AppNotes is a monthly publication from Novell for technical articles.

5. **Novell Professional Developer (NPD) Bulletins:** Contains all "Bulletins" a monthly technical publication.

6. **Novell Labs Bulletins:** Gives compatibility information about third party products. All product tests are performed by Novell engineers.

7. **Training:** Contain the latest course offering from Novell.

8. **Top Issues:** Provide answers for the questions most frequently asked of Novell's technical support engineers.

9. **Red Box Contents Listings:** Contain the CD ROM files listing for NetWare 3.12, NetWare 4.1 System, and NetWare 4.1 Documentation.

10. **Printing Decision Trees:** Contain troubleshooting tips for printing problems.

NetWire

NetWire is Novell's on-line information service available through the CompuServe Information System (CIS). To access NetWire you need an account on CompuServe, a modem, and communications software. NetWire may be the best place to get inexpensive technical support. Most of the questions are answered within 24 hours either by system operators (SysOps), Novell's technical support staff, or other expert users from all over the world. You also have access to Novell's product information, press releases, calendar of events, and forums. In addition, you can download files, patches, fixes, and updated utilities from the NetWire libraries.

Note: Readers should remember that NetWire's organization and content change from time to time. Consequently differences between this written material and NetWire may occur.

Two of the most important things in NetWire are forums to get specific technical support and libraries to download files.

NetWire Forums

Message forums are used to post technical questions. Questions are answered by System Operators (SysOps), Novell technical support staff, or other expert users. There are many forums available. Each forum focuses on a particular topic. For example, NetWare 2.x forum (NETW2X) deals with issues specific to the 2.x operating system. NetWare 3.x forum (NETW3X) focuses on issues specific to 3.x operating system. The Novell Information forum (NGENERAL) can be used to talk to other CNEs and get information about various Novell Programs. Novell Users forum (NOVUSER) is also popular among CNEs to get information about new uploaded files, job postings, and classifieds to buy or sell networking products such as CNE manuals. To go to any specific forum, you use the "GO" command with the forum name, for example, GO NETW3X.

See appendix for a list of NetWire forums.

The NetWire Libraries

The NetWire Libraries are used to get updated files, patches, and fixes. Currently there are two main library areas: NWOSFILES and NWGENFILES.

NetWare OS Files Forum

Libraries Available:

1. New Uploads
2. NetWare 4.x
3. NetWare 3.1x
4. NetWare 2.2
5. Pre 3.11, 2.2
6. SFT III 3.11
7. SFT III 4.1
8. NW Client OS2
9. NW Client DOS/Win
10. NW Client Win NT
11. NW Client Win 95
12. NetWare Utilities
13. General Information

NW General Files Forum

Libraries Available:

1. New Uploads
2. UNIX Connectivity
3. NW Connectivity
4. NetWare Messaging
5. Desktop Products
6. NetWork Management
7. NetWare for Mac
8. NW Navigator
9. Tuxedo
10. NW Telephony/Video
11. OracleWare
12. Educ/Labs/Other
13. AppWare
14. Translation
15. General Information

Using NetWire

To use NetWire connect and log in to CompuServe and use GO NETWIRE. You may want to use a CompuServe browser, such as WinCIM or OZWIN for easy access to NetWire (or other CompuServe services).

Using WinCIM

WinCIM is available to all CompuServe members free of charge. If you are not already a member of CompuServe, you can get an account by calling 1 800-848-8199 or 614-457-8600.

To get latest WinCIM release information use GO WinCIM. To get technical support, use GO WCIMSUPPORT on CompuServe.

To install WinCIM, insert Disk 1 in drive A or B, choose **Run** from **File** menu of Windows Program Manager, and type A:SETUP or B:SETUP. Press <Enter>. Follow on-screen instructions to install WinCIM.

Troubleshooting & Supporting Networks

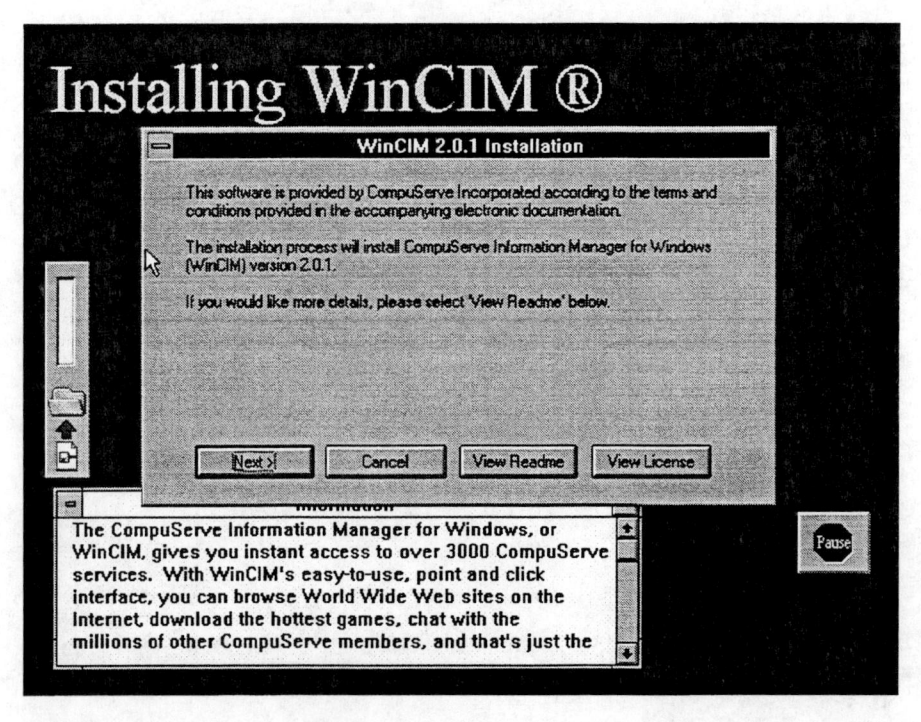

Figure 2-5: Installing WinCIM

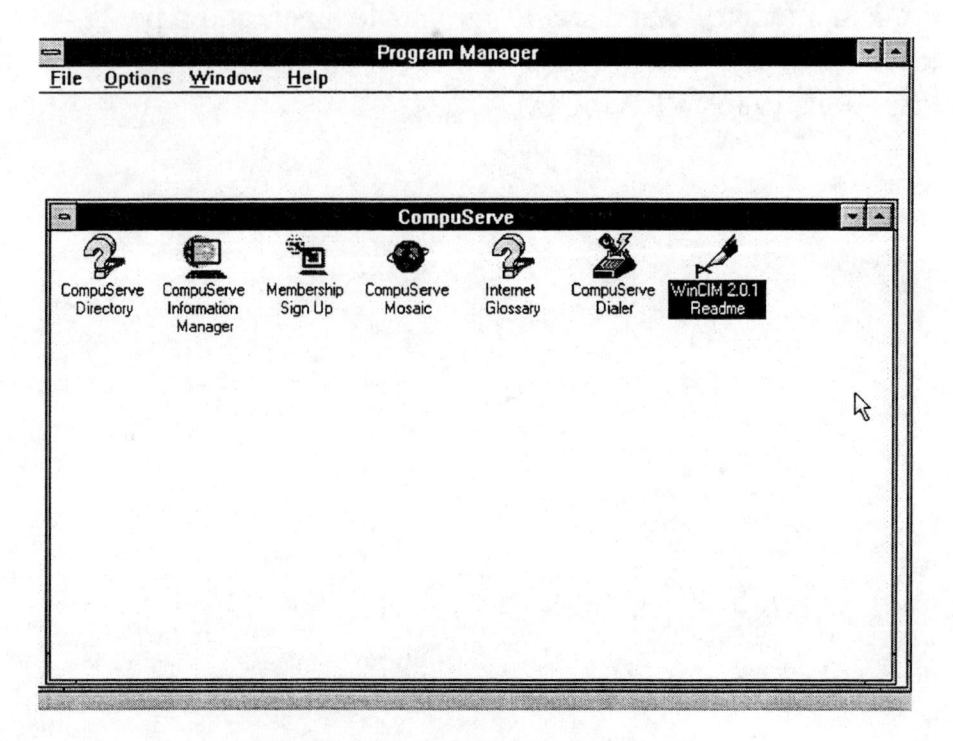

Figure 2-6: CompuServer Program Group

© 1993 - 96 · PC Age, Inc. All Rights Reserved · 20 Audrey Place · Fairfield, NJ 07004 · U.S.A. · Tel: 201-882-5370

Chapter 2: Troubleshooting Tools

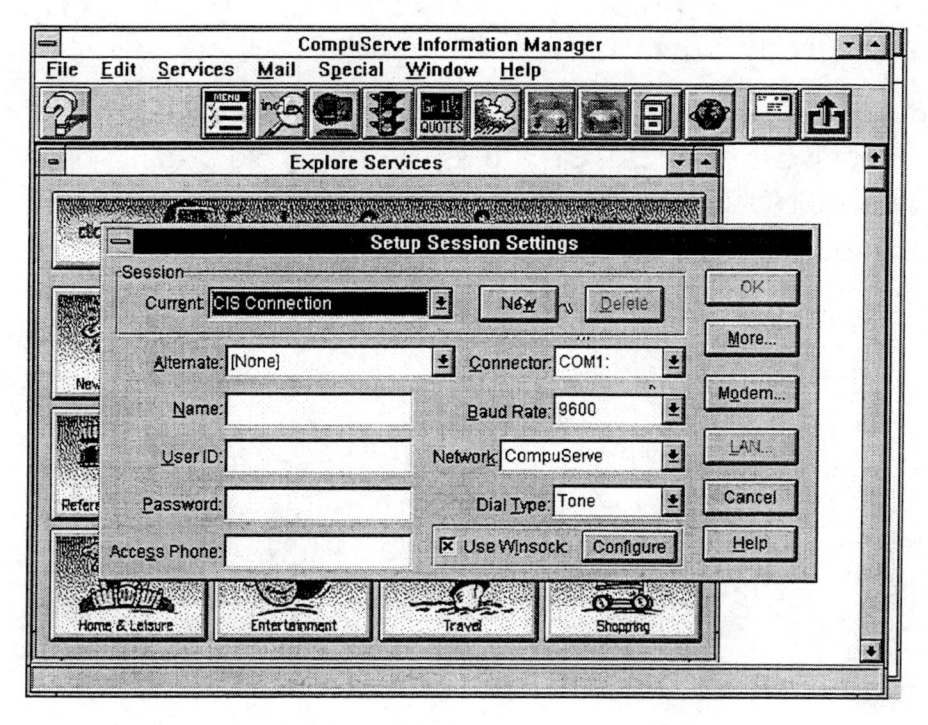

Figure 2-7: CompuServe Setup Session Settings

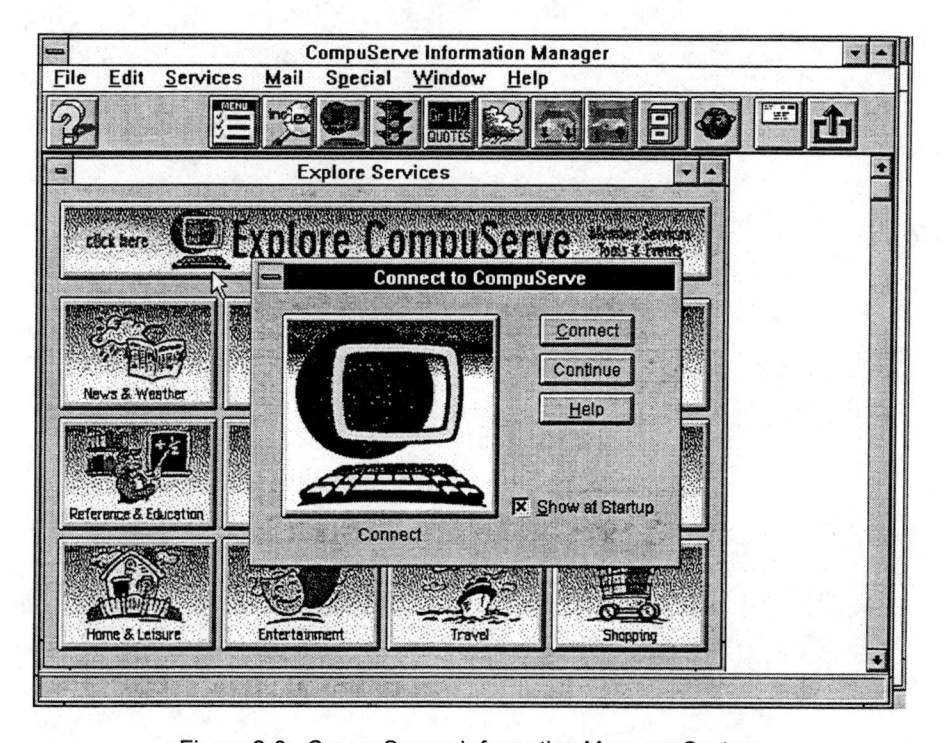

Figure 2-8: CompuServer Information Manager System

© 1993 - 96 · PC Age, Inc. All Rights Reserved · 20 Audrey Place · Fairfield, NJ 07004 · U.S.A. · Tel: 201-882-5370

2-15

Using NovCIM

NovCIM is a Novell customized version of WinCIM for NetWire users. NovCIM makes it easy to use NetWire. To install NovCIM, download NOVCIM.EXE from NetWire (Go NovCIM) or NSEPro. Run NOVCIM.EXE file in a directory to decompress files. Select Run from the Windows File menu, and type **Path:SETUP**; where path specifies the directory where you have decompressed NOVCIM.EXE file.

Novell On the Internet

Novell services are available on the Internet. Most users access the Internet through local Service Providers using a modem and communications software. Your workstation needs TCP/IP protocol to access the Internet. An Internet browser facilitates getting around on the Internet.

Users can obtain Novell Information through the World Wide Web (http://www.novell.com), Gopher (gopher.novell.com), and File Transfer Protocol (ftp.novell.com). The Novell services found on the Internet supply most of the information available from the NetWire forum on CompuServe and NSEPro.

Software tools that users find helpful are Netscape or Mosaic for the World Wide Web (WWW). These tools are also known as Web browsers as they help users navigate through the Web and browse information.

Like NetWire on CompuServe, NetWire on the Internet offers you Files, Patches, and Fixes; Technical Information Documents (TIDs); Novell Labs hardware and software test bulletins; What is New; and Novell programs.

Support Forums to ask technical questions are supported on CompuServe, but not on Internet. Application Notes and Developer Notes are also available on CompuServe, but not on the Internet.

Note that Novell on-line product manuals are not available on NetWire. They are available on NSEPro. NSEPro does not offer Support Forums.

Navigating Novell Internet Services

To access information or services on the Internet you use the following three methods: World Wide Web, File Transfer Protocol, and Gopher.

World Wide Web (WWW)

To give you easy access to information, companies develop their WWW pages.

The WWW page contains hypertext links, which you can use to navigate Internet services. Each link provides information as text, graphics, sounds, and digitized movies, points to a link on another page, allows you to download or upload files, initiate a search, or points to other Internet services.

Using your WWW browser such as NetScape or Mosaic you can go to Novell's home page by entering the following address: **http://www.novell.com**.

You can access NetWire from Novell's home page by clicking on **NetWire Technical Support Services** hypertext link.

File Transfer Protocol (FTP)

FTP is used to copy files from one computer to another on the Internet. Many companies maintain FTP servers or sites to provide you information. You use FTP client to access the information. Most FTP software is text-based rather than graphic, which makes FTP more difficult to use as compared to the WWW.

To find files that have information your are looking for, you can use a search tool called Archie. Using Archie you enter search terms and it returns a list of files on FTP sites that match your search terms.

The Novell FTP address is ftp.novell.com. Login as anonymous. World Wide Web browser for LAN WorkPlace for DOS and for UnixWare are available on ftp.novell.com in /pub/WWW.

Gopher

Gopher provides an easy to use interface to access information on Gopher Servers or Sites. Gopher client allows you to move from one site to another using menus or the address of a site.

With Gopher, you can use Veronica to find files that have information you are looking for. Like Archie, Veronica allows you to enter search terms and searches Gopher sites for files that match your search terms.

To visit Novell Gopher site use the address gopher.novell.com.

The Micro House Technical Library

The Micro House Technical Library (MTL) is a comprehensive set of technical information and troubleshooting reference books distributed on a single CD-ROM and updated quarterly. MTL is divided into the following four useful publications:

1- The Encyclopedia of Main Boards This database includes documentation and diagram covering more than a thousand microcomputer mainboards (motherboards). For each board there are jumper settings, memory configuration, cache settings, connections, and component locations.

Figure 2-9: Micro House Technical Library Main Menu

2- The Encyclopedia of Hard Drives — This includes documentation and diagrams covering hundreds of hard drives and controller cards with jumper settings, performance specifications, and component locations. In addition, it provides specifications on over 2000 hard drives including size, number of heads, cylinders, tracks per sector, write precompensation, and mean time between failures.

3- The Network Interface Technical Guide — This database has documentation and diagrams covering hundreds of network boards with jumper settings and other specifications.

4- The Encyclopedia of I/O cards — This database has documentation and diagrams covering hundreds of I/O cards with jumper settings and other specifications.

Searching the MTL

Four types of searches are available within the library: Key word, Encyclopedia of Hard Drives, Encyclopedia of Main Boards, and the Network Interface Technical Guide.

Note: Your version of the library may also have Encyclopedia of I/O cards.

Key Word Searches — Select this icon (upper right hand corner icon in main menu) to search for up to 10 words in all documents (or selected documents). For example, if you enter "IDE CABLE", all documents will be retrieved which have both IDE and CABLE.

Key word Search does not locate words that are contained in pictures. For those words you use criteria searches.

Criteria Searches — To search specifically for hard drivers, controllers, or network interface cards (NICs) first click on the book you want to search and then click on the icon of the item (hard drive, controller, main board or NIC) that is in the upper right hand corner of the dialog. For example, to search for a specific hard disk first select the Encyclopedia of Hard drives from the main menu and then click on the hard drive icon. Hard Drive Criteria Search screen will appear. Now you can enter hard drive parameters and then click on search icon. All hard drive documents will be searched and a listing of found items will be presented (the "hit list"). You may then view the individual items by clicking on your selection.

Hands-On Exercises

How to use NSEPro (Windows Version)

Information is located by selecting database headings/icons, by forming queries, or by a combination of the two. Each selection is a step along the path to the information.

1. If NSEPro is available on a network, login to the network and run Microsoft Windows.

   If NSEPro is available on a PC, run Microsoft Windows and insert the NSEPro CD if necessary.

2. Open the NSEPro group and select your topic of interest by double clicking on the appropriate icon, continue to make selections which narrow and refine your choice.

3. NSEPro menus include a Toolbar with various buttons.

   a) The **Query** button permits entry of criteria for searching the database and record hits are displayed to indicate matches.

   b) The **Next** hit button moves the cursor in the document to the next word that matches the query's specified criteria.

   c) The **Previous** hit button moves the cursor in the document to the previous word that matches the query's specified criteria.

d) The **Backtrack** button permits you to return to previous steps (one step at a time).

e) The **Show Trail** button presents a list of the steps you have taken. You can return directly to a particular step by selecting that step.

f) The **Contents** button switches between the reduced table of contents corresponding to the record hits, and the document locations corresponding to the table of contents.

Example 1:
Download a file called 312PT6.EXE using NSEPro.

1. Select the Network System Support icon.

2. Select **Service & Support** volume.

Chapter 2: Troubleshooting Tools

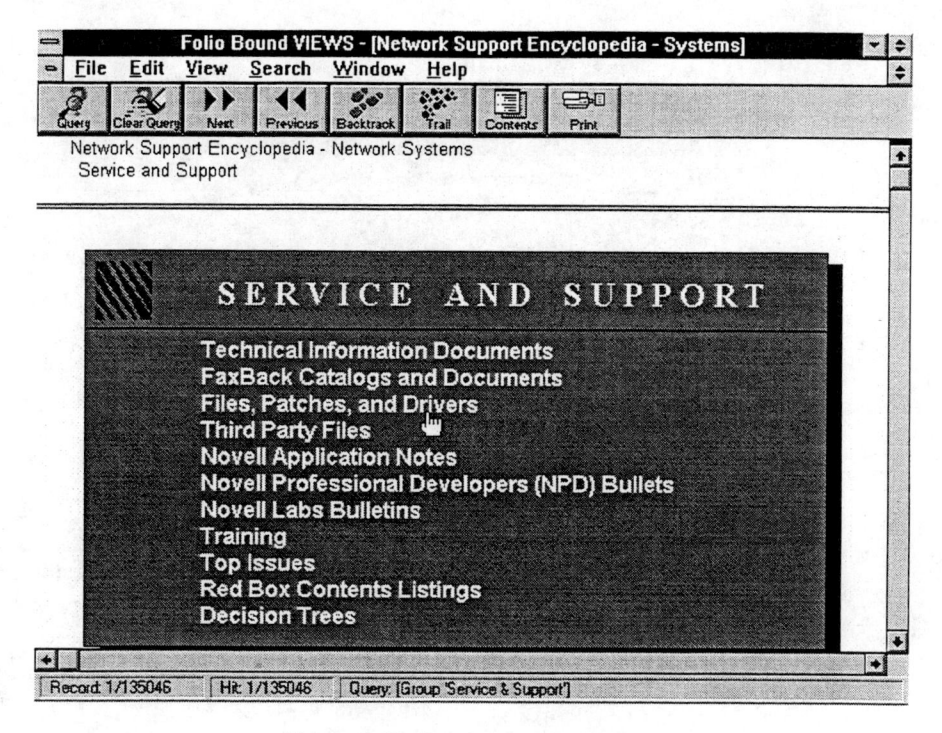

Figure 2-10: Service and Support menu

3. Select **Files, Patches and Drivers** (see Figure 2-10).

4. Select the **Query** button.

Troubleshooting & Supporting Networks

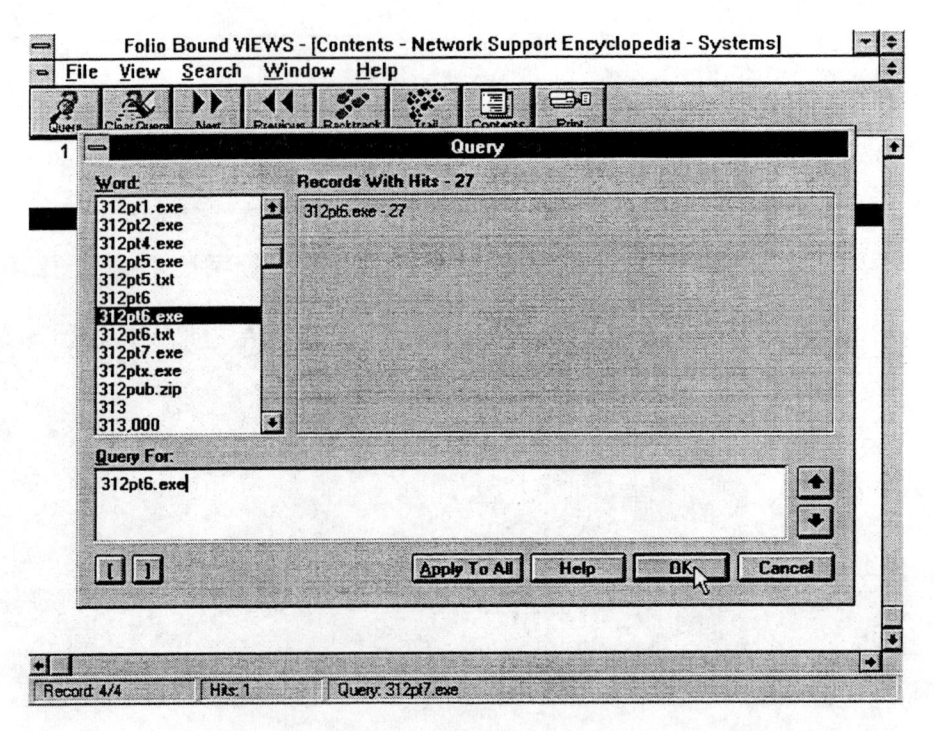

Figure 2-11: Query Screen

5. Enter the name of the file to search for, i.e., 312PT6.EXE (see Figure 2-11).

6. Click on **OK** button to display the headings of the hit record(s).

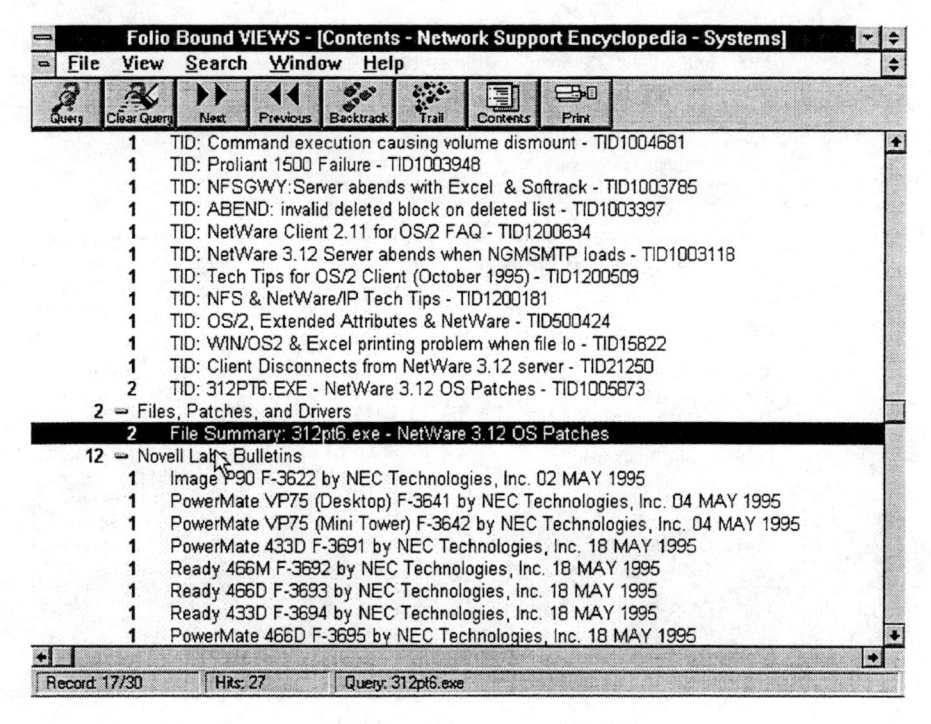

Figure 2-12: View Screen (Collection of hit records)

7. You can double-click on the heading title of a record to view its contents. To view contents of another record, click on the Contents button to move between the hit list and the contents of a record. Double-click on **File Summary: 312pt6.exe-NetWare 3.12 Operating System Patches** record title heading (see Figure 2-12).

Troubleshooting & Supporting Networks

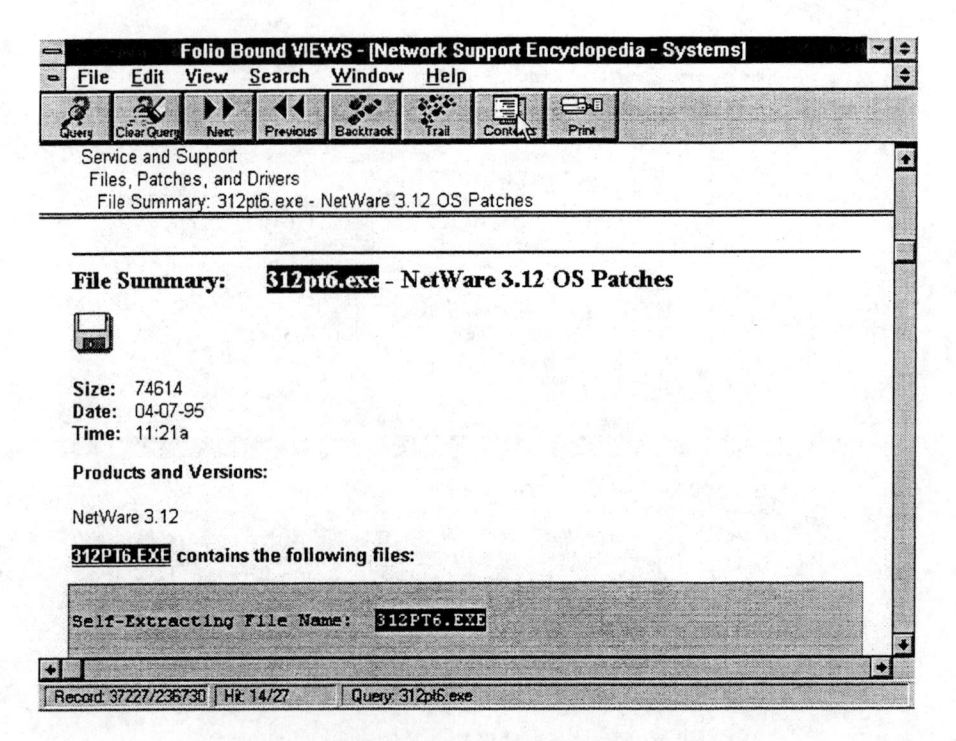

Figure 2-13: Contents of a record

8. View the contents of the record (see Figure 2-13).

To download the file, double-click on the floppy disk icon (see Figure 2-13).

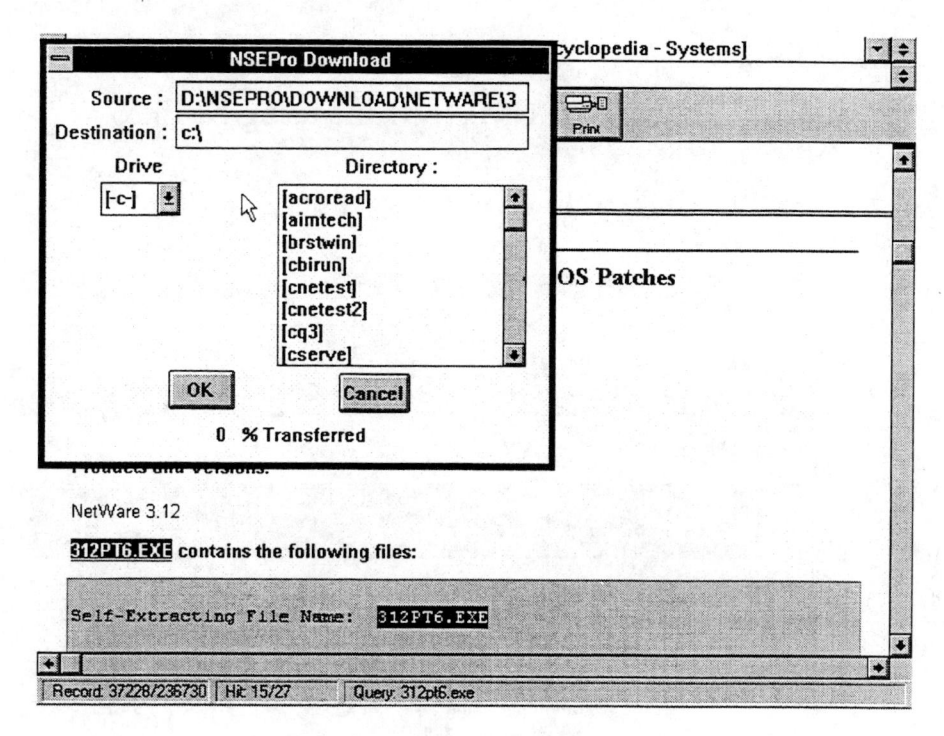

Figure 2-14: NSEPro Download Screen

Specify destination path and click on **OK** (see Figure 2-14).

Note: If the "NSE_DOWNLOAD" environment variable is not set, you will receive an error message when trying to download a file. NSEPro installation program puts the SET NSE_DOWNLOAD=D:\DOWNLOAD\ command in your AUTOEXEC.BAT file to set this variable. Make sure it is not deleted.

Troubleshooting & Supporting Networks

Example 2:

Download the latest CDROM.NLM file using NSEPro.

1. Double-click on File Updates volume.

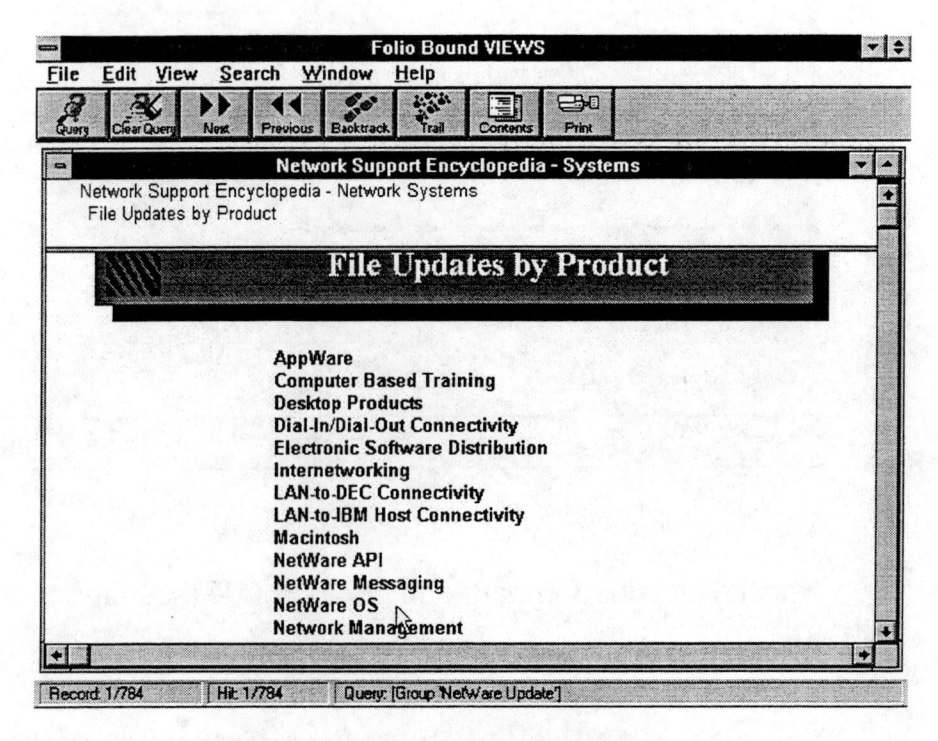

Figure 2-15: File Updates by Product name

2. Double-click on NetWare OS (see Figure 2-15).

Chapter 2: Troubleshooting Tools

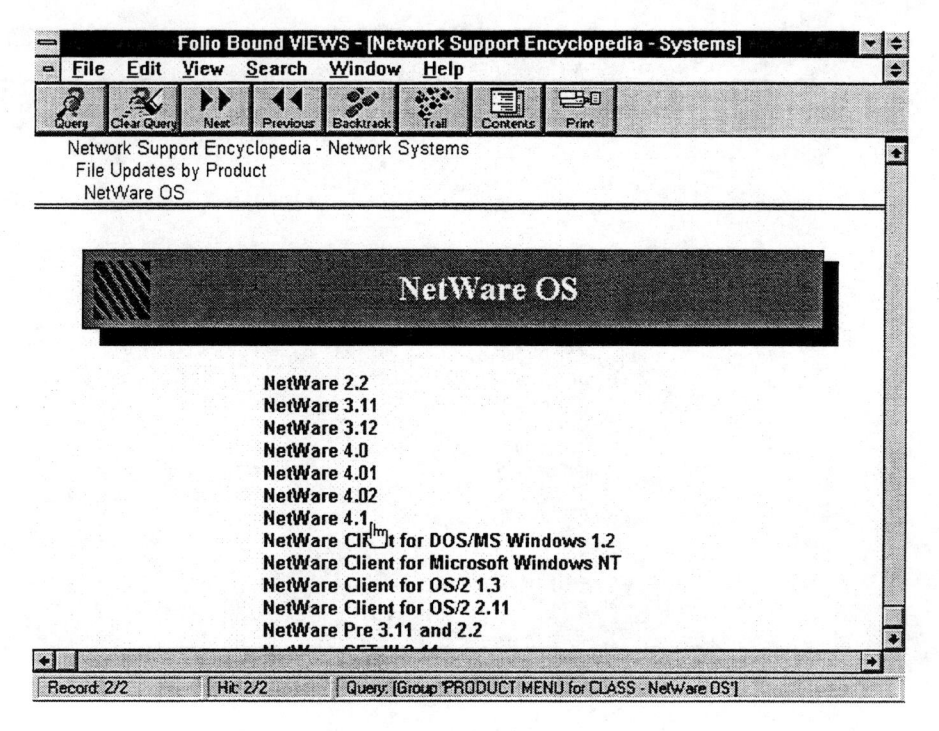

```
┌─────────────────────────────────────────────────────────────┐
│  Folio Bound VIEWS - [Network Support Encyclopedia - Systems]│
│  File  Edit  View  Search  Window  Help                      │
├─────────────────────────────────────────────────────────────┤
│  Query Clear Query Next Previous Backtrack Trail Contents Print│
│                                                              │
│  Network Support Encyclopedia - Network Systems              │
│    File Updates by Product                                   │
│      NetWare OS                                              │
│                                                              │
│              ┌──────────────────────────────┐                │
│              │        NetWare OS            │                │
│              └──────────────────────────────┘                │
│                                                              │
│                   NetWare 2.2                                │
│                   NetWare 3.11                               │
│                   NetWare 3.12                               │
│                   NetWare 4.0                                │
│                   NetWare 4.01                               │
│                   NetWare 4.02                               │
│                   NetWare 4.1                                │
│                   NetWare Client for DOS/MS Windows 1.2      │
│                   NetWare Client for Microsoft Windows NT    │
│                   NetWare Client for OS/2 1.3                │
│                   NetWare Client for OS/2 2.11               │
│                   NetWare Pre 3.11 and 2.2                   │
│                                                              │
│  Record: 2/2    Hit: 2/2   Query: [Group 'PRODUCT MENU for CLASS - NetWare OS']│
└─────────────────────────────────────────────────────────────┘
```

Figure 2-16: NetWare Operating System menu

3. Double-click on NetWare 4.1 (see Figure 2-16).

© 1993 - 96 · PC Age, Inc. All Rights Reserved · 20 Audrey Place · Fairfield, NJ 07004 · U.S.A. · Tel: 201-882-5370

Troubleshooting & Supporting Networks

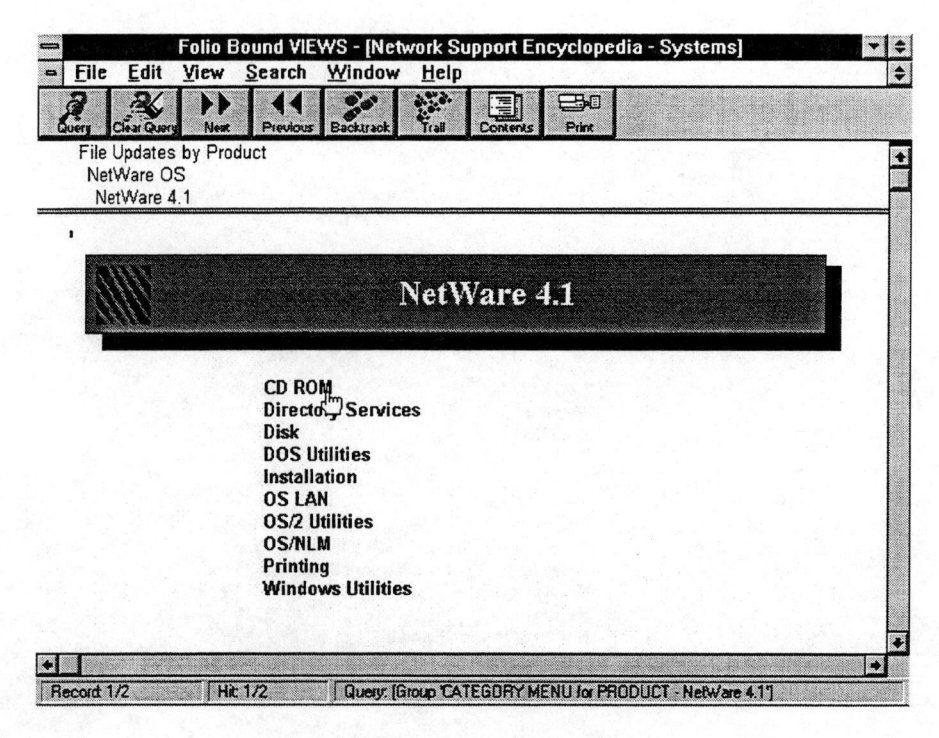

Figure 2-17: NetWare Operating System menu

4. Double-click on CD ROM (see Figure 2-17).

Chapter 2: Troubleshooting Tools

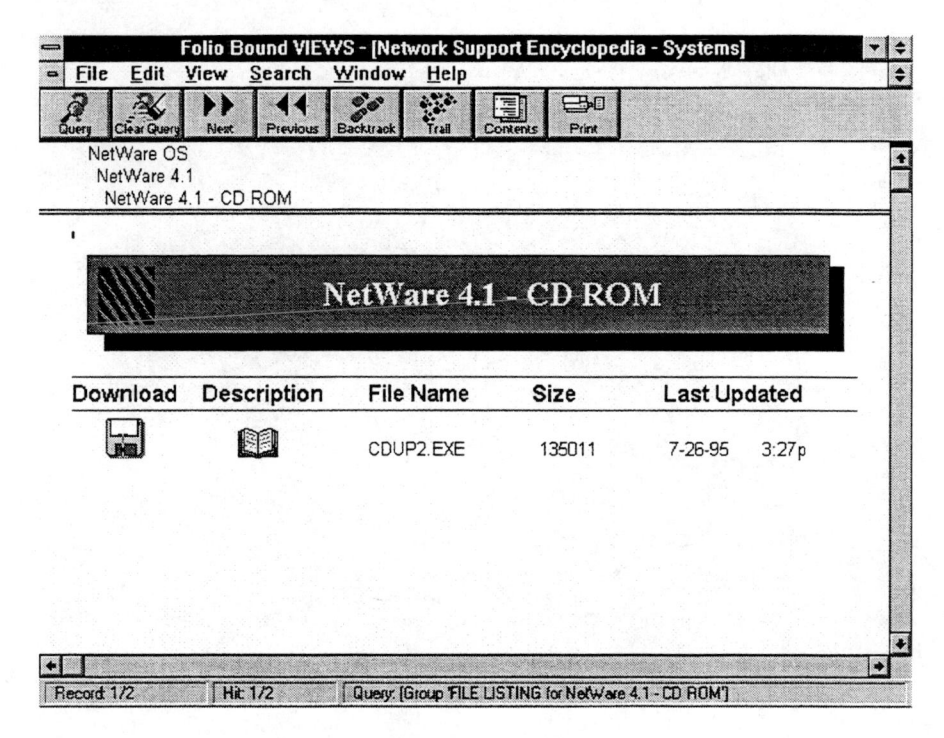

Figure 2-18a: NetWare 4.1 CD-ROM

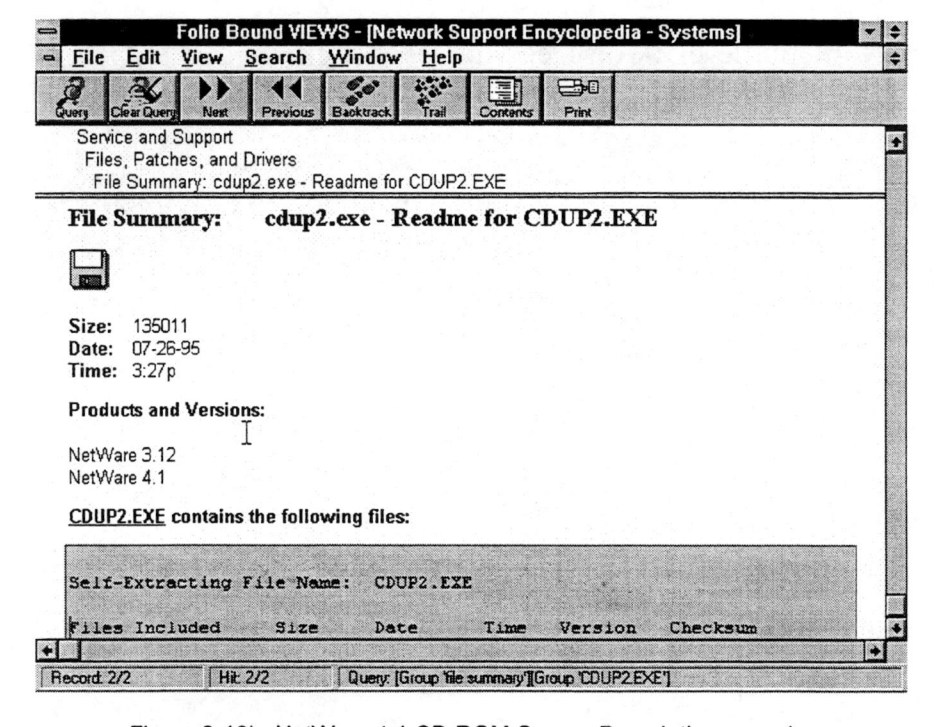

Figure 2-18b: NetWare 4.1 CD-ROM Screen-Description page 1

© 1993 - 96 · PC Age, Inc. All Rights Reserved · 20 Audrey Place · Fairfield, NJ 07004 · U.S.A. · Tel: 201-882-5370

2-33

Troubleshooting & Supporting Networks

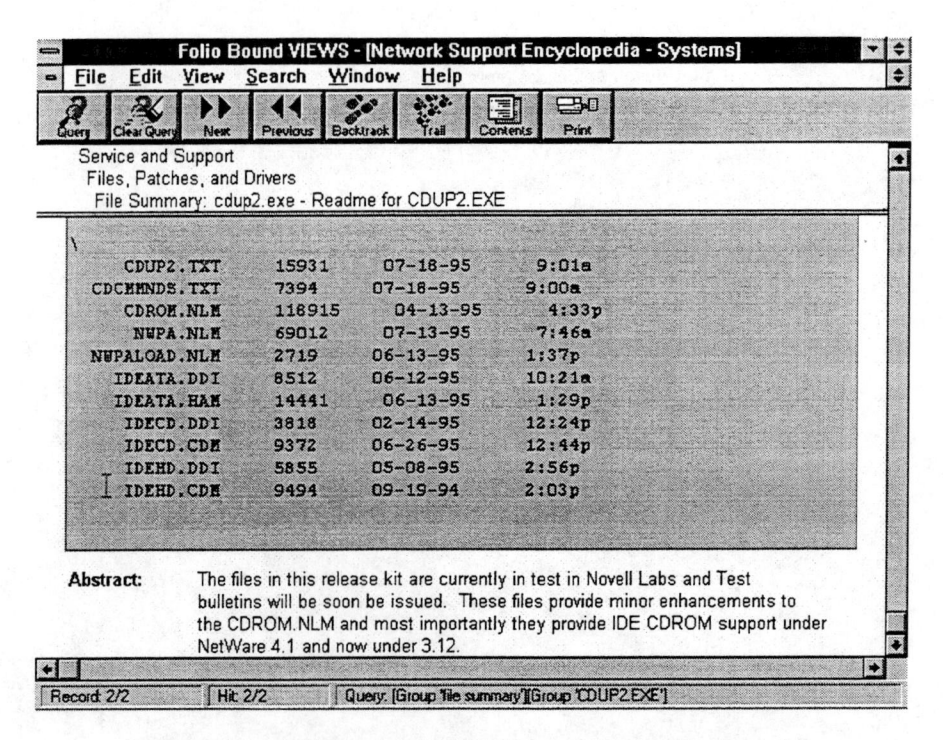

```
         Folio Bound VIEWS - [Network Support Encyclopedia - Systems]
  File  Edit  View  Search  Window  Help

  Service and Support
    Files, Patches, and Drivers
      File Summary: cdup2.exe - Readme for CDUP2.EXE

         CDUP2.TXT     15931    07-18-95     9:01a
         CDCHMNDS.TXT   7394    07-18-95     9:00a
         CDROM.NLM    118915    04-13-95     4:33p
         NWPA.NLM      69012    07-13-95     7:46a
         NWPALOAD.NLM   2719    06-13-95     1:37p
         IDEATA.DDI     8512    06-12-95    10:21a
         IDEATA.HAM    14441    06-13-95     1:29p
         IDECD.DDI      3818    02-14-95    12:24p
         IDECD.CDM      9372    06-26-95    12:44p
         IDEHD.DDI      5855    05-08-95     2:56p
         IDEHD.CDM      9494    09-19-94     2:03p

    Abstract:  The files in this release kit are currently in test in Novell Labs and Test
               bulletins will be soon be issued. These files provide minor enhancements to
               the CDROM.NLM and most importantly they provide IDE CDROM support under
               NetWare 4.1 and now under 3.12.

  Record: 2/2    Hit: 2/2    Query: [Group file summary][Group 'CDUP2.EXE']
```

Figure 2-18c: NetWare 4.1 CD-ROM Screen-Description page 2

5. Double-click on Description to confirm this is the right file (see Figures 18a, 18b, and 18c).

6. Double-click on the floppy disk icon to download the CDUP2.EXE file (it contains the latest CDROM.NLM).

NSEPro Exercise 1

What are the minimum PC hardware and software requirements to run WinCIM?

Steps:

1. Select the **Network Systems Support** icon.
2. At the main menu select the **Query** button.
3. Enter **NetWire hardware software WinCIM** as search criteria. Each word you enter will reduce the number of Records With Hits.
4. Click on **OK** button to display the headings of the hit record(s).
5. Select the **Contents** button.
6. Use the page down key to go to "Hardware And Software Requirements".
7. Requirements are listed there. You may print by selecting the **Print** button.

Answer:

- IBM or compatible with 1MB RAM (2MB recommended).
- 4MB of hard disk space.
- 80286 CPU or higher (80386SX or higher recommended).
- Pointing device (mouse) compatible with MS Windows.
- MS Windows 3.0 or later (3.1 or later recommended).
- EGA (or higher resolution) monitor.
- Hays or compatible modem.

NSEPro Exercise 2

You want to know what Novell Sales & Marketing events were scheduled for 1995.

Steps:

1. Select the **Network Systems Support** icon.

2. At the main menu select **Sales & Marketing**.

3. At the Sales & Marketing menu select **Novell Events Calendar**.

4. A listing of all Novell Sales & Marketing events for 1995 is given.

NSEPro Exercise 3

Locate and download a program that allows the user to scan the bindery for objects, properties, and values.

Steps:

1. Select the **Network Systems Support** icon.
2. At the main menu select **Service & Support**.
3. Select **Files, Patches, and Drivers**.
4. Select the **Query** button.
5. Enter **bindery scan objects properties values** as search criteria. Each word you enter will reduce the number of Records With Hits.
6. Click on **OK** button to display the headings of the hit record(s).
7. Highlight **File Summary: binscn.exe - Sample Bindery scanning program** heading title.
8. Select the **Contents** button.
9. Select the **Floppy Disk** icon.
10. Enter the Destination (C:\DOWNLOAD) in the Download window.
11. Select **OK**.
12. When the download is complete, the Download window closes.

Note: The DOWNLOAD directory must exist before doing the download.

NSEPro Exercise 4

You are running NetWare 3.11 and you find that there is a problem with the FLAGDIR command. The workstation hangs when a directory has a period in the name. What version of FLAGDIR corrects this problem?

Steps:

1. Select the **Network Systems Support** icon.

2. At the main menu select **Service & Support**.

3. Select **Files, Patches, and Drivers**.

4. Select the **Query** button.

5. Enter **3.11 FLAGDIR** as search criteria. Each word you enter will the reduce number of Records With Hits.

6. Click on **OK** button to display the headings of the hit record(s).

7. Double click on TID: FLAGDIR.EXE heading record to view contents.

8. You can download this file by double clicking on the **Floppy Disk** icon and proceeding as in the earlier exercise.

NSEPro Exercise 5

Find all Novell Authorized Education Centers (NAEC) in Orlando, Florida.

Steps:

1. Select the **Network Systems Support** icon.

2. At the main menu select **Novell Programs**.

3. At the Novell Programs menu select **Novell Education & Certification**.

4. At the Novell Education menu select **Education Center Referral** list.

5. At the Education Center Referral list select **Novell Authorized Education Center** (NAEC).

6. A listing of all NAEC course offerings is given arranged alphabetically by State name. Move to Florida using the mouse or page down key.

Troubleshooting & Supporting Networks

NSEPro Exercise 6

You want to download the latest Patch Kit for the NetWare 3.11 Operating System (OS) to your local C:\DOWNLOAD directory.

Steps:

1. Select the **Network Systems Support** icon.

2. At the main menu select **Service & Support**.

3. Select **Files, Patches, and Drivers**.

4. Select the **Query** button.

5. Enter **patch kit for NetWare 3.11 OS** as search criteria. Each word you enter will reduce the number of Records With Hits.

6. Click on **OK** button to display the headings of the hit record(s).

7. You can double-click on the heading title of a record to view its contents. To view contents of another record, click on the Contents button to move between the hit list and the contents of a record.

   Double-click on **TID:311PTD.EXE Patch kit for NetWare 3.11 OS-TID18** button.

© 1993 - 96 · PC Age, Inc. All Rights Reserved · 20 Audrey Place · Fairfield, NJ 07004 · U.S.A. · Tel: 201-882-5370

8. You will see a description of the hit you selected. You can download the file by double clicking on the Floppy Disk icon and proceeding as in earlier exercises.

Troubleshooting & Supporting Networks

How to use the Micro House Technical Library (MTL)

The following exercises use MS Windows. Select the Micro House Technical Library icon and answer the questions.

Using the MTL Encyclopedia of Hard Drives

You have a Hewlett Packard 97560E hard disk controller, and you want to add a second drive. Which switch would you use and what are the settings?

Steps:

1. From the Main menu click on The Encyclopedia of Hard Drives or you can click on the Hard Drives icon.

2. Click on Hard Drive Specifications.

3. Click on the Search icon.

4. Highlight the Name and Model. Then double click. A display of all hard drive settings is displayed. You may have to scroll through the screen to see the answer.

5. Clicking on the box "See Diagram #1" will show you the board layout.

Answer:	Switch		
	S6	S7	S8
	Off	On	Off

© 1993 - 96 · PC Age, Inc. All Rights Reserved · 20 Audrey Place · Fairfield, NJ 07004 · U.S.A. · Tel: 201-882-5370

2-42

Using the MTL Encyclopedia of Main Boards

You have a Leading Edge computer model WINPRO 486 and you want to use a monochrome monitor. Which jumper is used to select between monochrome and color? Which pins need to be closed to select monochrome?

Steps:

1. From the Main Menu click on The Encyclopedia of Main Boards.

2. Click on the Mainboards icon.

3. At the Mainboard Criteria Search menu you can either input the search information or click on the Search icon and select the Name and Model from the search list.

4. From the search list click on the Name and Model. Select your answer from the displayed information. You may have to scroll through the screen to find the answer.

Answer:

Jumper (JP1). Pins 1 and 2 are closed.

Troubleshooting & Supporting Networks

Using the MTL NetWare Interface Technical Guide

Q.1. You have a COMPEX ANET 16-1 ARCnet card. What are the jumper settings for an I/O base address of 300h?

Steps:

1. From the Main Menu click on the Network Interface Technical Guide.

2. Click on the NICs icon.

3. At the Network Interface Card Search Criteria menu, click on Search. At the hit list screen highlight the selection and double click.

4. Select the answer from the displayed information. You may have to scroll through the screen to see the answer. Click on the "See Diagram #1" box to display a layout of the board.

Answer:

P4	P5	P6	P7	P8	P9
closed	closed	closed	closed	open	open

Q.2. You have a Gateway Communications Inc. G/Ethernet 16 Combo NIC card and you want to set it for 10Base5 (AUI transceiver via DB-15 port). Which jumpers would you use and would they be open or closed.

Answer:

JP11	JP12	JP13
open	open	closed

Q.3. You have a Thomas-Conrad Corp. TC5143-T NIC and you want to enable the Boot PROM. Which jumper would you select ? Should it be open or closed?

Answer:

Jumper (P5) closed

Using NetWire

(The following steps assume that you are using NovCIM.)

To find a list of all NetWire forums
Steps:

1. Select CompuServe Information Manager icon.
2. Select New User Info icon (see Figure 2-19).
3. Select User Documentation icon (see Figure 2-20).
4. Select File It and then Save (see Figure 2-21).
   The User Documentation should be saved to
   C:\CSERVE\FCABINET\CABINET\FOLDER00.000
   directory.

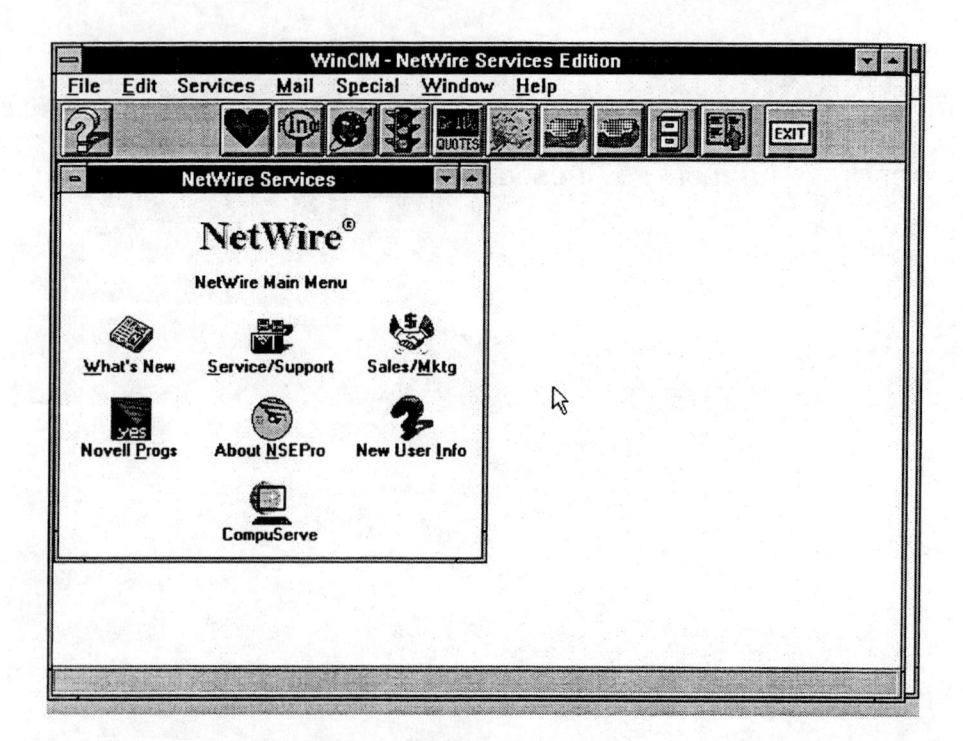

Figure 2-19: Novell version of WinCIM (NovCIM) - NetWire Main Menu

Chapter 2: Troubleshooting Tools

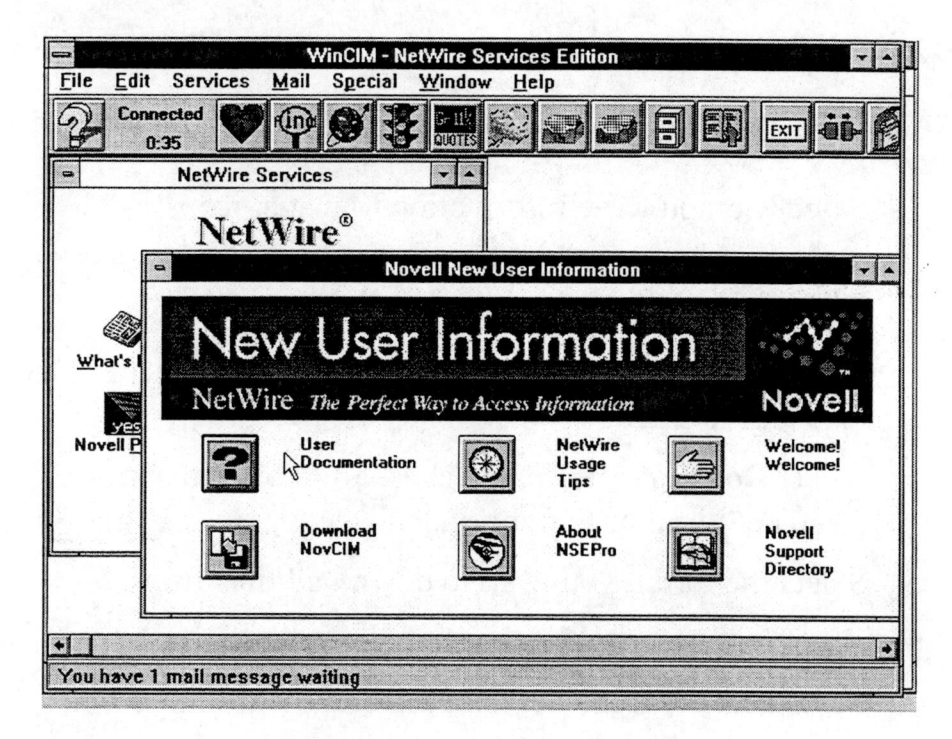

Figure 2-20: New User Information Menu

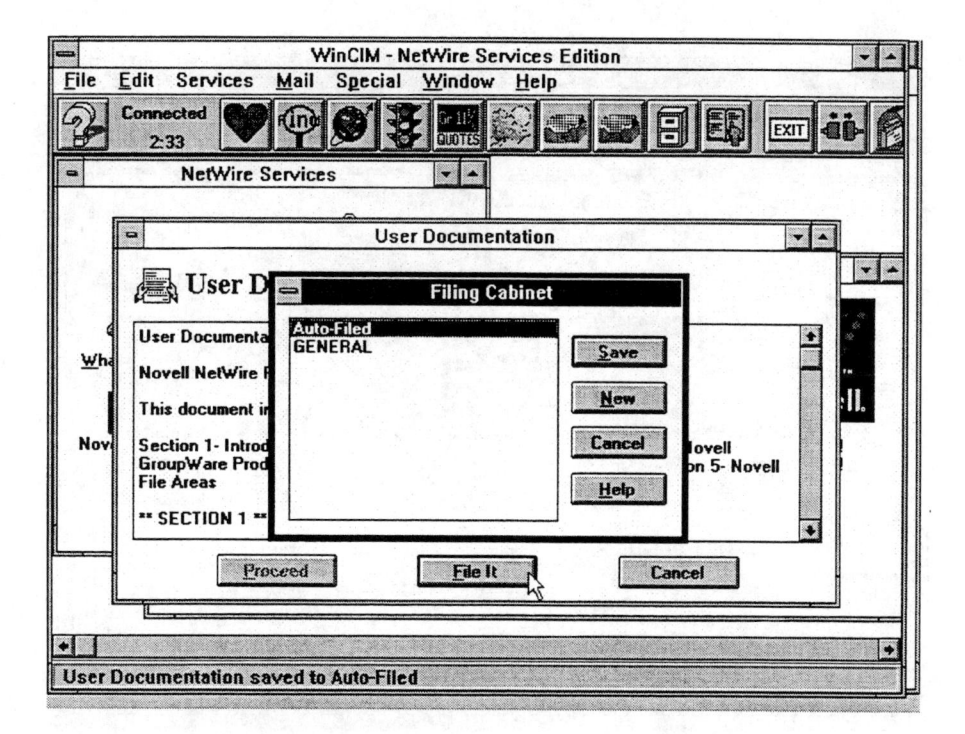

Figure 2-21: New User Information Menu

© 1993 - 96 · PC Age, Inc. All Rights Reserved · 20 Audrey Place · Fairfield, NJ 07004 · U.S.A. · Tel: 201-882-5370

2-47

To download or upload files
Steps:

1. Select CompuServe Information Manager icon.
2. Select Service/Support icon from NetWire main menu (see Figure 2-19).
3. Select **NetWare Products** from Technical Services menu (see Figure 2-22).
4. Select **Download Files, Patches, and Drivers** option from NetWare Systems Support menu (see Figure 2-23).
5. Select the forum you want to download files from.
6. Use icons on screen to search, download, or upload a file.
7. To disconnect from NetWire select the right-most icon from the top icon menu.

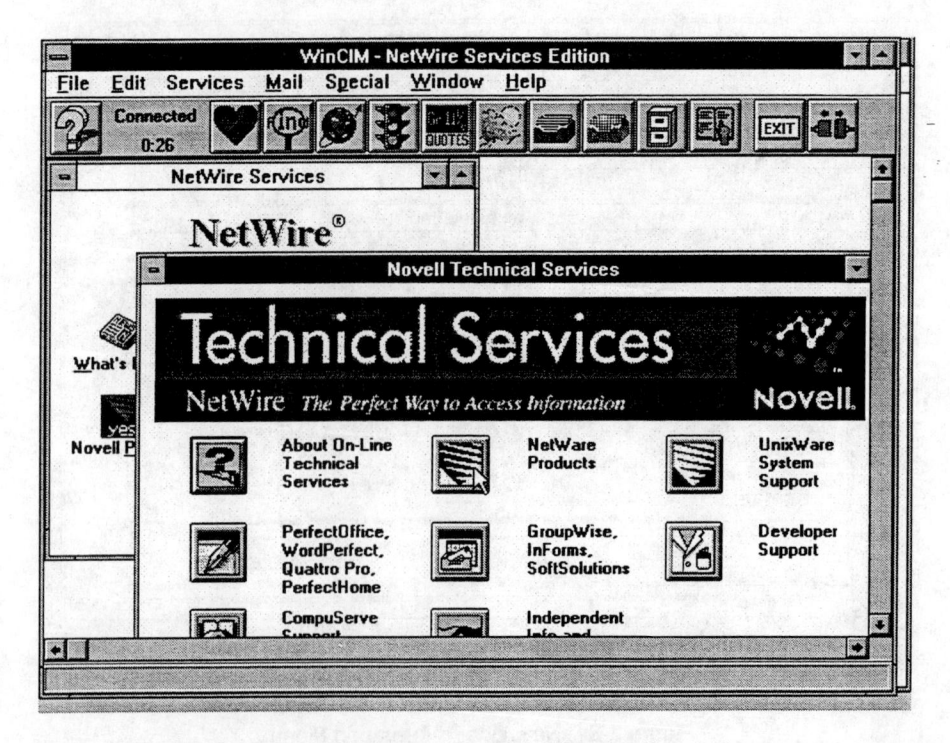

Figure 2-22: Novell Technical Services (Service/Support) menu

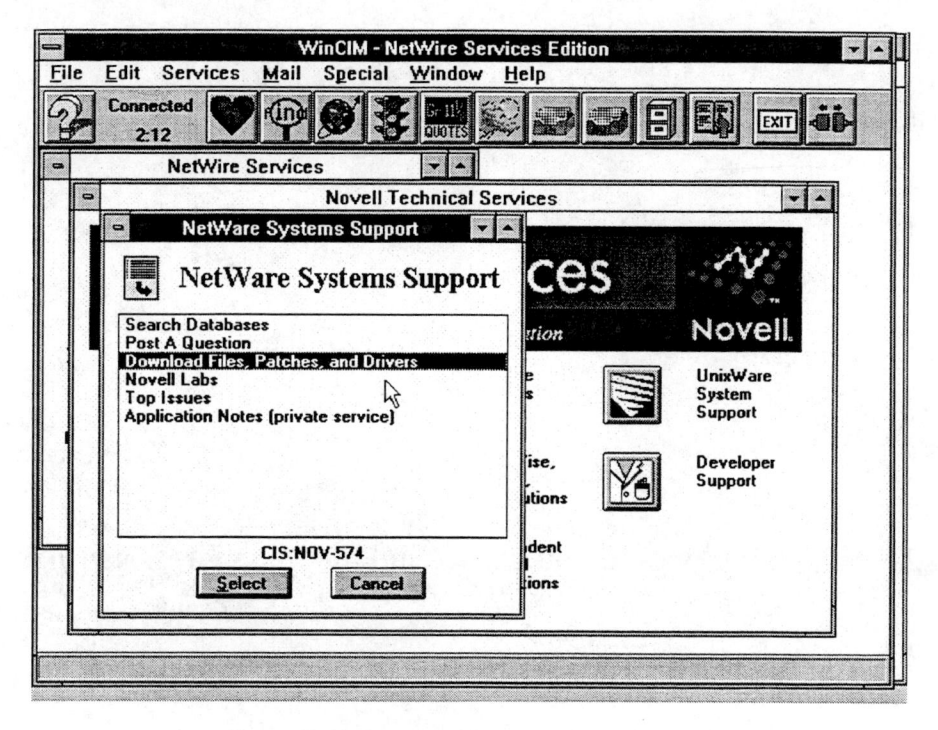

Figure 2-23: NetWare Systems Support menu

To leave or retrieve messages

Steps:

1. Select CompuServe Information Manager icon.
2. Select Service/Support icon from NetWire main menu.
3. Select **NetWare Products** from Technical Services menu.
4. Select **Post A Question** option from NetWire Systems Support menu.
5. Select a forum of your choice from Post A Question menu.
6. Use icons on screen to search, leave, or retrieve messages.
7. To disconnect from NetWire select the right-most icon from the top icon menu.

Review Questions

Q.1. Which tool would you use to download the very latest version of a file?

    a. NSEPro   b. NetWire
    c. MTL   d. Check It Pro

Q.2. Which tool would you use to find the I/O address settings of a NIC?

    a. NSEPro   b. MTL
    c. NetWire   d. Check It Pro

Q.3. Which tool would you use to download a file inexpensively?

    a. NSEPro   b. NetWire
    c. MTL   d. Check It Pro

Q.4. Which tool would you use to find out the model number of an HP I/O card?

    a. NSEPro   b. MTL
    c. NetWire   d. Check It Pro

Q.5. Which tool would you use to make a copy of your CMOS setup?

    a. MTL   b. COMCHECK
    c. Check It Pro   d. NSEPro

Q.6. Which tool would you use for low-level formatting for a variety of hard disks?

    a. MTL   b. Check It Pro
    c. NSEPro   d. DISKCHECK

Q.7. AppNotes are available on:

    a. Hard copy only
    b. NSEPro only
    c. Hard copy and NSEPro
    d. Hard copy, NSEPro, and NetWire

Q.8. To copy CMOS configuration from one PC to another, which one of the following can be used?

    a. Check It PRO   b. DOSGEN
    c. NSEPro   d. COMCHECK

Q.9. Which of the following commands are related to NSEPro? (select all that apply)

    a. PATH=D:\PROGRAMS\WIN
    b. LASTDRIVE=Z
    c. MAP S16:=NESPRO\PROGRAMS\WIN
    d. SET NESPRO= NETWORK
    e. SET NSE_DOWNLOAD =D:\DOWNLOAD\

Q.10. Which of the following is Novell's WWW address?

    a. http://www.novell.com
    b. ftp://www.novell.com
    c. gopher://www.novell.com
    d. www://http.novell.com

Q.11. Which of the following is used when using NetWire on Internet? (select all that are true)

    a. Go NetWire
    b. hypertext links and graphic
    c. Web browser
    d. NovCIM Internet browser

Chapter 3 Network Boards and Cabling

In this chapter we will first discuss the configuring elements of network boards and then discuss in detail the most popular network standards (network boards) for physically connecting a LAN: Ethernet, Token Ring, ARCnet, FDDI, and ATM.

Configuring Elements

Network boards or other computer devices are usually configured using jumpers and DIP (DiPolar) switches. Configuration involves setting up interrupt (IRQ), memory address, I/O ports, etc.

Most new devices come with configuration software. It is much easier to configure a device using software than to adjust the device's jumpers and DIP switches.

Jumpers

Jumpers are used to configure computer devices. The jumper consists of two pins that stick up out of the computer board. A tiny jumper block is used to establish an electronic contact between two pins. Jumpers are used on network boards to set interrupts, memory addresses, and I/O ports.

DIP Switches

DIP switches are used to configure expansion boards or the system board (motherboard). For example, on an Ethernet board, DIP switches are used to configure the appropriate I/O port or to set the board to use boot PROM (Programmable Read Only Memory).

On an ARCnet board, DIP switches are used to set the node address.

On the system board, they are used to configure internal hardware components such as video type, amount of memory, and numbers of disk drives.

There are two types of DIP switches: Rocker and Slide. Rocker switches are depressed for ON or OFF settings. Slide switches are moved to the ON or OFF position.

Most Popular Network Boards

Ethernet

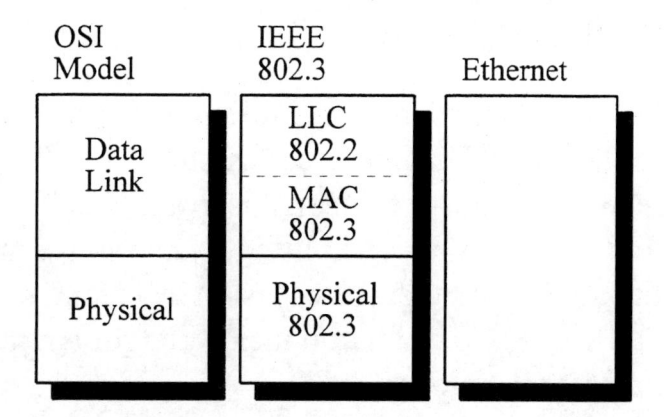

```
    OSI         IEEE
   Model        802.3        Ethernet
              ┌────────┐
              │  LLC   │
   ┌────────┐ │  802.2 │    ┌────────┐
   │  Data  │ ├╌╌╌╌╌╌╌╌┤    │        │
   │  Link  │ │  MAC   │    │        │
   │        │ │  802.3 │    │        │
   ├────────┤ ├────────┤    │        │
   │        │ │        │    │        │
   │Physical│ │Physical│    │        │
   │        │ │  802.3 │    │        │
   └────────┘ └────────┘    └────────┘
```

Terms used: OSI (Open Systems Interconnection), LLC (Logical Link Control), MAC (Media Access Control)

Figure 3-1: Ethernet, IEEE 802.3, and the OSI Model

Ethernet is currently the most popular network standard for physically connecting a LAN. It was introduced in the mid to late 1970s by Xerox corporation. Ethernet version 1.0 was jointly released by Digital Equipment Corp., Intel, and Xerox in 1980. Ethernet 2.0 was released in 1982.

In 1985, IEEE (Institute of Electrical and Electronics Engineers) made Ethernet a standard and released its Ethernet specifications called IEEE 802.3.

IEEE 802.3 is based on Ethernet, but supports multiple Physical Layer options. For data link services, 802.3 relies on the IEEE 802.2 LLC.

Note: In this chapter we will discuss IEEE 802.3 and refer to it as Ethernet.

Ethernet is an inexpensive 10 Mbps network standard that can be installed with bus or star topology. It supports coax, UTP, and fiber optic cable.

Ethernet performance is substantially affected under heavy load, which is a disadvantage.

Ethernet uses the Carrier Sense Multiple Access with Collision Detection (CSMA/CD) channel access method. In this method, any station can transmit if the channel is available. If a collision is detected, the station begins transmitting a jamming signal (32-48 bits long) that guarantees that the collision lasts long enough to be detected by all stations. The station then waits for a random interval before retransmitting.

General terminology used to describe CSMA/CD is contention. Ethernet is also referred to as the "contention-based" standard.

Different Types of Ethernet

10Base5 (Standard Thick-Ethernet)

10Base5 specifications are the same as the original Xerox Ethernet. It uses thick coax cable with bus topology. 10Base5 is also called Thick or Standard Ethernet. It supports a data rate of 10Mbps and a maximum segment length of 500 meters. 10Base5 uses a device called Medium Attachment Unit (MAU) to connect a computer (using a NIC) with the cable (media). This device is also called transceiver. A MAU or transceiver transmits and receives signals on the cable (media) and also detects collisions.

A MAU or transceiver is attached to a NIC using a cable called an AUI (Attachment Unit Interface) or transceiver cable. The AUI cable is also called a "drop cable".

```
        ┌─────┐
        │ NIC │
        └──┬──┘
       AUI │  Tranceiver cable
    ───────■───────
     MAU or Transceiver
```

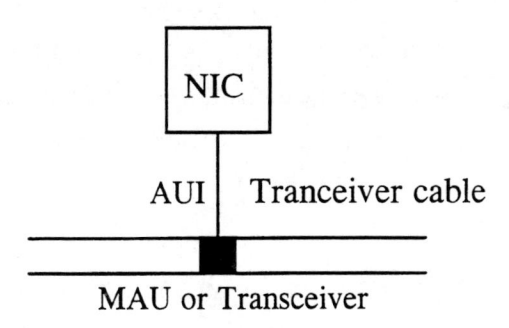

Figure 3-2: 10 Base 5 Ethernet

The drop cable attaches to the network cable by a clamp. One type of clamp that attaches to the network cable without cutting the network cable is called "Vampire Tap".

10Base5 is not popular anymore because the cable is inflexible and very difficult to work with and the bus topology is difficult to troubleshoot.

Thick-Ethernet Cabling

- 10Base5 uses RG-11 cable. The impedance of the cable is 50 ohms.

- The board must be set to use the external transceiver.

- Maximum distance from node (file server or workstation) to transceiver is 50 meters (164 feet). There is no minimum distance.

- Maximum trunk segment length is 500 meters (1640 feet).

- Maximum nodes per segment are 100 including repeaters.

- Maximum of 5 segments are allowed using 4 repeaters. You can put computers only on 3 of those segments. This is called 5-4-3 rule. The segments that have computers are called populated segments. Unpopulated segments are used to extend the network distance.

- Maximum entire network length is 2500 meters (8200 feet).

- Minimum distance between transceivers is 2.5 meters.

- Both ends of a segment must be terminated and one and only one end should be connected to ground.

- 10Base5 and 10Base2 networks can be connected together by using special adapters.

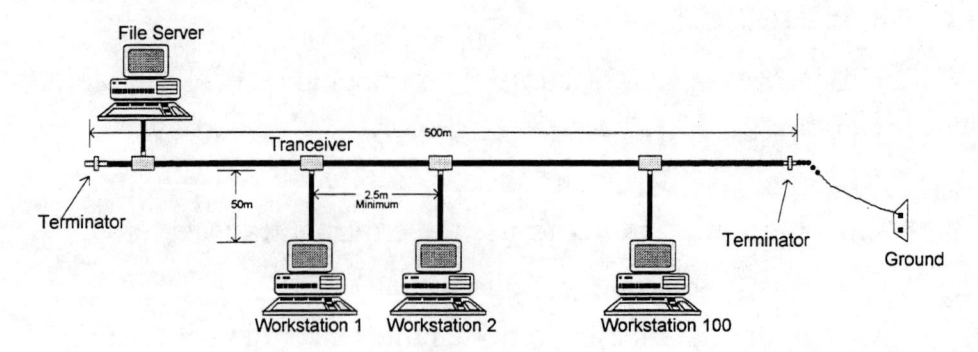

Figure 3-3: Thick Ethernet (10Base5)

10Base2 (Thin-Ethernet)

10Base2 is an inexpensive Ethernet standard that uses thin coax cable with bus topology and offers 10 Mbps speed. 10Base2 is easier to install and cheaper than 10Base5 because it uses thin coax cable and internal transceiver (transceiver is on the NIC).

10Base2 does not support long distances or a large number of stations, but it is a good choice for small LANs.

10Base2 Cabling

The following rules apply for 10Base2 Ethernet cabling:

- 10Base2 uses thin coax cable (RG-58A/U or RG-58C/U) with bus topology.

- Cable impedance is 50 ohms.

- RG-58U should not be used because it does not meet IEEE specification.

- The board is normally set to use the internal transceiver and stations are directly attached to the bus using the T-connectors.

- Minimum distance between two devices is 0.5 meters.

- Maximum length of a trunk segment is 185 meters (607 feet), although some vendors support up to 300 meters.

- Maximum number of nodes on a trunk segment is 30 including repeaters.

- Up to 5 trunk segments may be connected through 4 repeaters.

- Only 3 segments can be used for network nodes. The other 2 are to add distance only.

- Total network distance is 925 meters (3035 feet).

- Both ends of the trunk segment must be terminated with a 50-ohm terminating resistor. One and only one end of the cable should be grounded.

- Repeaters are used to mix 10Base2, 10Base5, and fiber-optic. If repeaters are used the Signal Quality Error (SQE), also called "heartbeat", test on the card must be turned off.

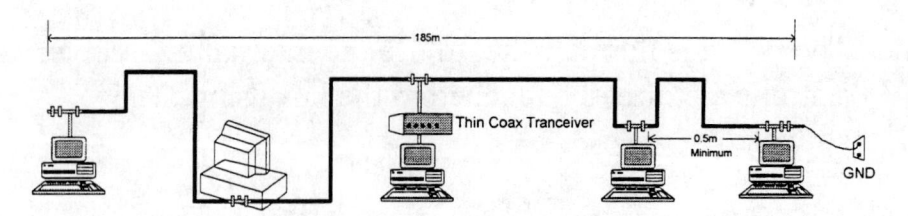

Figure 3-4: Thin-Ethernet (10Base2)

10BaseT (Twisted Pair Ethernet)

- 10BaseT offers a modular approach to the construction of a LAN. A 10BaseT network can be expanded in stages. 10BaseT uses inexpensive unshielded twisted pair (UTP) cable. Standard 10BaseT cables consist of two, three, four, or six twisted pairs with a solid copper core. Data-grade phone cabling (level 3 or better) may also be used.

- 10BaseT cables should have the proper number of twists per foot to prevent "crosstalk". 10BaseT is very susceptible to electromagnetic interference (EMI).

- Devices are connected to a central concentrator in a star configuration.

- Data rate is 10Mbps.

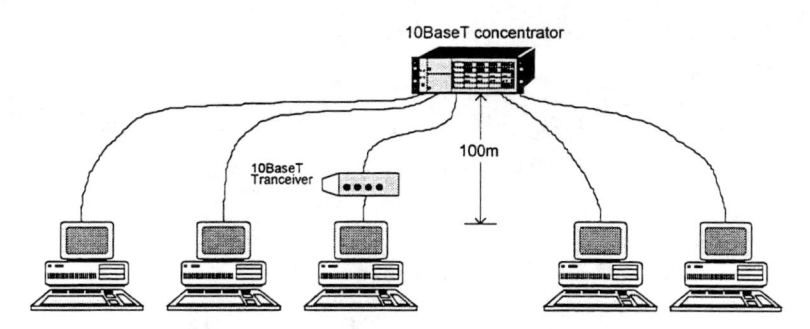

Figure 3-5: Twisted Pair Ethernet (10BaseT)

10BaseT Cabling

The wire used for 10BaseT should be AWG (American Wire Gauge) #22, #24, or #26. The impedance should be 85 to 115 ohms.

The length of a segment (cable from concentrator to node) must be between 0.6 to 100 meters.

A 10BaseT network can have 5 segments using 4 concentrators. It means between two PCs there may be up to four concentrators. This is called 5-4 rule. Note that 5-4-3 rule (only 3 populated segments) does not apply for 10BaseT. A segment can have up to 512 nodes. A network can have a maximum of 1024 nodes.

Note: UTP (10BaseT), thin coax cable (10Base2), and thick coax cable (10Base5) segments can be connected using special transceivers.

External transceiver is used with 10Base5 network but it may also be used with 10Base2 or 10BaseT network.

A new Ethernet Standard is called 10BaseF that uses fiber optic cable and supports greater distance.

Setting Ethernet Boards

You can buy Ethernet cards for 10Base5, 10Base2, or 10BaseT cabling. Some cards offer more than one cabling options (called combo cards). In this case you will set the card for the proper connector type. Ethernet NIC has one (or more) of the following connectors:

- A 15-pin DIX (Digital, Intel, Xerox) connector to work with thick cabling. This connector is for the external transceiver. Board must be set to bypass the internal transceiver.

- A BNC (Bayonet Neill-Concelman) T-connector to work with thin cabling. In this case, the board uses the internal transceiver.

- An RJ-45 connector for 10BaseT cabling.

Ethernet boards are pre-addressed from the factory. They have settings for interrupt level and base I/O address, but they do not use a base memory address setting.

Preamble	Start Frame Delimiter	Destination Address	Source Address	Length	LLC INFO. and Data	FCS
Bytes 7	1	2 or 6	2 or 6	2	46 - 1500	4

Figure 3-6: IEEE 802.3 Frame Format

Ethernet frame fields are described in Appendix A.

Ethernet Frame Types

In the networking world, networks often use a variation of Ethernet protocols (frame types). For example, NetWare 3.11 or below networks use the Ethernet_802.3 (raw) frame type by default while NetWare 3.12 uses the Ethernet_802.2 (Ethernet_802.3 with an 802.2 sublayer, the IEEE 802.3 standard) frame type by default. Ethernet_802.3 was developed before the IEEE 802.3 standard. It does not use the IEEE 802.2 sublayer and, therefore, is not fully IEEE 802.3 compatible. Many non-Novell networks, such as UNIX networks or DECnet, use the Ethernet II (Ethernet DIX II) frame type. Another variation of Ethernet frame is Ethernet_SNAP (Sub-Network Address Protocol) used on AppleTalk (EtherTalk) networks.

To communicate, server and stations must use the same frame type. NetWare v3.12 or v4.x supports different frame types to support different clients on the network. The frame types and transport protocols supported by NetWare are summarized in the following table.

Frame Type	Communication Protocols Supported
Ethernet_802.2	IPX, TCP/IP
Ethernet_802.3	IPX
Ethernet_SNAP	AppleTalk, TCP/IP
Ethernet_II	IPX/SPX, TCP/IP

Setting Up a NetWare Server for Multiple Frame Types

You specify the frame type with the FRAME option when loading the LAN driver. By default, it is Ethernet_802.2. You can use multiple network boards, each with its own frame type, or you can use one board to support multiple frame types.

To use the Ethernet_802.3 frame type, you would issue the commands at the console prompt like this:

    Load NE2000 INT=3 PORT=300 FRAME=Ethernet_802.3

    Bind IPX to NE2000 NET=AAA1

To support both the Ethernet_802.2 and Ethernet_802.3 frame types using the same board, you would issue the commands like this:

    Load NE2000 INT=3 PORT=300 FRAME=Ethernet_802.2

    Bind IPX to NE2000 NET=AAA1

    Load NE2000 INT=3 PORT=300 FRAME=Ethernet_802.3

    Bind IPX to NE2000 NET=BBB1

These commands should be placed in the AUTOEXEC.NCF file.

Note that although the two protocols are supported by the same board (INT and PORT settings are the same), the Network address (NET) is different.

Troubleshooting an Ethernet Network

- Make sure all the network parts are physically connected and within the manufacturer's specification.

- Terminators should be checked for proper resistance with a Volt-Ohm-Milliameter. It is a common mistake to use ARCnet 93-ohm terminators in place of Ethernet 50-ohm terminators.

- Cable continuity testing devices should be used to make sure cables are intact. The COMCHECK utility can also be used.

- A Time Domain Reflectometer (TDR) can be used to detect cable problems such as crimps, shorts, or breaks.

- A bad transceiver can create problems on the cable. Swap the transceiver or card (if transceiver is in the card) to isolate the problem.

- Make sure to set up the workstation and the file server for the same Ethernet frame type(s).

- Use the diagnostics disk that accompanies the NIC to test the card without having to remove it.

- To isolate the problem take out all the other cards except the network card from the PC and put one card back at a time.

- Make sure there is no interrupt conflict. Ethernet, by default, uses interrupt 3 that is also used for COM2. It can create problems if you are using COM2 (usually for modem). In this case, you may change Ethernet card interrupt to 5. Make sure you also change the interrupt in the NET.CFG file or in IPX so your software can communicate with your card.

Note: Protocol analyzers (such as LANalyzer for Windows) can be used to troubleshoot an Ethernet network for difficult problems.

Token Ring

The IEEE 802.5 Token Ring standard is a sophisticated LAN technology that uses the token-passing cable access method in a ring topology and offers 4 or 16 Mbps speed.

IBM played a major role in popularity of Token Ring networks. IBM's specifications for a Token Ring architecture differ somewhat from the official IEEE 802.5 specifications. Our discussion about Token Ring mostly refers to IBM Token Ring.

Up to 260 nodes (IEEE 802.5 standard supports a maximum of 250 nodes) can be connected in a ring using Multi-Station Access Units (MSAUs or MAUs) or Controlled Access Units (CAUs).

MSAUs are passive devices that do not require electrical power and do not have internal intelligence. CAUs need electrical power and have intelligence to participate in network management (called Active Devices).

Nodes are connected to a MSAU or CAU using lobe drop cables. Each node has its own dedicated cable. This configuration or topology looks like a star configuration and that is why it is also referred to as star-wired ring topology.

The IBM 8228 MSAU has eight ports to connect eight nodes (some vendors support more than eight ports). Each MSAU also has Ring In (RI) and Ring Out (RO) ports to connect multiple MSAUs. When you connect multiple MSAUs, you connect all of them in a physical ring using RI and RO ports. Connect the RO of the first MSAU to the RI of the second MSAU and so forth. Connect the RO of the last MSAU to the RI of the first MSAU.

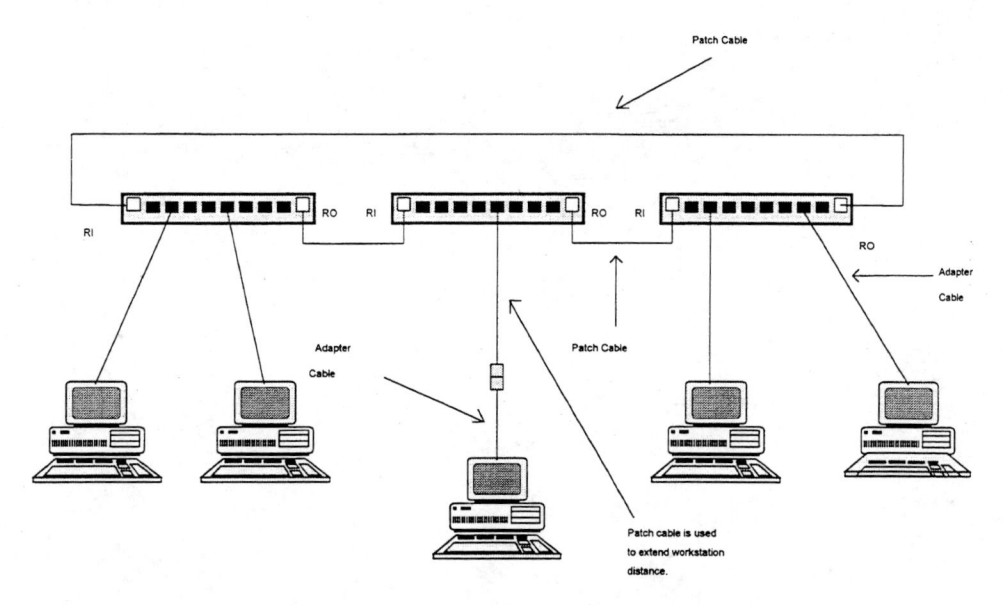

Figure 3-7: Token Ring Network

You do not use RI and RO ports if only one MSAU is used. In this case an internal (inside of MSAU) physical ring is used.

MSAUs have internal relays to maintain the continuity of the ring. An empty port, an off workstation or a failed workstation, is bypassed using a relay (relay is closed). When a station is connected and turned on, a five-volt signal (called a "phantom signal") is sent by the Token Ring card. This signal opens the relay for the lobe to become part of the ring, thus initializing the port. You will hear a click. In case the NIC is unable to open the relay, a set-up aid device (a device provided with the MSAU) can be used to initialize the port.

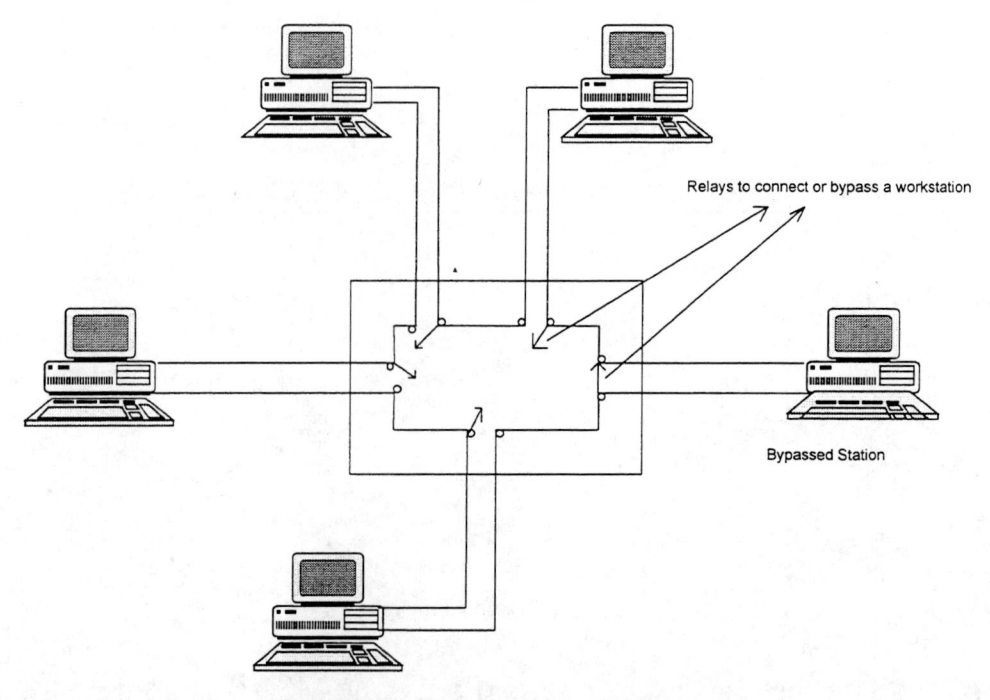

Figure 3-8: Star Wiring And Bypass Switches

Token Ring Advantages

1. It provides excellent throughput (performance) under heavy load conditions (heavy network usage).

2. It is easy to connect with IBM mainframe or mini systems.

3. It has built-in troubleshooting and fault tolerance features such as beaconing and automatic ring reconfiguration.

Token Ring Disadvantages

1. It is very expensive when compared to Ethernet and ARCnet.

2. Token Ring networks are complicated and difficult to troubleshoot. The major disadvantage is that each node on the ring must handle the data being transferred (each node is working as a unidirectional repeater). If by chance one node on the ring fails to transfer the data (malfunctioning), that failure could interrupt the network operation.

Token Ring Operation

Transmission on a Token Ring network is controlled by the token-passing media (cable) access method. In a Token Ring network a token (a three-byte packet) is circulated in the ring to give each node a chance to transmit. When a node receives a token (called a "free" token), it adds data to the token making it a data/command frame or packet. This packet may also be considered a "busy" token, but it is actually not a token anymore. Tokens are only needed to transmit not to receive.

Only one token is allowed in a ring at a time. Each node in the ring works as a unidirectional repeater and passes the data (token frame or data/command frame) to the next active node on the ring. The destination node also copies the data to its memory and reverses two bits of the frame to indicate that it has recognized the address and copied the data before regenerating it.

The original source node eventually receives the data/command packet and removes it from the ring. In a 4 Mbps Token Ring, the node first removes the data/command packet, regenerates the token, and then passes it on to the next node. In a 16 Mbps network, the node issues a new token after sending the last bit of its data/command frame. This is called the "early release of token". There may be multiple frames on the ring at the same time, but there is always only one token in the ring.

Active Monitor

One station in the ring acts as an active monitor. It performs ring maintenance functions like removing the frame that the original node has failed to remove, etc. Usually the first workstation is the active monitor. Automatic procedures can make any station an active monitor. Other stations in a ring are known as standby monitors.

IEEE 802.5 Frame Format

Data/Command Frame

Starting Delimiter	Access Control	Frame Control	Destination Address	Source Address	Data	FCS	Ending Delimiter	Frame Status
Bytes: 1	1	1	2 or 6	2 or 6	>=0	4	1	1

Token

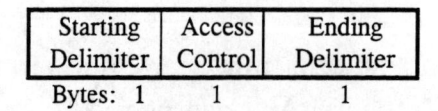

Starting Delimiter	Access Control	Ending Delimiter
Bytes: 1	1	1

Abort

Starting Delimiter	Ending Delimiter
Bytes: 1	1

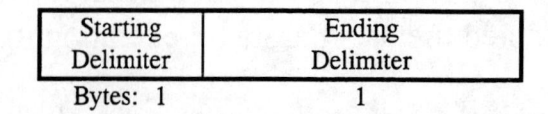

Figure 3-9: IEEE 802.5 Frame Format

Token Ring frame fields are described in Appendix A.

Token Ring Cabling

Two types of cables are used in a Token Ring network: adapter cables and patch cables.

Adapter Cable

Adapter cables are used to connect the workstation to the MSAU. Adapter cable is usually made of IBM Type 6 cable and has an IBM hermaphroditic cable connector on one side and an adapter card connector on the other side.

Adapter cables are also available with other types of IBM cables and connectors.

Patch Cable

Patch cables are used to connect MSAUs to each other (using the RI and RO ports). This cable is usually made of IBM Type 6 cable and has IBM's hermaphroditic cable connectors on both sides. It is also used to extend the adapter cable distance from workstation to MSAU.

Patch cables are also available with other types of cables and connectors.

Token Ring Over Unshielded Twisted Pair

IBM Token Ring originally supported only Shielded Twisted Pair (STP) cable. Now MSAUs are available that accept both Type 1 STP and Type 3 UTP cabling. A new IEEE specification for UTP (level 5 wire, not to be confused with IBM Type 5) at 16 Mbps is replacing the old 4Mbps specification. Token Ring over UTP is becoming very popular because most companies already have UTP installed. For sites where EMI is a problem and/or a greater distance is needed, Type 1 cable is still the media of choice.

Distance Limitations

- Maximum distance between MSAU and workstation is 100 meters.

- A typical maximum distance between two MSAUs is 45 meters (without repeaters or converters).

- The maximum length of patch cable connecting all MSAUs in a ring is 120 meters.

Token Ring Cable Types

Type 1 cable is made of braided cables shielded around two twisted pairs of #22 American Wire Gauge (AWG) copper. Type 1 is used for interconnection among terminal devices and distribution panels, and to connect wiring closets.

Type 2 is basically the same as Type 1 with one addition. It has four twisted pairs of telephone conductors so it can be used for data and voice communications. It is used for the same purpose as Type 1.

Type 3 is unshielded solid copper twisted pair (#22 or #24 AWG). It has at least two twists per foot. Type 3 is cheaper than STP cable but it is susceptible to EMI. Type 3 does not achieve 16 Mbps speed.

Type 5 is fiber-optic and is used on the main ring path only.

Type 6 is shielded twisted pair. The loss per unit length is higher than Type 1 or Type 2 (Type 1 or Type 2 supports greater distances than Type 6). It is mostly used for patch and adapter cables.

Type 8 is used for data communication under carpeted floors.

Type 9 is a fire-retardant version of Type 6.

Beaconing

We have briefly discussed before the role of the Active Monitor in ring maintenance. The Active Monitor sends out a frame to the next active computer in the ring every seven seconds. The next active computer sends this frame to the next active computer and so on. Therefore each computer in the ring knows who the Active Monitor is and that the ring is functioning O.K.

The computer that sends a frame to the next active computer is called the Nearest Active Upstream Neighbor (NAUN) of the next active computer.

If a computer does not receive a frame from its NAUN in seven seconds, it starts sending a beacon frame that defines a failure or fault domain.

The beacon frame includes the sending computer address, its NAUN address, and the type of beacon. The fault domain includes the computer reporting the failure, the NAUN, and everything in between.

The beacon frame also initiates a process called autoreconfiguration. The nodes within the fault domain attempt to reconfigure the network around the failed area without administrator intervention (the node disconnects itself from the ring if it finds error in itself).

Beaconing problems require administrator intervention, for example, to examine the addresses and diagnose the problem.

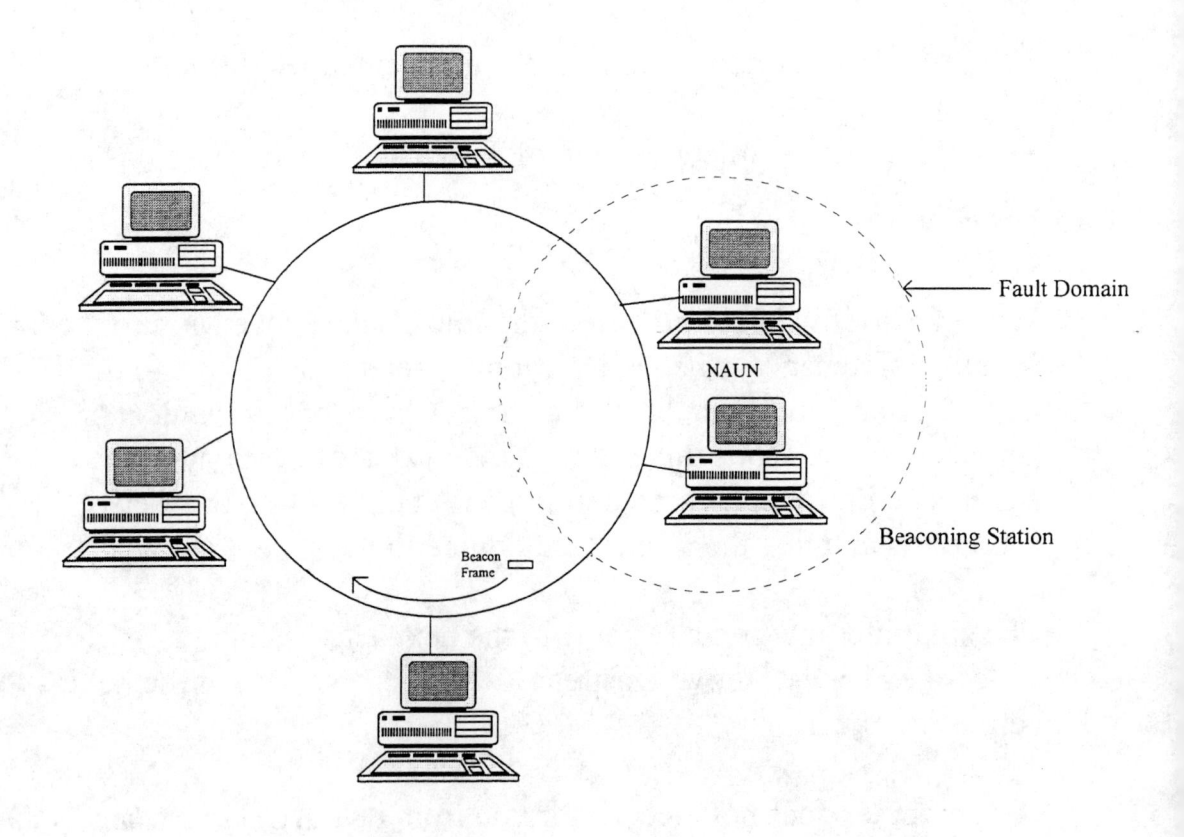

Figure 3-10: Beaconing Process

Troubleshooting Tips

- Do not mix 4 Mbps cards and 16 Mbps cards in the same ring. Speed is displayed on the workstation screen when you load the Token Ring driver.

- Avoid using MSAUs from different vendors on the ring.

- If you are using two Token Ring cards in a computer, make sure both cards are using different parameters.

- Make sure all ports in an MSAU are properly initialized. Use the Set-up Aid device if needed. To troubleshoot a small network that is not using any bridge or router, you should disconnect all cables from the MSAU and reset all the ports.

- Large Token Ring networks can be very difficult to troubleshoot. Maintain an up-to-date physical layout of your network and proper documentation to quickly isolate the problem. Documentation should include the addresses of nodes and their locations.

  Some companies use their own addressing scheme to quickly find out the location of a beaconing node. It is not recommended that you use your own addressing schemes. You should use the Token Ring card address burned into ROM at the factory. In case you are using your own address, make sure your address does not conflict with another node and is within the legal range of your card manufacturer.

Note: IEEE assigns the first three bytes to each NIC manufacturer. You can override the NIC factory address by using the NET.CFG file.

ARCnet

ARCnet (Attached Resource Computer Network) is a simple and reliable network architecture for small LANs. It specifies the lower two layers of the OSI model. ARCnet, the oldest of the popular LAN options, was introduced by Data Point Corporation in 1977. It was then licensed to Standard Microsystems Corporation (SMC). ARCnet is now an ANSI (American National Standards Institute) standard (878.1). It may be considered as a token-bus network because it uses the token-passing cable access method in a bus environment, but it should not be confused with IEEE 802.4 Token-Bus standard.

ARCnet's node address is an eight-bit numerical address from 1 to 255 that is usually set with DIP switches. The address "0" is reserved for broadcasts. Each station knows its address (Source IDentifier [SID]) and the address of the next station (Next IDentifier [NID]) to pass the token. The token goes from station to station in ascending address order and the highest address station passes the token to the lowest address station. To maintain a logical ring, ARCnet networks perform auto-reconfiguration or recon whenever there are any changes in the network (like connecting or disconnecting stations).

In **star topology**, active and passive hubs are used to connect nodes. Active hubs usually have 8 ports and passive hubs have 4 ports. Active hubs need electrical power and work like repeaters (that is, they regenerate the signal before distributing). Passive hubs do not need electrical power and merely distribute the signal to their four ports.

ARCnet Network Features

- ARCnet is very reliable and usually does not have vendor compatibility problems. It has been stable enough to provide interoperability, i.e., you can mix ARCnet components from different vendors.

- It is easy to install, expand, and modify.

- ARCnet supports coax RG-62A/U (93 ohm), UTP, and fiber optic cablings in bus and star topologies. Media and topologies can be mixed together.

- ARCnet active hubs are available with built-in diagnostics and LEDs with error troubleshooting.

- ARCnet allows one workstation to directly connect to the file server. To connect more than one station, you must use active or passive hubs (if using star topology).

- Inexpensive and very popular for small LANs.

Disadvantages

- ARCnet is not an IEEE standard, that is why not many third party networking products (management and troubleshooting products, for example) support ARCnet.

For example, LANalyzer For Windows supports Ethernet and Token Ring but not ARCnet.

- ARCnet's speed of 2.5 Mbps is slow.

- ARCnet was not designed to support large networks (maximum number of nodes per network is 255) and interconnectivity.

- ARCnet is not compatible with NetWare SFT III (server mirroring).

ARCnet frame types

ITT (Invitation To Transmit)

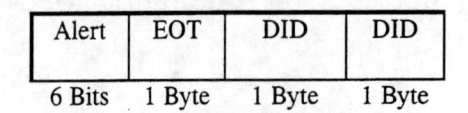

Alert	EOT	DID	DID
6 Bits	1 Byte	1 Byte	1 Byte

FBE (Free Buffer Enquiry)

Alert	ENQ	DID	DID
6 Bits	1 Byte	1 Byte	1 Byte

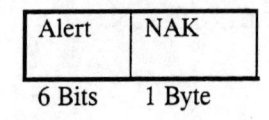

ACK (Acknowledgment)

Alert	NAK
6 Bits	1 Byte

NAK (Negative Acknowledgment)

Alert	NAK
6 Bits	1 Byte

PAC (Packet or Data)

Alert	SOH	SID	DID	DID	Count	Data	CRC
6 bits 1 Byte	1 Byte	1 Byte	1 Byte		1-2 Bytes	1-508 Bytes	2 Bytes

Figure 3-11: ARCnet Frame Types

ARCnet Transmission

Each ARCnet frame starts with an alert, six consecutive 1s, to synchronize all the receivers. To transmit the data, a node seizes the ITT frame (token) and sends the FBE frame to its destination. If the destination can accept the data frame, it replies with an ACK frame; otherwise it replies with a NAK frame. If the source receives an ACK, it sends a data (PAC) frame. The destination returns an ACK to the source for each data frame it receives correctly. No response is sent if the data frame is not received correctly.

ARCnet Frame Fields

The ITT frame starts with an ASCII EOT (End of Transmission), followed by two bytes for the destination address. The destination address (DID), which is actually the NID, is duplicated for error checking.

The FBE frame begins with an ASCII Enquiry.

The PAC or data frame starts with an ASCII SOH (Start Of Header). The 1 or 2 byte count field indicates the number of bytes in a data field.

ARCnet Cabling (Coax cable)

- The maximum distance from one network end to the other end (entire network length) is 20,000 feet.

- The maximum distance from active hub to node or from active hub to active hub is 2,000 feet.

- Unused active hub ports need not be terminated, but unused passive hub ports must be terminated with a 93 ohm terminator.

- A passive hub cannot connect to another passive hub.

- A passive hub cannot connect two active hubs. Passive hubs connect workstations to an active hub.

- Maximum distance from passive hub to active hub or workstation is 100 feet.

Twisted Pair ARCnet
- The maximum cable length can be up to 400 feet.

- The maximum number of stations on a cable can be 32.

- The cable should be #22-24 AWG made up of solid copper. The impedance should be 105 ohms.

- The minimum number of twists per foot is 2.

Fiber Optic ARCnet
Fiber Optic ARCnet supports greater distance.

ARCnet Bus with UTP
When using **bus topology** with UTP, you can daisy-chain it from node to node. In this case, the maximum length of the trunk cable can be 1000 feet. Remember to terminate both ends of cable when using bus topology. Some boards have built-in terminators that

can be set using jumpers for the last nodes on the cable (end nodes).

You can also use coax cable in bus topology using BNC T-connectors.

Setting ARCnet Boards

Each ARCnet board must be set to a unique node address with a DIP switch or using configuration software. Addresses may be from 1 to 255. Most boards have jumpers to set the base memory and the base I/O address. Usually you do not have to change these settings. The factory defaults work fine in most situations. ARCnet boards may have BNC connectors for coax cable and RJ11 telephone jacks for twisted-pair cable.

We may also set the time-out in ARCnet boards. The default is 31 microseconds. This is the time a board will listen before it assumes the next node is no longer there. Increasing this time will allow a network to be longer than 20,000 feet, but the network communication will be slower.

Note: Not all ARCnet boards support time-out settings.

How to set ARCnet Node Address using Switches

In an ARCnet NIC eight switches are used to set the node ID. Each node attached to the network must have a unique node ID. **A node ID of zero is not permitted.**

An explanation of how to set the switches to correspond to a particular node ID is given below:

Switch 1 serves as the least significant bit (LSB) for the node ID (for most cards). Note that the decimal value of each switch is shown below to simplify the conversion of the node ID from decimal to binary.

For example, to set the node ID to 23 decimal, find the numbers in the "Decimal Value" row in the box below that add up to 23 (23 = 16 + 4 + 2 + 1). Set those switches to the OFF position and the remaining switches to the ON position.

Example: Set a node ID of 23

Node ID = 23 (decimal) = 1 + 2 + 4 + 16 = 11101000

LSB ⇩

Switches	1	2	3	4	5	6	7	8
Off/Open	1	1	1	-	1	-	-	-
On/Closed	-	-	-	0	-	0	0	0
Decimal Value	1	2	4	8	16	32	64	128

Example: Set a node ID of 183.

Node ID = 183 (decimal) = 1 + 2 + 4 + 16 + 32 + 128 = 11101101

Switches	1	2	3	4	5	6	7	8
Off/Open	1	1	1	-	1	1	-	1
On/Closed	-	-	-	0	-	-	0	-
Decimal Value	1	2	4	8	16	32	64	128

© 1993 - 96 · PC Age, Inc. All Rights Reserved · 20 Audrey Place · Fairfield, NJ 07004 · U.S.A. · Tel: 201-882-5370

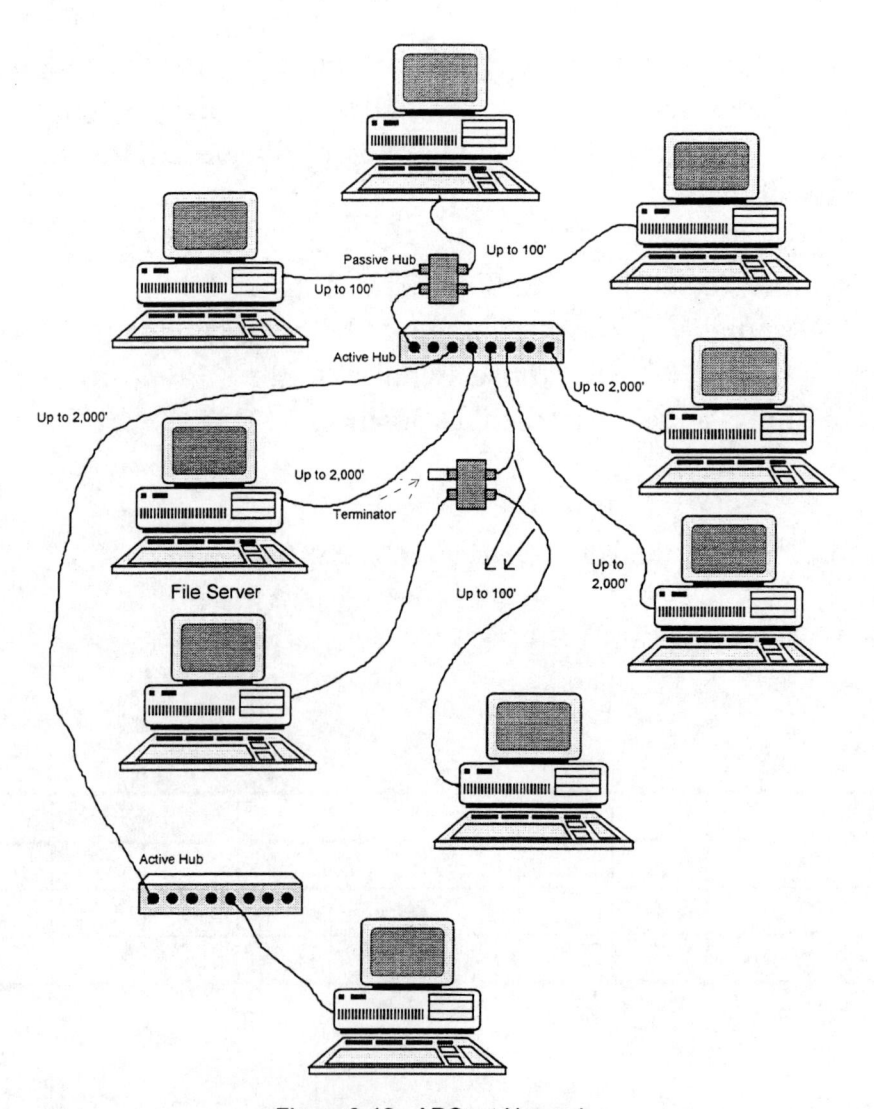

Figure 3-12: ARCnet Network

Troubleshooting Tips

- Major problem with ARCnet networks is duplicate node addresses. If only two workstations are having network access problems, check the node addresses of both workstations. To set node addresses, check your vendor's documentation.

- Always terminate unused ports on a passive hub using 93 ohm resistors.

- Active hub ports are self-terminating if unused and you do not need to terminate them. It is a good idea to terminate unused ports using 93 ohm resistors to avoid difficult to find errors.

- A good advantage of ARCnet is the use of inexpensive passive hubs. Some vendors do not support passive hubs, so avoid using ARCnet hardware from these vendors.

- Do not connect two active hubs in a ring.

ARCnet Plus

ARCnet Plus is a 20 Mbps version of ARCnet. It is backward compatible with ARCnet and uses the same coax cable.

Thomas Conrad Network System (TCNS)

A high speed derivation of standard ARCnet is TCNS. TCNS uses the same coax cabling (RG-62 A/U) and provides speed up to 100 Mbps. It is the least expensive solution if you are looking to upgrade a 2.5 Mbps ARCnet to a 100 Mbps network specially because it uses the same type of coax cabling. TCNS is also much less expensive than 100 Mbps FDDI.

FDDI

The FDDI (Fiber Distributed Data Interface) was developed by the ANSI X3T9.5 committee. It is based on the use of optical fiber cable and a token-passing ring configuration operating at the data rate of 100 Mbps.

Like IEEE 802.3 (Ethernet), 802.4 (Token Bus), and 802.5 (Token Ring), FDDI includes Physical layer and MAC sublayer specifications and assumes the use of the IEEE 802.2 (LLC) standard operating above the MAC layer (it can also use other upper layer protocols).

A new form of FDDI is CDDI (Copper Distributed Data Interface) which uses copper (UTP) instead of fiber and supports shorter distances as compared to FDDI. CDDI is also known as TP-PMD (Twisted Pair - Physical Medium Dependent). There are yet no official standards for CDDI. CDDI is much less expensive than FDDI but it does not offer the same security or immunity to interference as FDDI does.

The FDDI standard was developed to deal with the requirements associated with three types of networks:

- Backend Local Networks or Computer-Room Networks. These networks are used to interconnect mainframes, minicomputers, and large data storage devices.

- High speed office networks. These LANs connect engineering workstations and computers with image and graphics processing applications.

- Backbone Networks: These high-capacity networks, can be used to interconnect lower-capacity LANs.

FDDI Characteristics

- FDDI is very similar to IEEE 802.5 (Token Ring) and uses ring topology (Star-wired ring topology like Token Ring).

- Uses dual counter-rotating rings. The primary ring is for data, the secondary ring is idle under normal conditions. If the primary ring fails, FDDI automatically routes traffic in the opposite direction on to the secondary ring. This fault tolerance feature is called wrapping.

- Stations (file servers, workstations, bridges, routers, etc.) can be connected to both rings (called class A stations) or to only one ring (called class B stations). Only class A stations participate in the ring reconfiguration process if there is a primary ring failure.

- Maximum number of stations is 1000 and maximum cable length is 200 Kilometers. Recommended maximums for Class A stations is 500 stations and 100 Kilometers. Because in case of primary ring failure each Class A station will be counted as two and length of the entire ring will double (primary + secondary).

Troubleshooting & Supporting Networks

FDDI

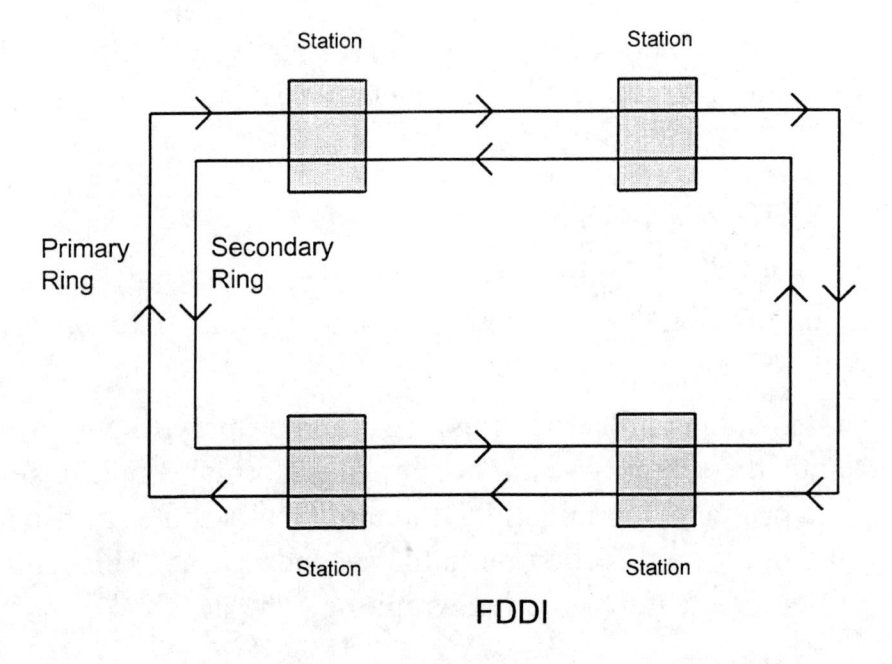

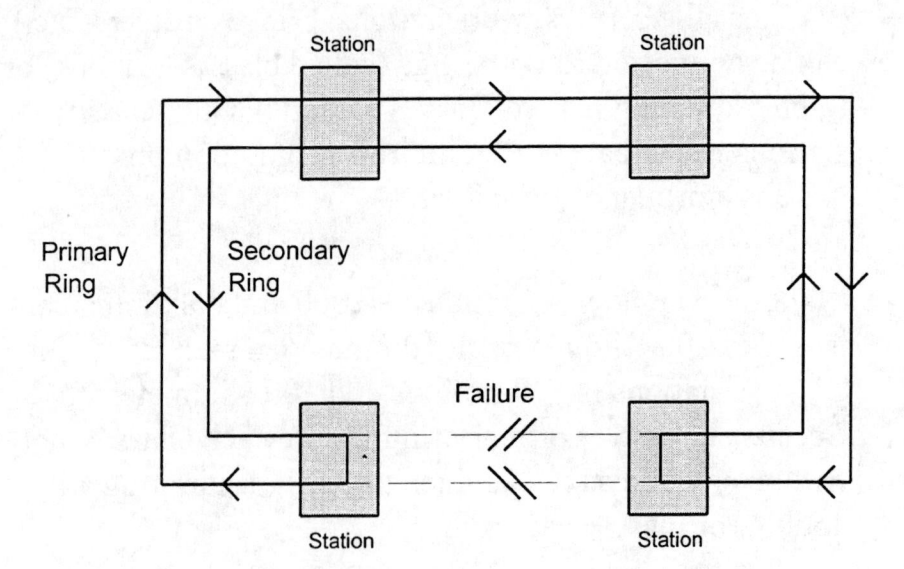

Figure 3-13: FDDI Failure and Network Reconfiguration

Advantages of FDDI

- FDDI is a fast network (100 Mbps) and supports large distances (up to 200 Km).

- It has built-in management features.

- The medium (fiber-optic cable) is extremely reliable and secure.

- Immune to electrical interference or EMI because it uses light for transmission. It also maintains ground isolation between buildings.

Disadvantages of FDDI

- FDDI is very expensive.

- Special expertise is needed to install and maintain the FDDI network.

FDDI Token-Passing Process

The FDDI token-passing process is similar to that of IEEE 802.5. FDDI releases a new token at the end of the transmitted frame to provide a high data-rate. There may be multiple frames on the network at a given time. However, there is only one token on the network. FDDI frames can vary between 17 and 4500 bytes in length.

Management Features

Like IEEE 802.5, FDDI supports the "claim token" process and beaconing.

Troubleshooting Tips

- Select the type of fiber optic cable according to your needs. The type of fiber optic cable varies with the distance. Multimode fiber is the most popular for LAN cabling. Single-mode fiber is the most expensive and is used to cover longer distances and higher speeds.

- Optical Time Domain Reflectometer (OTDR) is used to test fiber optic cables. A less expensive optical power meter and a known source of light energy can also be used. To test for a complete break in the cable, a flashlight can be used.

- If OTDR or optical power meter shows a loss of optical power greater than 13.0 decibels, check for bad connections or an open cable condition.

- Looking at the active fiber optic cable can damage the eye.

- Dirty connectors can cause problems because FDDI uses light for data transmissions.

- Plastic Fiber Optic cable is much more flexible than glass cable but cannot be used for a distance greater than 50 meters or when a throughput of over 10 Mbps is desired.

ATM

ATM (Asynchronous Transfer Mode) is an emerging packet-switching standard. ATM provides very high bandwidths (155.52 Mbps to 2.488 Gbps) for a variety of traffic (voice, data, video) over LAN/MAN/WAN.

ATM supported only fiber optic cables in the beginning. It now also supports UTP.

ATM proposals, as applied to a LAN environment, include use as a backbone connecting servers and as a switch (router) connecting LANs. Eventually ATM could move into individual computers on the network in which case the computer could connect to a WAN. Speeds such as 25 Mbps, 51 Mbps, and 100 Mbps have been mentioned for LANs. ATM for LANs is still under development and standards do not exist right now.

NETWORK SPECIFICATIONS

	ARCnet	Ethernet 10BASE5	Ethernet 10BASE2	Ethernet 10BASET	TOKEN RING	FDDI
Topologies	Bus/Star	Bus	Bus	Star	Ring	Ring
Speed	2.5 Mbps	10 Mbps	10 Mbps	10 Mbps	4 & 16 Mbps	100 Mbps
Transmission Type	Baseband	Baseband	Baseband	Baseband	Baseband	Baseband
Cable Access Method	Token Passing	CSMA/CD	CSMA/CD	CSMA/CD	Token Passing	Token Passing
Hardware (Not Incl. Computers)	NIC Cable Active Hub Passive Hub 93 Ohm Terminator	NIC Repeater External Transceiver DIX Connector Drop Cables 50 Ohm Terminator	NIC with internal transceiver Repeater Cable BNC Connector T- Connector 50 Ohm Terminator	NIC Cable Concentrator	NIC MSAU (IBM 8228 Units) Adapter Cable Patch Cable Setup Aid	NIC Concentrator Fiber Optic Cable
Cabling Options	RG-62 Coax UTP Fiber Optic	RG-8 & RG-11 Thick Ethernet Coax	RG 58A/U or RG 58C/U Thin Coax	UTP	STP UTP	Fiber Optic Multi-mode Single-mode
Network Length (Total)	20,000'	2,500 m (8200 feet)	925 m (3035 feet)	500 m (1640 feet)	120 m (400 feet)	200 km
Segment Length	AH-AH = 2,000' AH-WS = 2,000' AH-PH = 100' PH-WS = 100' PH-PH = Not Allowed	Segment = 500 m	Segment = 185 m	Concentrator-WS = 100 m	Max. Distance MSAU-WS = 100 m MSAU-MSAU = varies	
Nodes (Max. incl. FSs & WSs)	255	300 (incl. repeaters)	90 (incl. repeaters)	1024	260 nodes, 33 MSAUs	1000

Table 3-1

FS	=	File Server	MSAU	=	Multistation Access Unit
WS	=	Workstation	NIC	=	Network Interface Card
AH	=	Active Hub	m	=	Meter
PH	=	Passive Hub	km	=	Kilometer
UTP	=	Unshielded Twisted Pair	Mbps		Mega bits/sec
STP	=	Shielded Twisted Pair			

Computer Bus Architecture and Card Compatibility

When you buy computer cards (NIC or controller, etc.) you buy according to your computer's bus architecture to avoid incompatibility problems and to get the best performance.

Important points about bus architecture and card compatibility are :

- The Industry Standard Architecture (ISA) was introduced by IBM with IBM PC/AT computer. The AT ISA bus offers 8-bit or 16-bit data transfer slots. ISA bus is backward compatible with 8-bit IBM XT bus so IBM XT 8-bit card can be used in ISA slots. Each ISA slot supports an 8-bit card with one edge connector. 16-bit cards are supported through a slot extension connector (a second shorter edge connector). 16-bit slots support 8-bit cards but you can not fit 16-bit cards in 8-bit slots.

    Note: some older cards are 4.8 inches tall and may not fit in new computers that support only 4.2 inches tall cards.

- EISA (Extended Industry Standard Architecture) computers use 32-bit slots that are downward compatible with 16-bit and 8-bit ISA cards. You can use ISA cards in EISA computers but you will not get the full benefit of EISA computers unless you use 32-bit cards.

- MCA (Micro Channel Architecture) cards are totally incompatible with ISA, EISA, and other non-MCA standards. MCA computers have both the 16-bit short and 32-bit long slots.

- The new bus architecture called **Local Bus** allows display (video) devices and disk controllers to communicate with the processor and system RAM at the speed of the processor (the actual I/O speed; for example, if a system is using 66 MHz 486DX2 chip, its I/O speed is 33 MHz. VESA local bus can only run at up to 33 MHz. PCI local bus can run at up to 66 MHz currently. VESA local bus and PCI are discussed below). ISA 16-bit and EISA 32-bit bus architectures are limited to 8 MHz of the main bus speed.

Two local bus standards are **VESA Local Bus (VLB)**, from the Video Electronics Standards Association (VESA) and **PCI** (Peripheral Component Interconnect), from Intel.

The VLB connectors are placed in line with existing ISA connectors on the system board.

VLB slots are downward compatible with both 8-bit and 16-bit ISA boards. It means you can put ISA cards in local bus slots, but then the cards will not be using local bus. A VLB card in VLB slot bypasses the main system bus.

VLB does not offer software setup of boards or bus mastering as offered by MCA and EISA. In general, bus mastering is a bus-access method in which a board or device takes control of the bus to send data onto the bus directly, without help of CPU. It greatly increases the performance.

Intel's PCI is a newer and faster 64-bit bus standard. An ISA or EISA card can not fit in PCI slot, but a PC can support ISA, EISA, and PCI slots all on the same motherboard. PCI supports bus mastering boards and software setup like MCA and EISA.

Local bus 32-bit designs (VLB v1.0 or PCI (32-bit)) provide a data transfer throughput of about 132 MB/second at 33 MHz processor speed (which is also the speed of the bus). Local bus 64-bit designs (VLB v2.0 or PCI (64-bit)) can transfer data at up to about 264 MB/second at 33 MHz processor speed. Compare this with 8 MB/second ISA, 33 MB/second EISA, 40 MB/second MCA data transfer throughputs.

Currently local bus designs are used to speed up computer graphic displays and disk I/O, very soon local bus will be used for full-motion video and network interfaces.

- The **PCMCIA** (Personal Computer Memory Card International Association) bus standard allows small (credit card) size boards in a notebook (laptop) or low power desktop computer.

  Unlike other buses, PCMCIA bus allows to remove or install a PCMCIA card on the fly, without rebooting the computer.

  PCMCIA requires software setup. It does not support bus mastering.

  PCMCIA data path is only 16-bits (version 2) and speed is limited to 33 MHz.

Troubleshooting & Supporting Networks

Exercise 3-1

Q.1. What is wrong in the following figures ?

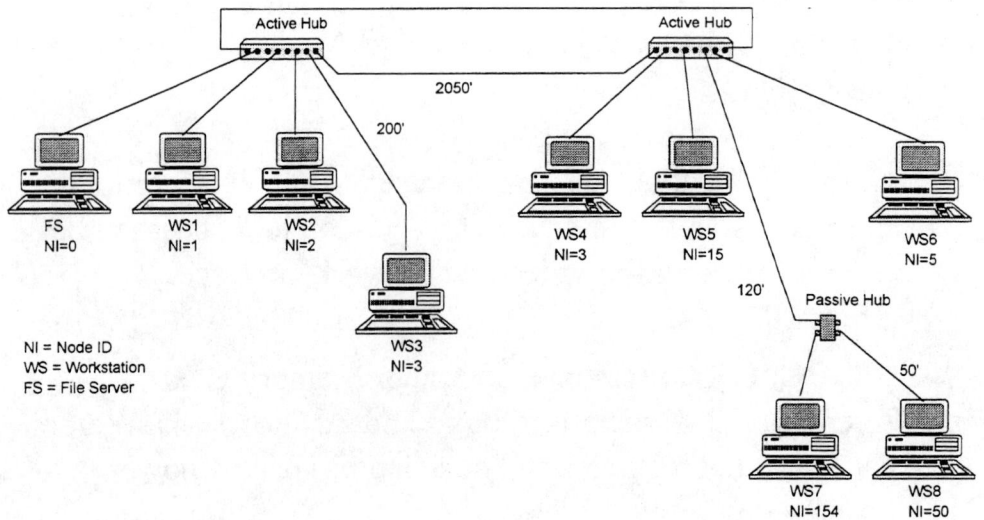

A.

- Distance between the two Active Hubs is 2050' (exceeds maximum allowed).
- WS3 has NI=3, which is a duplicate of WS4 (NI=3).
- WS5 has NI=15 (duplicate not required, but check valid range).
- FS has NI=0 (invalid node ID).
- WS7 has NI=154 (exceeds valid range).
- Distance from Passive Hub to Active Hub is 120' (exceeds maximum allowed for passive hub segment).
- Passive Hub connected to another Passive Hub / or cascaded improperly.

NI = Node ID
WS = Workstation
FS = File Server

B.

- Trunk segment is 180m (exceeds maximum 185m? — check length).
- Only one end of the trunk is terminated/grounded; the other end missing terminator.
- Multiple grounds on the same segment (should be grounded at only one point).
- 250m segment exceeds the maximum allowed length (185m for thin Ethernet).

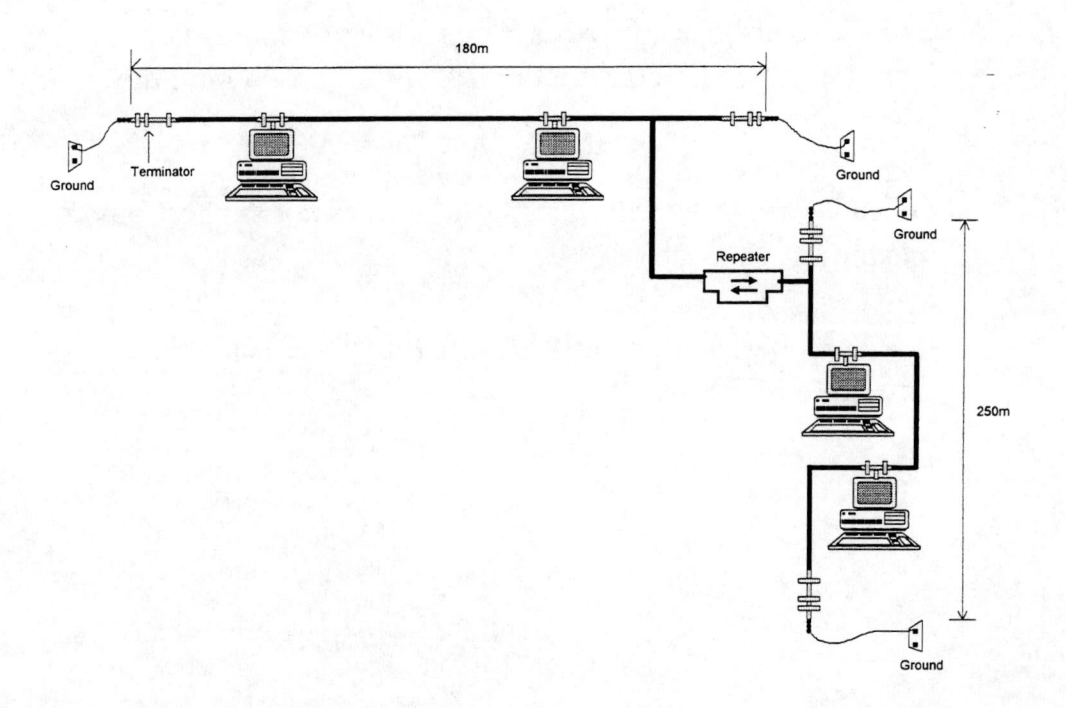

Chapter 3: Network Boards and Cabling

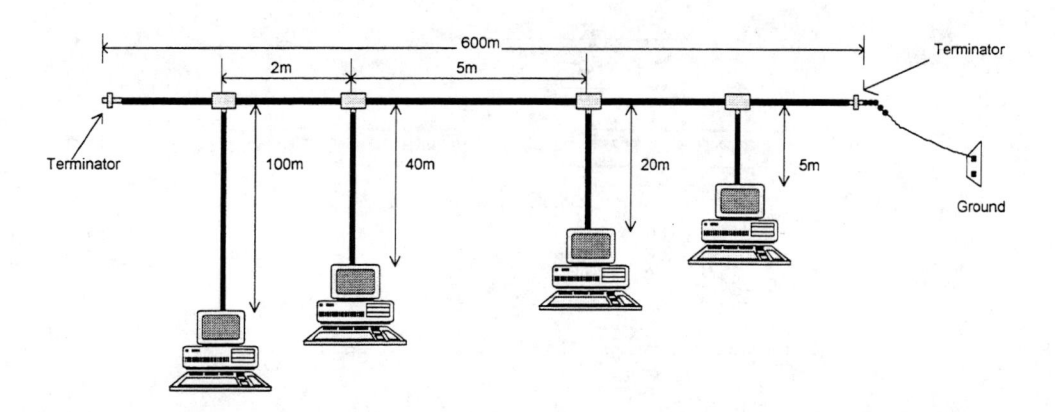

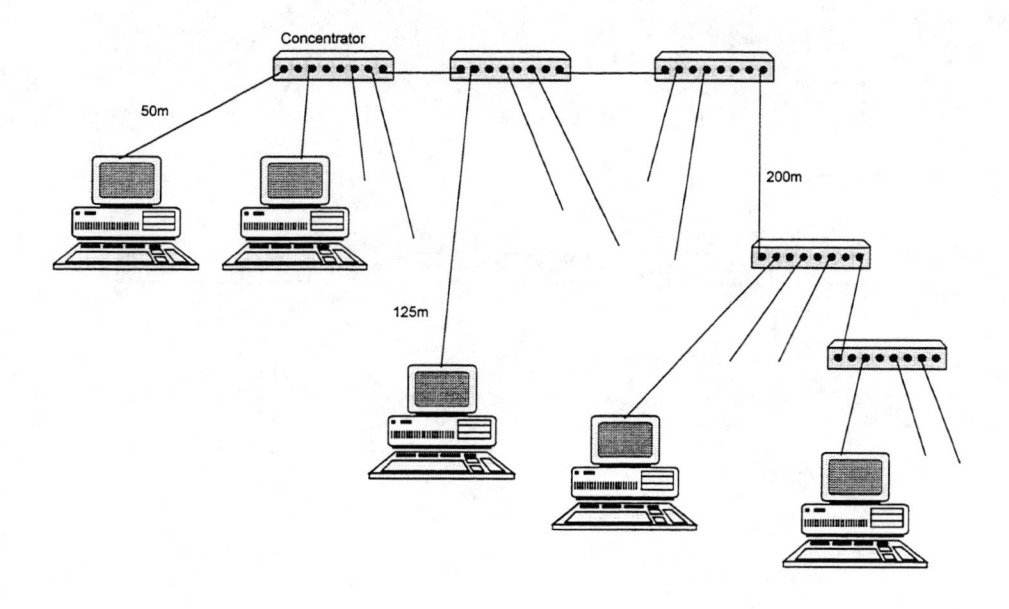

C.

D.

Q.2. Which of the following configurations are correct ?

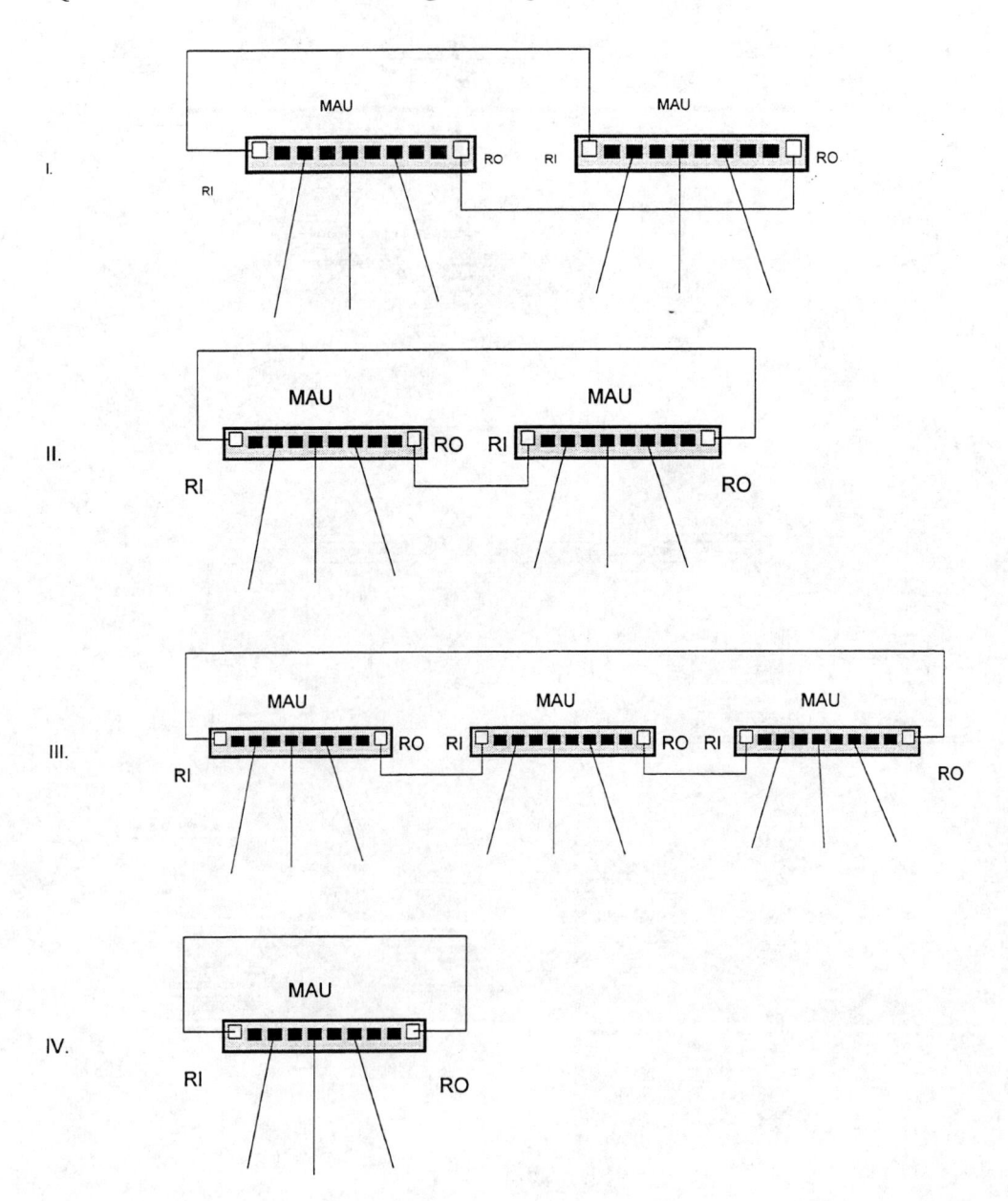

I.

II.

III.

IV.

Exercise 3-2

Set an ARCnet node ID of 56.

Troubleshooting Exercises

Problem 1: File server and workstation are directly connected without using a hub in 10BaseT network.

Procedure:

1. Connect workstation directly to the RJ-45 port on the file server's NIC.

2. Use COMCHECK on both computers (file server should not be up and running). You will see that both computers are not communicating.

3. Bring up the server and try to connect the workstation to the server. You will have errors.

Go through the same procedure with an ARCnet network. It should work fine (you can directly connect a workstation with a file server in an ARCnet network).

Problem 2: IRQ specified in NET.CFG file does not match with the IRQ set on the NIC.

Procedure:

1. Make a copy of your NET.CFG using a different name. Rename NET.CFG to NET.OLD. Rename copy of NET.CFG to NET.CFG. Change IRQ in NET.CFG file to a different IRQ from what you have set on the NIC. You may need to find out the IRQ setting of your NIC. Use your NIC's configuration software, Check It Pro, or jumpers on the NIC.

2. Try to load the ODI files. If ODI files are loaded already, unload VLM, IPXODI, and LAN driver with -U option. Load LAN driver. You will get an error message.

3. Correct the problem by deleting NET.CFG and renaming NET.OLD to NET.CFG. Try to load the LAN driver. You should not have the problem now.

4. Try the same procedure with the wrong I/O port address.

Problem 3: IRQ conflict.

Procedure:

1. Set the same IRQ for your NIC as used by another device (mouse or modem, for example) on your workstation. You will use Check It Pro to check for IRQs used on your computer. Use your NIC's configuration software (or jumpers) and NET.CFG file to set the IRQ for your NIC.

2. Connect your workstation to the server and log in. You will see either the other device or your NIC is not working properly.

3. Change your NIC's IRQ setting (in the card and in NET.CFG). Now use your workstation. You should not have any problem.

Problem 4: Frame type mismatch (Ethernet network).

>   **Note:** If you are modifying any files, make sure you have a copy of the original.

Procedure:

1. Find out which frame type is used on your workstation. You may want to unload and load the LAN driver for this.

2. Modify (or create) NET.CFG file to specify a different frame type. For example, if your workstation is using Ethernet_802.2, add a line for Ethernet_802.3 in NET.CFG as follows:

   ```
   LINK DRIVER NE2000
       FRAME Ethernet_802.3
       FRAME Ethernet_802.2
   ```

3. Now try to load workstation files. You can do this by first unloading VLM, IPXODI, and NE2000 with -U option and than loading them again. You will not be able to connect to the server.

4. Reverse the problem (delete the line you added) and try to connect. You should not have any problem.

   Note: If your server is setup to support multiple frame types, you may not get any errors. You may check which frame type(s) is supported by your server by using the CONFIG console command.

5. You can also configure your server to support multiple frame types. Use the commands similar to the following and try to connect your workstation with both frame types (first with Ethernet_802.3 and then with Ethernet_802.2, for example):

   Load NE2000 INT=3 PORT=300 FRAME=Ethernet_802.2
   Bind IPX to NE2000 NET=AAA1

   Load NE2000 INT=3 PORT=300 FRAME=Ethernet_802.3
   Bind IPX to NE2000 NET=BBB1

Problem 5: Workstation is connected to Ring Out (RO) port of MSAU (Token Ring).

Procedure:

1. Make sure your workstation is connected to a MSAU and you are able to log in.

2. Disconnect your workstation connector from the MSAU and connect to the RO port of the MSAU.

3. Try to log in to the server now. You will see errors.

4. Reverse the problem

Note: If you try COMCHECK you will not see any problems.

Problem 6: Memory address range used by Token Ring NIC is not excluded.

Procedure:

1. With MS DOS 5.0 or above, expanded memory manager is used to save base memory for applications. If memory manager is using memory needed by your NIC, the LAN driver will not load. To exclude the memory range you use command similar to the following command in your CONFIG.SYS

    DEVICE=C:\DOS\EMM386.EXE /FRAME=NONE /X=CC00-DFFF

2. Modify your CONFIG.SYS file to remove the option that excluded the memory range (make sure you have a copy of the original CONFIG.SYS). Save the file.

3. Reboot the computer and load the workstation files. Your Token Ring LAN driver will not load.

4. Reverse the problem and make sure it is working O.K.

Problem 7: Speed mismatch on the Token Ring network.

Procedure:

1. Make sure your Token Ring network is working fine at a speed of 4 or 16 Mbps. You will be able to see the speed of your NIC on the screen when loading Token Ring LAN driver.

2. Set speed of your workstation's NIC different from the server (if server is using 16 Mbps, set workstation's speed at 4 Mbps). You may use software configuration program or DIP switch(es) for this purpose.

3. Load workstation files. Your LAN driver will give an error message.

4. Reverse the problem and make sure it is working O.K.

© 1993 - 96 · PC Age, Inc. All Rights Reserved · 20 Audrey Place · Fairfield, NJ 07004 · U.S.A. · Tel: 201-882-5370

Problem 8: Duplicate address on an ARCnet network.

Procedure:

1. Make sure your ARCnet network is working fine.

2. Note the node address of server and the workstation.

3. Set node address of the workstation same as the server's (if you have two workstations, you may set same node addresses for both workstations.

4. Try to connect the workstation to the server. You will get errors.

5. Reverse the problem and make sure it is working O.K.

Review Questions

Q.1. You must use terminators with
_____.

    a. Unused active hub ports
    b. Unused passive hub ports
    c. Both unused active hub and passive hub ports
    d. Termination is not necessary with unused ports

Q.2. Vampire tap is used with a(n) _____ network.

    a. 10Base2   b. 10Base5
    c. 10BaseT   d. ARCnet

Q.3. How would you recognize if a card is 8-bit or 16-bit?

    a. A 16-bit card has one large edge and one small edge
    b. An 8-bit card has one large edge and one small edge
    c. A 16-bit card has only one edge
    d. A 16-bit card is 4.8 inches tall

Q.4. You can install an ISA card in an MCA computer?

    a. Never
    b. Only if you use the IBM setup disk
    c. Always
    d. Only if the ISA card is 32-bit

Q.5. If your client wants to install a network for graphic applications and they want good throughput, which network would you suggest?

    a. ARCnet   b. FDDI
    c. Token Ring   d. Ethernet

Q.6. For four circuits with one closed and three open you can have:

    a. 8-pins with one pair closed with a jumper
    b. 4-pins with one pin closed with a jumper
    c. 8-pins with two pairs closed with a jumper
    d. 8-pins with one pair closed with a jumper and one pin with a jumper
    e. Both a and d are true

Q.7. If your modem uses IRQ 3, and you want to use an Ethernet card, what would you do?

    a. Change the IRQ on the NIC and in the NET.CFG file
    b. Change the IRQ on the NIC
    c. Change the IRQ in the NET.CFG file
    d. No change is necessary

Q.8. If your modem uses IRQ 3, and you want to use the ARCnet card, what would you do?

    a. Change the IRQ on the NIC and in the NET.CFG file
    b. Change the IRQ on the NIC

c. No change is necessary
d. Change the IRQ in the NET.CFG file

Q.9. 10Base2 and 10BaseT segments can be connected by using:

a. Special NICs
b. Special transceivers
c. Special cabling
d. They cannot be connected

Q.10. How many nodes can you have on a 10BaseT network?

a. 512 using 4 repeaters
b. 1024 using 5 repeaters
c. 1024 using 4 repeaters
d. Unlimited using repeaters

Q.11. How would you set a node address of 182 if switch 1 serves as the least significant bit (LSB)?

a. OFF OFF OFF ON OFF OFF ON OFF
b. ON OFF OFF ON OFF OFF ON OFF
c. OFF OFF OFF ON OFF OFF ON ON
d. ON ON OFF ON OFF OFF ON ON

Q.12. Which of the following networks does not support fiber optic cable?

a. Ethernet
b. ARCnet

c. Token Ring
d. All of them support fiber optic cable

Chapter 4   Working with Storage Devices

Hard Drives

Computer hard drives are devices used for data storage and retrieval. Hard drives are classified according to the type of interface they use. There is a wide difference in performance between older drive types, like the ST-506, and the more current types like the SCSI. As a LAN technician you will most likely have to deal with many types of hard drives. The following is a description of the common hard drive types from the oldest to the most current.

ST-506

This early interface was developed by Seagate. The encoding techniques used were Modified Frequency Modulation (MFM) and Run Length Limited (RLL). RLL could record data at a higher density.

IDE -- Integrated Drive Electronics

With this type of drive the controller is placed on the drive itself. By placing the controller on the drive, the performance is increased. The IDE drive uses RLL encoding and is widely used today. It does not support multitask I/O, or bus mastering, and has a drive capacity limit of 528 MB (larger IDE drives use a non standard BIOS). IDE is inexpensive and a good choice to use in workstations but should not be used in servers.

ESDI -- Enhanced Small Drive Interface

ESDI is an enhanced version of the ST-506 interface. This drive type was standardized by ANSI. It incorporates the bus, controller, and drive in the same hardware. This interface was once very popular for high performance, larger capacity drives. ESDI is not popular anymore. SCSI drives are replacing ESDI drives in servers.

SCSI -- Small Computer Systems Interface

SCSI (pronounced "SCUZZY") drives use high speed parallel interfaces standardized by ANSI that allows multiple devices to be daisy-chained on a single cable. Each address on the cable can support a SCSI controller with up to two drives. This high performance interface can support high capacity drives and other devices such as CD-ROM and tape drive.

SCSI II

This new SCSI interface provides increased speeds by reducing overhead. Fast SCSI II offers transfer rates of up to 10 Mbps by using different timing and overhead. Wide SCSI II can theoretically provide speeds of 20 to 40 Mbps by providing a second data path.

Setting Up Hard Drives

Following five major steps are needed to set up hard drives on a NetWare server.

1. Configuring the drive.
2. Physical installation.
3. Hard drive cabling.
4. Setting the drive type in CMOS.
5. Preparing the disk for use.

1. Configuring the drive

The following items may need to be set up using jumpers on the disk controller card:

Base I/O address — Normally the factory setting is OK unless you are using two controller cards. The second controller must be given an I/O address that does not conflict with any other device.

Interrupt (IRQ) — Use factory defaults if possible. If not select an IRQ that does not conflict with other devices. Most PCs have IRQs 14 and 15 available for hard disks.

Base BIOS — This setting is for controllers that use ROM BIOS. Avoid addresses over E000h since they are not supported by many system cards.

DMA Channel Address — This setting is only used on some SCSI and ESDI controllers. Sharing a DMA channel is not recommended when using NetWare.

Drive Select — This setting is for the number of drives and the types of cable (flat or twisted) you are using. Drive Select applies to MFM, RLL, and ESDI drive only. This setting is on the drive itself.

SCSI Address — Addresses 0 through 7 are normally set using three jumpers. In most cases the SCSI disk controller, called the Host Bus Adapter (HBA), uses number 7 and other devices use addresses 0 through 6. Number 0 has the highest priority and 6 has the lowest priority.

Note: IBM Micro Channel Architecture (MCA) machines (e.g., PS/2) use number 7 for the HBA and the first drive starts with the number 6 (highest priority). The lowest priority number is 0 (the reverse order of the industry standard).

IDE Disk Configuration — Your IDE hard disk must be set to "Single drive only", "Master", or "Slave".

When using only one IDE disk, configure the disk as "Single drive only". If using two IDE disks, configure the boot disk as a "Master" and other disk that is not boot disk as "Slave".

If you get an error message similar to "Disk Controller Failure", check if you have configured a disk as "Slave" when you have only one hard disk.

C/D or DS — This jumper is used to indicate drive C: or D:. This setting is only required with IDE drives.

DSP — This is used to designate Master or Slave (IDE only).

ACT — This jumper is used to activate the external LED to indicate drive activity. Used only with IDE and SCSI drives.

© 1993 - 96 · PC Age, Inc. All Rights Reserved · 20 Audrey Place · Fairfield, NJ 07004 · U.S.A. · Tel: 201-882-5370

Figure 4-1

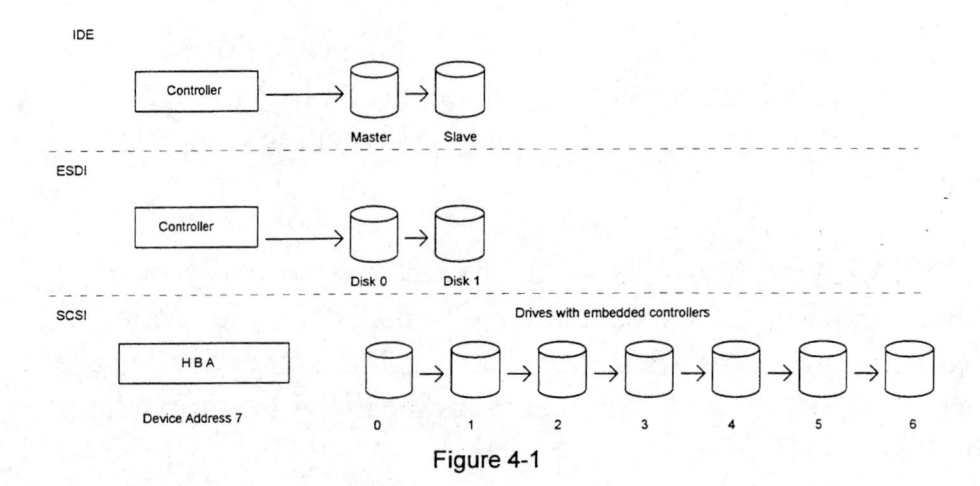

2. Physical Installation

To read or write data from hard disk, NetWare uses disk drivers (*.DSK) to communicate with the Host Bus Adapter (HBA). HBA communicates with the disk controller and the disk controller communicates with the physical drives. These three physical components (HBA, controller, and drive) are implemented for each interface type.

ST-506 or ESDI Installation

These drives use the ISADISK driver and have the HBA and controller on the same card.

IDE Installation

These drives can use either the ISADISK.DSK or IDE.DSK driver and the HBA is either a part of the system board (motherboard) or a separate card installed in an expansion slot. The controller is embedded on the hard drive.

Note: It is recommended that you use IDE.DSK instead of the standard ISADISK.DSK driver. If you are having problems with ISADISK.DSK, you may need to switch to IDE.DSK and recreate your NetWare partition.

SCSI Installation

SCSI device drivers are supplied by the manufacturers of the hardware because the drivers are unique to their devices. Some of the most popular SCSI drivers are incorporated in NetWare. SCSI and DCB (Disk Coprocessor Board)boards (referred to as HBAs) normally use an expansion slot. Up to seven devices, including disk controllers, can be attached to the HBA.

Be careful about hardware, software, and firmware revision levels of HBA and drives. Not every HBA will work properly with your SCSI drive.

Using impedance-matched cables with external disks will provide a more stable SCSI bus. When using an HBA and internal SCSI drives, the HBA and the last drive on the chain must be terminated.

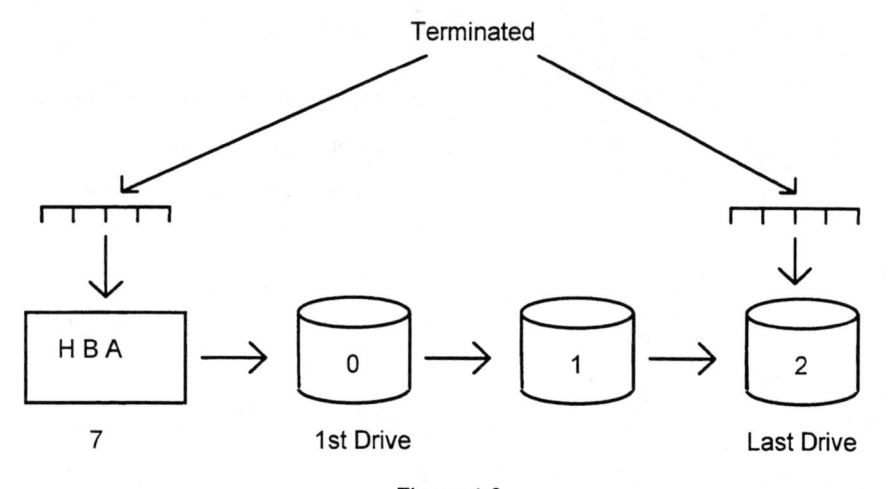

Figure 4-2

When using an external cabinet, the HBA is terminated and the last drive on the chain is either terminated internally or terminated by terminating the external cable. Terminating the external cable is the preferred method. This way when you add more drives you do not need to remove the terminator from the previous last drive.

If you are using both internal and external drives, you need to terminate the last drive on the internal chain and the last drive on the external chain. You do not terminate the HBA in this case.

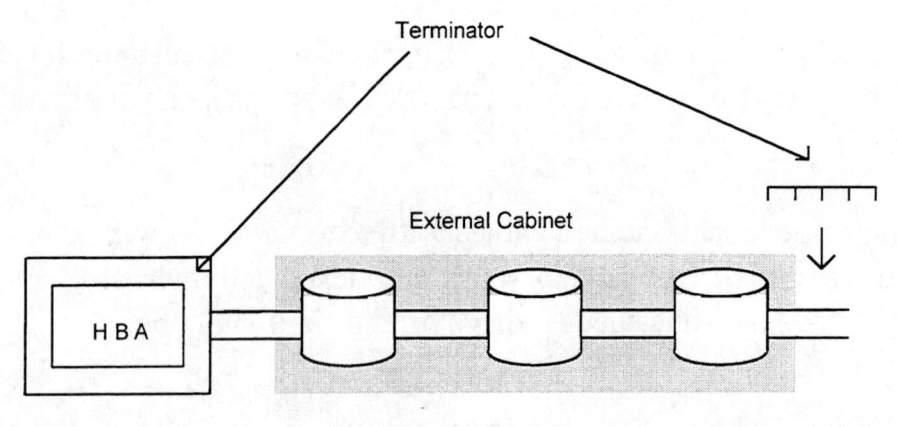

Figure 4-3

Check the manufacturer's documentation when setting up HBAs and SCSI drives. Some settings vary depending on the manufacturer. As an example, IBM PS/2 and some Hewlett-Packard machines use a SCSI address of 7 for the HBA but the devices start with an address of 6 and work down to 0.

Caching Controllers

Caching controllers provide better performance because of using cache. They are, however, not recommended to be used with NetWare. The reasons are:

- If system hangs or crashes before the data is written out to the drive, you have corrupted data.

- Some disk drivers do not flush the cache buffers (writing to the disk) when unloading. This can corrupt the data. Also DOWNing or rebooting the server can corrupt the data.

If you are using a caching controller and have corrupted data, try to turn off the cache.

3. Hard Drive Cabling

Drive cabling provides the communications path between the disk controller and drive. Important points about drive cabling are:

- For IDE hard drives a 40-pin cable is used. You can attach one or two IDE drives to one cable. Maximum cable length is 18 inches.

- The SCSI bus can use 25- or 50-pin cable. There must be only two terminators on the bus regardless of the number of devices used. The maximum distance between connectors on a SCSI cable is 18 inches. The minimum distance between connectors is 12 inches.

- MFM, RLL, and ESDI drives use two cables: one for control information and one for data. Dual hard drive twisted (5 wires) 34-pin cable is used as a control cable. Data cable is 20-pin and used for each MFM, RLL, or ESDI hard drive. For example, if you are connecting two MFM or RLL drives to one controller, you will use one control cable and two data cables.

- Pin 1 on the cable (identified with a colored strip) must be attached to the special end receptor on the controller card marked with a number 1 or a square dot. If the cable is attached in the reverse position, it can damage all components involved.

- Floppy and hard disk cables in ISA computers look similar but they have different cable twists (floppy drive cables have 7 twisted lines and hard drive cables have 5). These cables can not be interchanged.

4. Setting The Drive Type in CMOS

CMOS stands for Complementary Metal-Oxide Semiconductor. It is a battery-operated memory chip that contains firmware that stores your PC device and memory configuration. CMOS can normally be accessed through a SETUP program that can be invoked by pressing a key during startup. Some PCs such as the IBM PS/2 have the SETUP program on a reference diskette. The SETUP program has a list of drive types by number that you can choose from. You select the number that matches, or closely matches, the drive types you are installing.

Each drive type will display the number of cylinders, number of heads, capacity in MB, and write precompensation. Write precompensation deals with the fact that cylinders that are closer to the center of the disk have shorter tracks than those further away. If write precompensation is used, it is usually the maximum number of cylinders divided by two.

For SCSI drives select disk type "0" or "Not Installed" because the BIOS on the controller handles the drive configuration. ESDI drives generally use disk type "1" that corresponds to a 10MB drive, but it is overwritten by the ESDI controller BIOS.

The following rules apply to drives other than SCSI and ESDI:

- Select a drive type equal to or less than the number of cylinders on your drive.
- Select a drive type where the number of heads is equal to or less than the number of heads on your drive.
- Select a drive type where the capacity is equal to or less than your drive.
- If you cannot find a drive type that closely resembles the drive you are installing, you may select drive type 47. Most SETUP programs have a drive type 47 where you can enter your own parameters.

5. Preparing the Disk for Use: Formatting and Partitioning

Low Level Format

This is the first step in preparing the hard disk for data and usually done at the factory. Low level format takes the following steps:

1. The disk surface and heads are tested.
2. Disk tracks are set and each track is divided into sectors, each with a sector ID.
3. Sectors that test bad are marked as such.
4. The disk interleave ratio is set.

You may need to run a low level format to re-mark bad sectors or to change the interleave ratio.

Interleave Ratio

On a hard disk logical sectors are read in sequence order. If every sector that passes under the R/W heads is read by the CPU, this is called an interleave ratio of 1:1. An interleave ratio of 1:1 is now standard in most new drives due to improved electronics and faster processors. If the CPU (slow CPU) is not able to keep up with the sectors passing under the R/W heads, a time delay would result before the next sector to be read came around. To prevent this type of bottleneck a different interleave ratio should be used, such as 2:1 (skips every other sector). By changing the interleave ratio you can set the disk sectors so that a sector will be read then one or more sectors are bypassed before the next sector is read.

Interleave ratios are normally set during a low level format. Software is also available to reset interleave ratios without destroying the data.

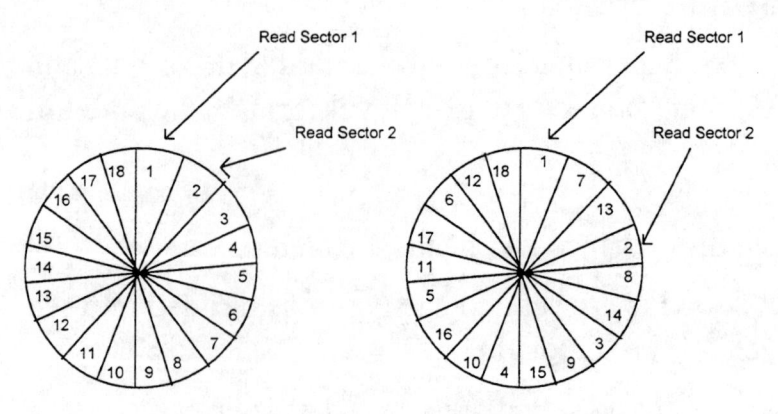

Figure 4-4. Interleave Ratio 1:1   Figure 4-5. Interleave Ratio 3:1

High-level Format

Different operating systems have different formats to prepare a disk for use. The following can be accomplished with high-level format with DOS:

1. Check the disk for bad sectors.

2. Create a boot sector.
3. Create the File Allocation Table (FAT).
4. Create a root directory.
5. Copy the system files to disk (if the /s option is used).

High-level formatting destroys (erases) all data on the disk.

Formatting Tips

- Disk drives are susceptible to both temperature and gravity. Always low level format a drive in the orientation it will be used (sideways or flat).

- When drives are manufactured normally a bad sector error rate of 1% or less is acceptable.

- Always back up the hard drive before formatting. Data can never be recovered after a low level format. There are some third party utilities that can recover data after a high-level format.

Partitioning The Drive

Partitioning divides the hard drive into physical sections. This is usually done when you need to run more than one operating system, such as DOS and NetWare, from the same disk drive. NetWare sees the DOS partition as physical partition 0 and the NetWare partition as physical partition 1.

Within the NetWare partition the Hot Fix redirection area (default 2%) is created first. The data area is a logical partition within the NetWare physical partition. A logical partition can be part of a physical partition or span physical partitions. Each logical partition will have a logical number. Physical partition numbers are used in error messages. Logical partition numbers are used for mirroring. Non-NetWare partitions cannot be mirrored by NetWare.

Note: When NetWare finds a bad block in data area, it marks that block as bad block and redirects the data to the Hot Fix redirection area. If your Hot Fix area is being filled up and unable to accept data, you may need to replace your hard disk.

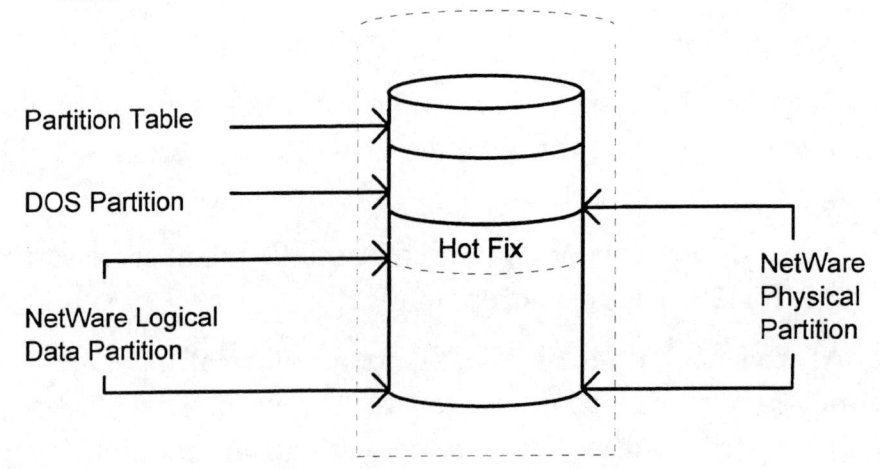

Figure 4-6 Physical and Logical Partitions

Volumes

Data is written to volumes in NetWare partitions. A volume destination table is used to keep track of volumes in each partition. NetWare keeps four copies of this table in the partition. Sixty-four (64) volumes can exist on a server with a maximum total size (all volumes) of 32 terabytes. Volumes are created using the INSTALL.NLM utility. When creating a volume you set the volume size by first setting the block allocation size then the initial segment size in blocks. NetWare will then calculate the volume size in MB. A volume can span multiple disks. This is called **Spanning**. The parts of the same volume on different disks are called volume segments. There can be a maximum of 32 segments per volume and up to 8 segments on a disk.

Note: If a volume is distributed over multiple disks and one disk fails, you will not be able to access the volume. If you have volumes on separate disks (one volume on one disk), a disk failure will only affect the volume on that disk. You should be using mirroring or duplexing when spanning the volume.

Hard Drives Tips

- Use hard drives with care. Bumping or shaking a drive can damage a disk.

- Majority of problems (about 95%) with SCSI hard drives are because of improper termination or ID settings.

- Certain older 386 system boards do not correctly support 16-bit memory transfers. You will need to use ESDI rather than SCSI drives with those boards.

- The minimum cable length between SCSI connectors is 12 inches. You may get corrupted data because of signal reflections if devices are placed too close together.

- Most SCSI drives are shipped with the "Parity-Enabled" jumper set. Check your vendor documentation to determine whether you need to change this setting.

Mirroring and Duplexing

Mirroring protects the data on your hard drive by duplicating the data on another drive that is connected to the same channel. NetWare 3.1x supports four disk channels (0-4). Both disk mirroring and duplexing are a part of NetWare System Fault Tolerance II (SFT II). Duplexing adds another level of security by using two disk channels. With both mirroring and duplexing, if a failure occurs on one drive, NetWare will automatically switch to the other drive without an interruption in service.

Mirroring protects against the loss of a disk while duplexing protects against the loss of a disk channel or a disk. Mirroring and duplexing are setup using the INSTALL.NLM utility (either process is called mirroring in the INSTALL utility). To enable mirroring the logical data partition on both disks must be the same size. If your disks are different physical sizes, the logical partition area can be adjusted by increasing or decreasing the Hot Fix redirection area.

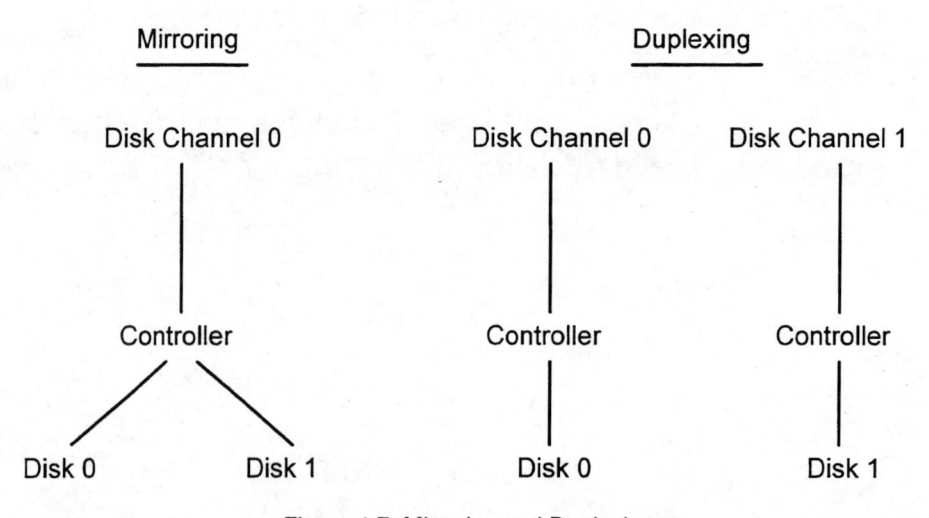

Figure 4-7 Mirroring and Duplexing

Mirroring and Duplexing Troubleshooting Tips

- Keep a record of your hard drives' 5 digit device codes. It will help to troubleshoot mirroring or duplexing problems.

- Disk drivers should always be loaded in the same order. This can be set in the STARTUP.NCF file.

- Periodically check to ensure the disks are "IN SYNC". It means both disks have the same data.

- Always ensure that timely backups are performed. Mirroring or duplexing does not replace a backup system. It protects from disk failure, but if a user by mistake deletes a file from one disk, it will be deleted from the mirrored disk too.

- Remember that duplexing is a special type of mirroring so the NetWare messages will be the same.

- When IDE drives are run in pairs they are setup as master and slave. Since the slave controller is disabled, when the master fails the slave will not function. IDE drives should only be used in a duplex configuration.

Other Network Storage Devices

The following three technologies are also used to store network data :

- RAID
- CD-ROM
- Magneto-Optical Drives

RAID

RAID (Redundant Array of Inexpensive Disks) is defined as any disk architecture that uses two or more physical disks to form one logical disk to achieve **data reliability** and **improved performance** with **increased capacity**. The idea is that more disks will give faster speed and more reliability than just one big disk (more disk heads are working and data can be redundant).

The key concept behind RAID is a technique called **data striping**. Striping means data blocks are written to each drive in the array in succession. For example, if there are three disks in the disk array and you are storing a file, the first block will be written to disk one, the 2nd block to disk two, and the 3rd block to disk three. This method provides better I/O performance because the I/O requests are not queued up behind one busy disk. Each drive operates independently of the others, allowing data to be transferred in parallel from each drive. This means that if you are using an array of n disks operating in parallel, the data will be transferred in 1/n the time compared to data transferred using a single disk.

Reliability in RAID is achieved by using a method called checksum or parity checking (check byte). In this method, a check byte is constructed in such a way that should one of the drives fails, the data in that drive can be reconstructed from the remaining data drives.

There are between five and seven RAID levels of architecture. The level you select should depend on the number of users, the maximum transfer rate of the system, the size of the data blocks, whether the data is stored in sequential or random order, and the proportion of reads to writes.

The following is a six-level RAID model:

Level 0: Block-Interleave Data Striping

This level provides improved performance by using data striping with block interleave, but does not use check bytes for data fault tolerance. A single drive failure brings down the entire disk system.

Level 1: Block-Interleave Data Striping with Disk Mirroring or Duplexing

RAID Level 1 uses disk mirroring or duplexing along with striping to provide data redundancy. Disks are paired and each block is written to both disks. If one disk fails, the other continues without interruption. This level provides real time data fault tolerance and uninterruptable service but is expensive (you are using two disks to store the same amount of data).

Level 2: Bit-Interleave Data Striping with Fault Tolerance (Checksum)

In Level 2 data is written one bit at a time instead of one block at a time. This method provides extremely fast data transfers (reading from the disks). Bit-interleave striping provides fast read operation but slow write operation. RAID levels that use bit-interleave are good if the system has many read operations and few write operations. This level uses a separate reserved disk for data recovery and uses the checksum method to isolate faulty bits. This level is not used with PCs but it is common in the mainframe world. It is not used with NetWare because NetWare writes data in 4 KB blocks, rather than in bits.

Level 3: Byte-Interleave Data Striping with Fault Tolerance (Parity Checking)

Level 3 provides striping at the byte level, with one disk reserved for data recovery called the parity drive. This is more reliable than Level 2.

In RAID Level 3, if a single drive fails during a write operation, the array controller will use the parity drive to reconstruct the contents of the failed disk and will write to the next disk. The failed disk will be skipped. This level has the disadvantage of low write performance because the parity drive must be accessed for every write, and there is also a high computer overhead for calculating the parity. (The same applies to RAID Level 2.)

This level can be used with PCs but not with NetWare.

Level 4: Block-Interleave Data Striping with Fault Tolerance (Parity Checking)

This level is same as Level 3, except it uses block interleave like Level 0. A block is the amount of data transferred in a single read/write operation. Block-interleave is not as fast as bit-interleave (Level 2) for read operations, but faster for write operations. This level can be used with NetWare.

Level 5: Block-Interleave Data Striping with Distributed Check Data

RAID Level 5 uses block data striping on all drives for a balanced fast read and write operations. It uses a distributed check data method. In the distributed check data method, parity checking is done in part on every drive that increases efficiency. Level 5 is more reliable but slower than Level 0 because of using parity checking. It is more efficient than Level 4 because of distributed error checking. It is slower than Level 3 in data transfers because of using blocks instead of parallel bits (for read operations). Overall it is the best choice and most popular to date and can be used with NetWare.

CD-ROM (Compact Disk-Read Only Memory)

CD-ROM is a format for storing digital data on a compact disk. A single CD-ROM can store approximately 682 MB of data. The standard used for almost all CD-ROMs is the ISO 9660 or its subset called the High Sierra standard.

CD-ROM extensions allow an MS DOS computer to read from an ISO 9660-Complaint CD-ROM disk. Some CD-ROMs come with their own drivers.

Some CD-ROM advantages are: instant access to large volumes of information, light weight, standardization, and common file formats. Its disadvantages are: it is slower than a hard drive and CD-ROM recording is very expensive.

CD-ROM Tips

- The CD-ROM should always be stored in its plastic container called caddie to prevent contamination from handling.

- SCSI connections are preferred over proprietary connections because the SCSI standard makes expansion simple.

- CD-ROM drives should not be installed above hard drives because CD-ROMs create a magnetic field that could destroy data on the hard disk.

© 1993 - 96 · PC Age, Inc. All Rights Reserved · 20 Audrey Place · Fairfield, NJ 07004 · U.S.A. · Tel: 201-882-5370

- It is possible to have performance degradation if CD-ROMs and hard drives are installed on the same SCSI controller.

- Load the correct CD-ROM device drivers at the server. Also make sure that the required NLMs are loaded. At the workstation, make sure to use the most recent version of drivers and extensions.

NetWare CD-ROM support

NetWare 3.12 and above now support CD-ROMs as additional volumes. Keep in mind that Microsoft's CD-ROM extension MSCDEX is not compatible with NetWare, but there are third party software solutions allowing CD-ROMs to work with NetWare.

NetWare 3.12 and above can be installed from CD-ROM. NetWare supports CD-ROM as a Read-Only volume. It makes it easier for network users to access any information available on CD-ROMs as a NetWare volume.

To install NetWare from CD-ROM, you need a DOS-based CD-ROM device. To use a CD-ROM as a NetWare volume, make sure you have a CD-ROM driver that works with NetWare. Adaptec controller is a good choice to use with CD-ROMs.

NetWare 3.12 and above comes with Adaptec drivers.

Here are steps to mount a CD-ROM as a NetWare volume:

1. Load the driver for the Host Bus Adapter (HBA) the CD-ROM is attached with (AHA1740.DSK, for example, if using Adaptec HBA).

2. Load ASPICD.DSK provided by Adaptec for Adaptec HBAs or CDNASPI.DSK provided by Novell for non-Adaptec HBAs.

    Note: You can add commands to your STARTUP.NCF to automatically load the above drivers. Some HBAs do not require ASPICD.DSK or CDNASPI.DSK.

3. Load the CDROM.NLM, type the following at the console prompt:

    LOAD CDROM

4. To list the volume name of the CD-ROM, type the following command at the console prompt:

    CD DEVICE LIST

   If a volume does not appear, you may try again by unloading and reloading the CDROM.NLM. If a volume name still does not appear, your CD-ROM may not be compatible with ISO 9660 or HIGH SIERRA and may not be used as a NetWare volume.

   To mount the volume, type the following at the console prompt:

    CD MOUNT volume_name
            or
    CD MOUNT device_number

   The volume_name or device_number can be found as in step 4.

CD-ROM Troubleshooting Tips:

1. Make sure your CD-ROM is ISO 9660-compliant. The Novell CDROM.NLM supports ISO 9660-compliant devices. Not all CD-ROM devices can be configured as NetWare read-only volumes.

2. Make sure you have the latest CDROM.NLM.

3. If your server hangs when loading the CD-ROM driver, you may have your CD-ROM device and hard disk attached to the same controller and the DOS CD-ROM drivers may already be loaded. DOS CD-ROM drivers and NetWare drivers may conflict with each other and both try to control the controller board.

    To solve this problem, down the server and modify server's CONFIG.SYS file so that it will not load DOS CD-ROM drivers (you needed these drivers to install NetWare from CD-ROM). Now you can bring up the server and load NetWare drivers for CD-ROM.

4. You may need to set SET RESERVED BUFFERS BELOW 16 MEG=200 command in the STARTUP.NCF file (and reboot the server) before mounting the CD-ROM. This command specifies the number of file cache buffers reserved for device drivers that cannot access memory above 16 MB.

5. If your CD-ROM driver shares a SCSI bus with a disk subsystem, the server's keyboard may lock up during installation of NetWare. It may be because you are copying

NetWare installation files to SYS volume that is created on the subsystem disk. To solve this problem you may need to do the following:

a. Create the SYS volume on the internal hard disk of the server rather than on the disk subsystem. Also load the NetWare SCSI driver after NetWare is installed.

b. If the CD-ROM drive has a parallel-to-SCSI board, configure it (under DOS) to use this board instead of the shared SCSI bus.

c. Install a separate SCSI board for the CD-ROM. Load the NetWare SCSI driver for the disk subsystem SCSI board only.

Magneto-Optical (M-O) Drives

M-O drives are the next step after CD-ROMs. This technology allows you to store huge amounts of data with random access read/write capability. Remember CD-ROMs do not allow the user to store data files — they are read only drives.

The M-O medium is a circular disk coated with multiple layers of magnetic media. An optical lens is used for the reading and writing of data through a laser beam.

M-O drives can be used in place of hard drives and tape drives to store archived data, graphics, and scanned documents. They can be used as internal drives, as removable media, or as "juke boxes" handling multiple M-O disks through robotics.

An M-O disk can withstand over one million rewrites because data is recorded by laser beam and there is no physical contact between media and recording head. There are no head crashes with M-O technology. On the down side, M-O drives are not as fast as SCSI or ESDI drives because they need two passes to write data: one to erase the surface and another to write. M-O drives are faster than Digital Audio Tape (DAT).

Initial setup for M-O drives is expensive because it is a new technology. They may not be cost effective for small capacity environments (drives cost about $3000 to $5000), but for high capacity environments M-O drives will eventually cost less than hard drives.

Exercise: Mirroring and Spanning

In this exercise you will do mirroring and spanning on the server.

Procedure:

a- Mirroring:

- This exercise assumes that you have one hard disk on your server and it is up and running. Down the server and install a similar, second hard disk (same type and size) in your server.

- Bring up the server.

- Load INSTALL.NLM

- Create NetWare partition on second disk (Device #1) as you created on first disk. Make sure both NetWare partitions have same size of data areas. If they have different sizes, change the number of blocks of larger data area to the same size as the smaller one. It will increase the Hot Fix Redirection Area of that NetWare partition. You can do this by selecting **"Change Hot Fix"** option of "Partition Options" menu.

- Go back to the **"Available Disk Options"** by pressing <Esc> and select **"Mirroring"**.

- Select Logical Partition #1 (this is the partition you want to mirror).

- Press <Ins> to add a partition to the set.

- Select available partition. You will see "Mirrored NetWare Partitions" screen showing like this:

    In Sync -   NetWare Partition #1 on Device #0
    Out Of Sync -   NetWare Partition #2 on Device #1

NetWare will start copying information from device #0 to device #1 to mirror them. After some time device #1 should also say "In Sync".

b- Spanning:

This exercise assumes that you have created SYS volume on one disk (Device #0) and it is mirrored with partition on device #1. In this exercise, you will first unmirror your hard disks and then add the second hard disk's space to the SYS Volume (spanning the SYS volume over two disks).

1. Unmirroring the disks.

   To unmirror the disk, follow the following steps:

   i. From the INSTALL **Installation Options**, select **Disk Options**.

   ii. Select **Mirroring** from **Available Disk Options**.

   iii. Press <Enter> to select the only entry for the mirrored pair from **Partition Mirroring Status** screen.

   iv. Highlight the NetWare Partition on Device #1 and Press <Del>. Device#1 will disappear from the screen.

   v. Press <Esc> to go to **Partition Mirroring Status**.

   vi. Highlight "Out Of Sync" Partition and Press <F3> to restore it. You will see a warning screen; press <Esc>. Select "No" for "Rename the volume segment?". Select

Chapter 4: Working with Storage Devices

"No" for "Salvage Volume SYS Segment 0 ?" Now you will see both partitions as "Not Mirrored".

vii. Press <Esc> twice to go back to **Installation Options** menu.

2. Select **Volume Options**. select the SYS volume.

3. Highlight **Volume Segments:** and press <Enter>.

4. Press <Insert> to add disk space to SYS volume. Press <Enter> to select **New Volume Segment Size.**

5. Press <Enter> to select "Yes" to add new segment to the volume. Now you will see that there are two segments on SYS volume. Now you can press <Esc> to go back to **Installation Options**. You have done spanning.

© 1993 - 96 · PC Age, Inc. All Rights Reserved · 20 Audrey Place · Fairfield, NJ 07004 · U.S.A. · Tel: 201-882-5370

4-31

Review Questions

Q.1. If you are installing an IDE drive and you do not find your drive type in the CMOS setup, which type would you usually select?

    a. Type 0   b. Not Installed
    c. Type 47   d. Type 1

Q.2. When installing a SCSI drive which drive type you would select in the CMOS setup?

    a. Type 0 or "Not Installed"   b. Type 47
    c. Type 1   d. Type 48

Q.3. When installing an ESDI drive which drive type you would select in the CMOS setup?

    a. Type 0 or "Not Installed"   b. Type 47
    c. Type 1   d. Type 48

Q.4. For which kind of hard disk do you have a master/slave relationship?

    a. IDE   b. SCSI
    c. ESDI   d. Master Disk

Q.5. For hard disks that have master/slave relationship, you use:

a. A 40-pin cable
b. A 50-pin cable
c. A 25-pin cable which can connect to two disks
d. A 34-pin cable which can connect to one disk only

Q.6. For an RLL disk you use:

a. A 50-pin control cable   b. A 40-pin control cable
c. A 34-pin control cable   d. A 50-pin data cable

Q.7. If the drive type is lost from the CMOS setup, a probable cause is:

a. The computer power supply is not working
b. The controller electronics has failed
c. The battery that supports CMOS has failed

Q.8. Which utility can be used to set up the interleave ratio of a disk without destroying the data?

a. NSEPro   b. MTL
c. Check It Pro   d. None of the above

Q.9. If you have corrupted data because of using caching controller, you should:

    a. Disable NetWare caching   b. Turn off controller caching
    c. Flush buffers by hand   d. Add more RAM

Q.10. You should replace your hard disk _____

    a. when the Hot Fix redirection area is unable to accept data
    b. when the hard disk is almost full
    c. when the SCSI controller is not working properly
    d. when the NetWare SYS volume is almost full

Q.11. 34-pin cable is used with which of the following drives? (select all that are true)

    a. MFM   b. RLL
    c. ESDI   d. SCSI

Q.12. Floppy and hard drive cables can be interchanged.

    a. true
    b. false
    c. only on IBM AT computers
    d. only with IDE drives

Chapter 5   Troubleshooting the Workstation

Connecting Workstations

To convert a stand-alone PC into a network workstation, we first plug a network interface card (NIC) into the PC's expansion bus (available slot). We then connect a cable to the NIC, giving the PC a physical connection to the network.

After the hardware connections, we need the following workstation software to get services from the network:

- IPX.COM or ODI (Open Data-Link Interface) Files
- NETx.EXE or NetWare DOS Requester

The above files establish the connection with the server and provide transparent access to network resources. We will discuss these files in detail.

Working with IPX and NETx

IPX and NETx files have been used since the first version of NetWare. You generate the IPX.COM file; the NETx file is provided to you by Novell.

IPX.COM (Internetwork Packet eXchange)

IPX.COM is generated using the WSGEN program (found on the WSGEN disk of NetWare 3.11 and earlier versions). You generate this file for the NIC you are using. The WSGEN program allows you to select a LAN driver for your NIC and set its configuration (IRQ, I/O Port, etc.). This LAN driver is then linked to the IPX.OBJ to generate IPX.COM. You can use the same IPX.COM file in each workstation as long as all are using the same NIC with the same configuration.

For example, if you generated IPX.COM for an Ethernet card with IRQ=3 and Port=300, you can use the same IPX.COM in each workstation so long as they have Ethernet NICs with the same configuration. If one workstation's NIC is using IRQ 5 (because of a conflict with another device), you need to generate the specific IPX.COM for that workstation.

IPX.COM generated for an Ethernet card cannot be used for any other type of NIC (ARCnet, Token Ring, etc.).

NETx

NETx, also called the NetWare shell, can be found on the WSGEN disk or downloaded from NetWire. The "x" in NETx represents the version of DOS. NET3, NET4, and NET5 were available to work with DOS 3, 4, and 5 versions. NETx.EXE file for DOS 6 replaces the older NETx.COM (for conventional memory), EMSNETx.EXE (for expanded memory), and XMSNETx.EXE (for extended memory). The most current version of NETx (NETx.EXE; here x represents "x") is DOS version-independent.

When you run NETx.EXE (after running IPX.COM), it establishes a logical connection with the first server that responds (usually the nearest server). Then the user can use that server's LOGIN directory to login to the same server or to another server (using LOGIN.EXE program).

How IPX and NETx Work

IPX and NETx provide transparent services from the server. To connect to the server and get services, you first run IPX.COM and then NETx.EXE. The NetWare shell establishes, maintains, and terminates the connection with the server. The shell intercepts all requests coming from the user (or application) to determine whether a request requires network access or not. If the request does not require network access, the shell passes it to DOS and DOS handles the request. If the request requires network access, the shell converts the request to NCP (NetWare Core Protocol) packets so that programs at the server can understand the request. The NCP packets are given to IPX.

IPX is Novell's proprietary communication protocol. A protocol is simply the rules or conventions for communication. If two systems want to communicate, they must use the same protocol (same language) to understand each other. IPX assigns source and destination addresses (logical, software, or network addresses) to a packet and uses the services of the LAN driver (which is linked into the IPX.COM) to communicate to the NIC for data (packet) transmission.

The NIC has on-board firmware that implements the low level of protocol. The NIC assigns the hardware or node address to the packet and implements a cable-access scheme so that packets enter the network in an orderly manner without colliding with other packets on the network. When the network cable is available for transmission, a transmitter on the NIC sends the packet on to the network cable. Incoming packets are received by a receiver on the NIC and handled in reverse order.

Note: When you load IPX, SPX is automatically loaded and used whenever necessary. SPX is the Novell Transport level communication protocol.

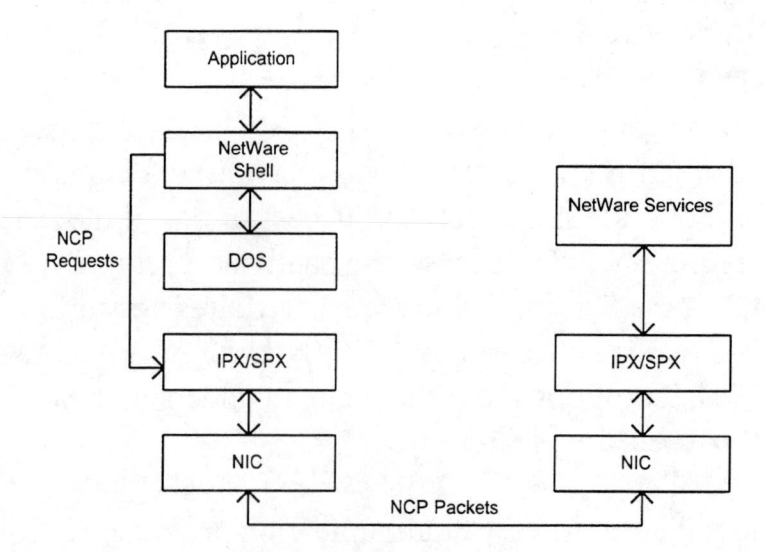

Figure 5-1 NetWare Architecture

Open Data-Link Interface

In the late 80's when more and more companies started using networking, the large organizations were having problems supporting different computer systems. For example, if a user wanted to access a Novell file server and a UNIX server using one PC, he had to have two NICs in the computer to support the two different communication or transport protocols (IPX/SPX for Novell and TCP/IP for UNIX). He also had to reboot the PC to load the desired protocol stack. The problem was worse if the same user wanted to connect to an AppleTalk server or any other networking system. The NICs were manufactured to support only one communication protocol.

To solve this problem Microsoft and 3COM introduced the NDIS solution in 1988 and Novell and Apple Computers developed the ODI (Open Data-Link Interface) specification in 1989. Now newer NICs manufactured according to NDIS or ODI specifications support multiple transport protocols. Users can now access different network systems using only one NIC and without rebooting the computer. The server can now provide services to different types of clients (DOS, Macintosh, UNIX workstation, etc.).

```
┌─────────────────────────────────────────┐   Protocol
│      NetWare Services and Server        │   Dependent
└─────────────────────────────────────────┘   Services

┌─────────────────────────────────────────┐
│                   TLI                   │
├─────────────────────────────────────────┤
│              NetWare Streams            │
│                                         │   Protocol
│   ┌─────────┐ ┌────────┐ ┌──────────┐   │   Stack
│   │ IPX/SPX │ │ TCP/IP │ │ AppleTalk│   │   Layer
│   └─────────┘ └────────┘ └──────────┘   │
│                                         │
├─────────────────────────────────────────┤
│          Link Support Layer (LSL)       │
├─────────────────────────────────────────┤
│   Multiple-Link Interface Driver        │
│   Network Board (Ethernet, Token-Ring,  │
│                             ARCNET...)  │
└─────────────────────────────────────────┘
```

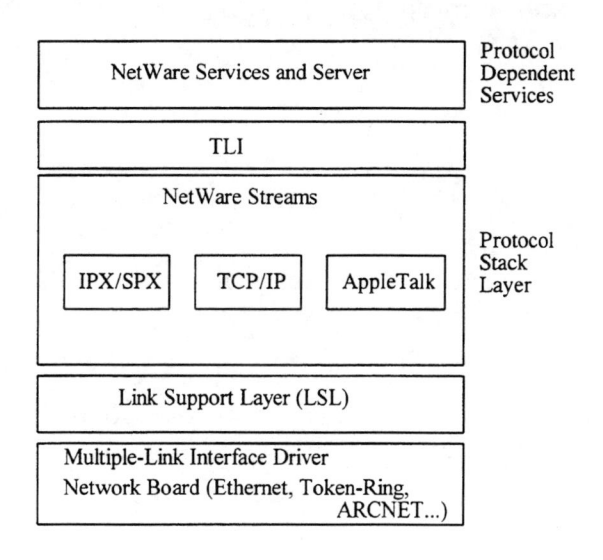

Figure 5-2: Open Data-Link Interface.

ODI supports multiple transport protocols (e.g., IPX/SPX, TCP/IP) in a single workstation or on a single server. ODI allows multiple transport protocols to share the same network board without conflict. For example, ODI provides TCP/IP support (traditionally limited to Ethernet) over ARCnet or Token Ring networks. It means that both IPX and TCP/IP can run on the same workstation using the same board. ODI specifications allow network boards to support different transport protocols.

Using the ODI specification, NetWare server's services and applications are available to all workstations regardless of the transport protocols they are using. At this level (NetWare server's services), this uniform transport interface is provided by a Streams interface — an interface developed by AT&T in UNIX System V.

ODI provides a standard interface for transport protocols by using the following layers (depicted in Figure 5-2):

- Network board and MLID (Multiple Link Interface Driver) Layer
- Link Support Layer (LSL)
- Protocol Stack Layer

All these layers are used to communicate with the NetWare operating system.

The ODI LAN drivers are different from previous drivers. They are called Multiple Link Interface Drivers because they can accept any type of packet, such as IPX, AppleTalk (from Macintosh workstations), or TCP/IP (from UNIX workstations).

The Link Support Layer (LSL) identifies the type of packet it receives and then passes the packet to the appropriate protocol in the protocol stack layer (like a switchboard).

The Protocol Stack Layer contains protocol stacks such as IPX/SPX, AppleTalk, and TCP/IP. When a specified protocol stack receives a packet, it passes it on to communicate with the

NetWare OS or sends it back through the layers to another network.

For DOS ODI workstations, you need to load ODI files (found on the DOS/DOS ODI disk) in the following order:

LSL
NE2000   (or any other MLID)
IPXODI
NETx   (or VLM)

Note: These files must be unloaded in reverse order.

NetWare DOS Requester

DOS Requester comes with NetWare 3.12 or higher. NetWare DOS Requester provides an interface between local DOS applications and the NetWare operating system. If any requests from the user or programs require network access (NetWare services), the DOS Requester converts these requests to NCP packets and then hands them to IPX for transmission. The DOS Requester replaces the NetWare Shell (NETx) which is used in previous versions of NetWare.

The NetWare DOS Requester is composed of multiple files called Virtual Loadable Modules (VLMs) that can be loaded and unloaded as needed.

To load the NetWare DOS Requester into the workstation memory, run VLM.EXE. When VLM.EXE is executed, it loads the VLMs from the current directory or another specified directory. A directory can be specified at execution or in NET.CFG (NetWare's workstation Configuration File).

Like the older NetWare Shells (NETx, XMSNETx, EMSNETx), The DOS Requester can be loaded in conventional, extended, or expanded memory.

Examples:

C:>VLM

Loads the DOS Requester using VLMs found in the current directory or as specified in NET.CFG.

C:>VLM /c=path

Loads the DOS Requester using VLMs found in the directory specified in the path.

C:>VLM /mc

Loads the DOS Requester in conventional memory.

C:>VLM /mx

Loads the DOS Requester in extended memory.

C:>VLM /me

Loads the DOS Requester in expanded memory.

The NetWare DOS Requester has several new features that the old NetWare shell did not have:

Modular Design: The Requester is a collection of VLMs that provides the flexibility of loading and unloading VLMs as needed. It also allows other companies to provide NLMs with other functionality.

Better Memory Usage: It can be loaded into expanded or extended memory and unnecessary modules can be unloaded.

DOS Redirection: The Requester includes a redirector that is called by DOS to provide network file and print services. It eliminates duplication of effort between the Shell and DOS. (The NETx shell previously performed these functions without involving DOS).

Enhanced Performance: Provides support for packet burst and large Internet packets.

Compatibility: Provides compatibility with previous versions of NetWare through NETx.VLM, and with NetWare 4.x through NDS.VLM.

DOS Requester Installation

The NetWare DOS Requester comes with NetWare 3.12 or higher.

NetWare 3.12 Workstation Software Installation

The DOS Requester installation program, INSTALL.BAT, comes on the NetWare 3.12 Client for DOS WSDOS_1 diskette.

To install the DOS Requester insert the WSDOS_1 diskette into drive A. At the prompt, type INSTALL. Follow the installation steps on the menu screen.

The steps are as follows:

Steps:

1. Select the default directory for client installation C:\NWCLIENT.

2. Answer "No" to allow changes (default), if the workstation CONFIG.SYS and AUTOEXEC.BAT files have already been modified. If "Yes" is answered the LASTDRIVE=Z parameter is placed at the end of the CONFIG.SYS file. A file called STARTNET.BAT is created for loading the ODI files, and a CALL is placed in the AUTOEXEC.BAT file to invoke the STARTNET.BAT file.

3. Answer "Yes" to "Do you wish to install support for Windows?" and select the default directory C:\WINDOWS.

4. a. Insert the NetWare 3.12 WSDRV_2 diskette into drive A: and press <Enter>. This diskette contains the NetWare supplied LAN drivers.

   b. Highlight a LAN driver, for example, Novell/Eagle NE2000. Press <Enter>.

   c. Accept the default settings by pressing the <Esc> key.

5. Press <Enter> to start the DOS Requester install process. You will see the install file being loaded. After the installation of the DOS Requester, restart the workstation and the Requester should load automatically from the STARTNET.BAT file. This file will look similar to the following:

   ```
   @ECHO OFF
   C:
   CD\NWCLIENT
   SET NWLANGUAGE=ENGLISH
   LSL
   NE2000
   IPXODI
   VLM
   ```

   Note: All the above files must be in the correct order. The above commands may also be placed in AUTOEXEC.BAT

   If you have workstations on Token Ring networks with IBM bridges, you may need to use ROUTE.COM. For workstations that require IBM LAN support programs, use LANSUP.COM.

NetWare 4.1 Workstation Software Installation

The workstation software for NetWare 4.1 is installed from the files on the server or floppies.

When installing from diskettes:

1. Insert the NetWare Client for DOS and MS Windows disk 1 into a disk driver
2. Get the proper prompt for the drive and type INSTALL <Enter>
3. Answer the questions on the INSTALL screen (see below)

When installing from a network Directory:

1. Change directory to CLIENT/DOSWIN subdirectory under SYS:PUBLIC
2. Type INSTALL <Enter>
3. Answer the questions on the INSTALL screen

Chapter 5: Troubleshooting the Workstation

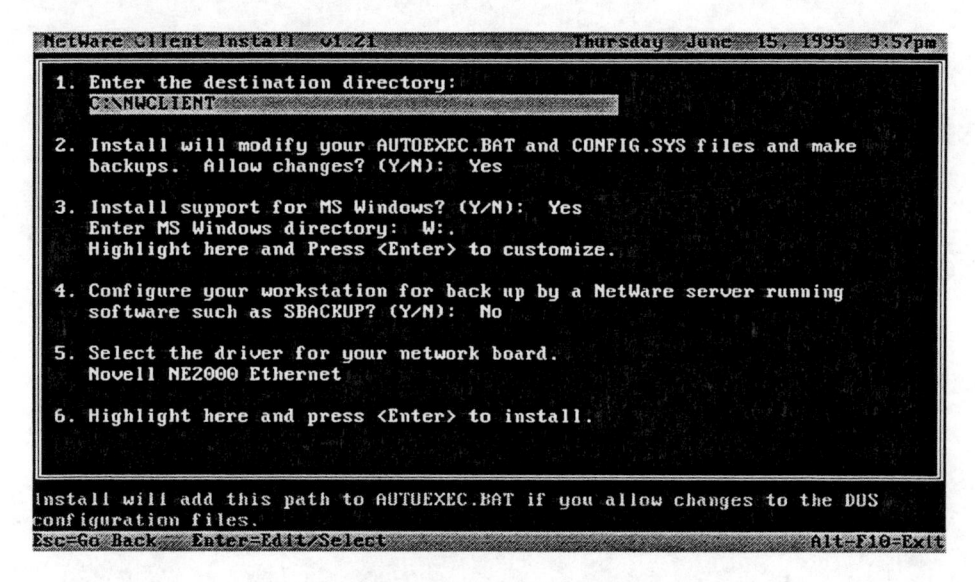

```
NetWare Client Install  v1.21                    Thursday June 15, 1995  3:57pm

   1. Enter the destination directory:
      C:\NWCLIENT

   2. Install will modify your AUTOEXEC.BAT and CONFIG.SYS files and make
      backups.  Allow changes? (Y/N):  Yes

   3. Install support for MS Windows? (Y/N):  Yes
      Enter MS Windows directory:  W:.
      Highlight here and Press <Enter> to customize.

   4. Configure your workstation for back up by a NetWare server running
      software such as SBACKUP? (Y/N):  No

   5. Select the driver for your network board.
      Novell NE2000 Ethernet

   6. Highlight here and press <Enter> to install.


Install will add this path to AUTOEXEC.BAT if you allow changes to the DOS
configuration files.
Esc=Go Back   Enter=Edit/Select                                Alt-F10=Exit
```

Figure 5-3 Install Screen

INSTALL program requires you to enter configuration values for your NIC. You can get EISA, MCA, or PCI local bus network boards values by using the setup or reference program. For ISA network boards, get the specific setting from the network board or its documentation.

The INSTALL command:

- Copies all the necessary files to the workstation in C:\NWCLIENT directory.
- Puts LASTDRIVE=Z in CONFIG.SYS file.
- Creates a STARTNET.BAT file to load workstation files.
- Places @CALL C:\NWCLIENT\STARTNET in AUTOEXEC.BAT.
- Creates a NET.CFG file which should be edited to specify user context.

NET.CFG File

NET.CFG is a configuration file for the ODI files/VLM or IPX/NETx. We can use any DOS editor to create the file. We need to create NET.CFG only if not using default options used by NetWare workstation files.

Conventions

- Main section headings are left justified and options are indented.
- Options and main headings are not case sensitive.
- Start a comment with a semicolon (;) or pound sign (#).
- All numbers specified are decimal, except where noted otherwise.

The following are main section headings in the NET.CFG file:

Link Driver

Link Support

NetWare DOS Requester

Protocol

Link Driver Section

This section is used to specify LAN driver and options used by the driver. Some important options are:

Link Driver drivername
    DMA [#1| #2] channel_number
    INT [#1| #2] interrupt_request_number
    MEM [#1| #2] hex_starting_address [hex_length]

PORT [#1| #2] hex_starting_address_[hex_number_of_ports]
NODE ADDRESS hex_address
SLOT number
FRAME frame_type

Link Support Section

This section is for configuring the receive buffers, the size of the memory pool buffers, and the number of boards and stacks. Some important options are:

Link Support
    BUFFERS number [size]
    MEMPOOL number
    MAX BOARDS number
    MAX STACKS number

NetWare DOS Requester Section

This section is used to specify VLMs loading and to set up client environment. Important options are:

NetWare DOS Requester
    PREFERRED SERVER = server_name
    FIRST NETWORK DRIVE = drive_letter

Note: When using NETx, specify parameters related to NETx such as PREFERRED SERVER and FIRST NETWORK DRIVE at the top of NET.CFG file (left justified) without using any section heading.

Protocol Section

This section is used to specify options used with protocols such as IPX, SPX, and TCP/IP. Important options for IPX protocol are:

Protocol IPX
   INT64 [ON/OFF]

   INT7A [ON/OFF]

   IPX RETRY COUNT number

A Sample NET.CFG File

Link Driver NE2000
  INT 5
  PORT 320
  FRAME ETHERNET_802.2

NetWare DOS Requester
  FIRST NETWORK DRIVE = F
  SHOW DOTS = ON
  MAX TASKS = 45
  CACHE BUFFERS = 15
  LONG MACHINE TYPE = COMPAQ
  PREFERRED SERVER = PCAGE

Note: The Novell old workstation configuration file is SHELL.CFG. If you are using IPX/NETx files you may be using SHELL.CFG file. If you want to create a NET.CFG file to use with ODI files/VLM, copy all commands from SHELL.CFG to the top of NET.CFG. All commands must be left justified. Now you can delete the SHELL.CFG file. Note that not all SHELL.CFG commands are valid for ODI files/VLM — invalid commands will be ignored.

Workstation Troubleshooting Techniques

General Troubleshooting Tips

- Make sure all hardware is installed properly (NIC is seated properly, cable is connected, etc.). Use the COMCHECK utility to check whether a good physical connection exists. To run COMCHECK, the server does not have to be up and running. Just run IPX.COM or ODI files on all connected workstations and then run COMCHECK on all workstations. The COMCHECK screen will show you information about all communicating workstations.

- If only one workstation is having problems, check for TSRs (Terminate-and-Stay Resident programs) and other programs like a disk space doubler program. These programs may have some conflict with NetWare workstation files. Also check AUTOEXEC.BAT and CONFIG.SYS files for any conflicting commands. You should have a bootable disk with only NetWare workstation files to help troubleshooting the workstation.

- Make sure the correct frame type is used on both the workstation and the file server.

- Make sure the correct LAN driver is loaded and bound to the protocol at the server. Use the TRACK ON utility on the server to check communication between workstations and the server.

- If two workstations are having network access problems, check for duplicate addresses.

- Check for any possible hardware configuration conflicts. For example, if your workstation locks up at random, you may have an IRQ conflict between two devices (between the mouse and NIC, for example). Use Check✓It Pro to check hardware settings for the devices.

- If you have more than one server and want to connect to a specific server, either use server name with the LOGIN command, or use the "PREFERRED SERVER" command in NET.CFG. Note that, if your "PREFERRED SERVER" is not available, you will be connected to the server that responds first. One of my users once was connected to a backup server when the preferred server was temporarily unavailable. She actually entered some data in the backup server without knowing it. This kind of situation can be very undesirable.

  (The DISABLE LOGIN console command can be used on the backup server so users will not be able to log in to the backup server if the preferred server is not available .)

Troubleshooting Tips When Using IPX/NETx

- Make sure the IPX.COM file is for the NIC you are using and has the proper configuration of the card. Run IPX with /I option to check configuration.

- Make sure that NETx is for the version of DOS you are using. Download the latest NETx.EXE from the NetWire (DOSUPx.ZIP).

- If you cannot change to the network drive after running NETx, check for the LASTDRIVE command in CONFIG.SYS file. Your first network drive will be the next alphabet letter after the letter specified in the LASTDRIVE command. For example, if your LASTDRIVE command is:

    LASTDRIVE=E

The first network drive will be F:.

Note: You must not have the LASTDRIVE=Z command in CONFIG.SYS when using NETx.

Troubleshooting Tips When Using ODI Files/VLM

- Make sure you are using the latest version of the DOS Requester. Many bugs have been fixed since the first version.

- Make sure the main headings in the NET.CFG file are left justified and the parameters are indented. If a main heading is not left justified it will be ignored.

- Make sure the LASTDRIVE=Z command is in the CONFIG.SYS file. The DOS Requester will not connect to the network if it is missing.

- VLMs load from the current directory. Make sure the directory is correctly specified in the configuration file if VLMs are not to be loaded from current directory.

- VLMs must load in their proper order. Make sure all VLMs are ordered correctly.

- Do not load the NETX.COM or NETX.EXE program with VLMs. These shells are not compatible with the DOS Requester. NETx.VLM is used to provide backward compatibility.

- Do not include VLMs that you do not want to load in the NET.CFG file or comment them out by using the semi colon (;) before the VLM name.

Working With Diskless Workstation

A diskless workstation is a computer with no floppy or hard disk. A diskless workstation is not a "dumb" terminal. It is a complete computer without any drive. Diskless workstations have the following advantages:

- Security And Virus Prevention: Users cannot copy company data to floppy disks and cannot introduce virus from floppy disks.

- Diskless workstations may cost less.

- They have fewer maintenance problems.

- Offer centralized management of DOS boot files.

To use diskless workstations, you install a remote boot PROM chip on the NIC. The Boot PROM chip must be compatible with the NIC you are using. Buy it from the NIC manufacturer or use a recommended compatible PROM. You need to have at least one workstation on the network with a floppy or hard disk to run the NetWare DOSGEN utility.

DOSGEN copies all NetWare startup files from the workstation disk to a file called NET$DOS.SYS in the SYS:LOGIN directory. The NET$DOS.SYS file is called the boot image file. When you boot a diskless workstation, the PROM in the NIC establishes a connection with the server and boots the workstation from the DOS files in the boot image file.

You can create one boot image file (NET$DOS.SYS) if all diskless workstations have similar boot requirements or you can create one boot image file for each diskless workstation. The BOOTCONF.SYS file is used to manage boot image files. This file has the node address and boot image file name for each workstation.

Steps To Use DOSGEN Utility

1. Install remote boot PROM in the NIC and configure your NIC to recognize it. To configure the NIC, you may have to use jumpers on the card or setup software. You will do this for each diskless workstation.

2. Login to the network as a Supervisor from a workstation that has at least one drive.

3. Insert the boot disk for the remote boot workstation into the drive A. This boot disk should have only the files necessary to boot a workstation. These files are usually COMMAND.COM, IO.SYS, MSDOS.COM, AUTOEXEC.BAT, CONFIG.SYS, and the NetWare workstation files (VLMs, ODI files, etc.). DOSGEN copies all files from the boot disk to the boot image file on the file server.

4. Change to the SYS:LOGIN directory and run the DOSGEN utility (if there is no search mapping for the SYS:SYSTEM directory, you must specify the complete path). Type:

    F:\login>DOSGEN
          or
    F:\login>\SYSTEM\DOSGEN

    DOSGEN creates a boot image file called NET$DOS.SYS in the SYS:LOGIN directory. This file has a copy of all the files on the boot disk.

Chapter 5: Troubleshooting the Workstation

5. Copy the AUTOEXEC.BAT file from the boot disk in drive A into the SYS:LOGIN directory. If the user default directory is specified in the login script also copy it to the user's default directory (where the user will be after logging in).

   Note: If AUTOEXEC.BAT is not copied to both SYS:LOGIN directory and the default directory, the user will get a "Batch file missing" error.

6. Flag the NET$DOS.SYS file in SYS:LOGIN shareable by typing:

   Flag NET$DOS.SYS s

   Note: NET$DOS.SYS has some problems with DOS 5.0 and above. If you are using DOS 5.0, you have to run RPLFIX on NET$DOS.SYS. Type:

   F:\login>a:RPLFIX NET$DOS.SYS <Enter>

   Note: Make sure you place the disk with the RPLFIX program in drive A. RPLFIX can be downloaded from NetWire.

   If you are using the Novell Enhanced or IBM RPL PROMs, you need to load the Remote Program Load NLM RPL.NLM) at the file server and bind it to the server's LAN drivers (RPL works with the 802.2 frame type only.) before booting the workstation. You also need to load the RPL.COM file (after LSL and before the LAN driver) on the workstation if you are using ODI drivers. Make sure your boot PROM supports ODI.

To create multiple boot image files (if every diskless workstation needs to have its own boot image file), you can use BOOTCONF.SYS file. Check Novell product manuals for more information.

TRACK ON Command

The TRACK ON command is used at the server to investigate problems with servers, routers, and workstation connection.

The TRACK ON display information is formatted according to whether the server is receiving information (IN), broadcasting information (OUT), or handling a connection request. Figure 5-3 shows a sample TRACK ON screen.

TRACK ON displays three types of information:

Routing Information Protocol (RIP)

RIP is used by routers and servers to inform each other about the networks they know.

Workstation Connection Request

The Service Advertising Protocol (SAP) request/response information is displayed when a workstation is connecting to a server.

Service Advertising Protocols (SAP)

SAP is used by servers, routers, and gateways to advertise their services.

```
1 RIP        IN [0000AAA1:008013F54C3D] 4:52:13pm  00000A01 1/2
             OUT [00000A10:FFFFFFFFFFFF] 4:52:21pm  00000A01 2/3   000AAA10 1/2
             0000AAA1 1/2
2 RIP        OUT [000AAA10:FFFFFFFFFFFF] 4:52:21pm  00000A01 2/3   00000A10 1/2
             0000AAA1 1/2
             OUT [0000AAA1:FFFFFFFFFFFF] 4:52:21pm  00000A10 1/2   000AAA10 1/2
             IN [00000A10:000000000001] 4:52:39pm       PCAGE10   1
3 SAP        IN [0000AAA1:008013F54C3D] 4:52:43pm       PCAGE01   1
4 SAP        IN [00000A10:000000000001] 4:52:46pm       PS1   1
5 S          IN [0000AAA1:008013790C12] 4:52:47pm       Get Nearest Server
6 A          OUT [0000AAA1:008013790C12] 4:52:47pm      Give Nearest Server PCAGE10
7 P          IN [0000AAA1:008013790C12] 4:52:47pm       Route Request
8 SAP        OUT [00000A10:FFFFFFFFFFFF] 4:52:51pm       PCAGE01   2 PCAGE01   3
```

Figure 5-3 TRACK ON Screen.

Line 1 is an inbound RIP message. Line 2 is an outbound RIP message. Lines 3 and 4 are inbound SAP messages. Lines 5, 6, 7 are workstation SAP connection request/response messages. Line 8 is an outbound SAP message.

Following is a brief explanation of each of TRACK ON's display components:

IN : Indicates that the message is incoming to the server.

OUT : Indicates that the message is outgoing from the server.

First number in the bracket (AAA1 or A10, note that the leading zeroes are filled in by the system) indicates the internal IPX number or network address. In the screen the internal IPX number is A10 and network address is AAA1. NetWare 3.1x file servers use both their internal IPX numbers and their network addresses to send messages.

Second number in the bracket (for example 008013F54C3D in line 1) indicates the node address of the server, router, or workstation. Number FFFFFFFFFFFF indicates a broadcast message. NetWare 3.1x servers also use 1 as a node address when using internal IPX numbers in messages.

Line 1 A01 is the internal IPX network number. 1/ means number of hops from the sending server to this network. In this case it is 1. A hop is one internal or external router that has been crossed by the packet. /2 indicates the number of ticks that a packet would take to reach this network from the sending server. In this case it is 2. A tick is 1/18th of a second.

Line 3 In this SAP message, PCAGE01 is the name of the server and this server is 1 hop away from the sending network (AAA1).

Line 4 is also a SAP message from the print server, PS1.

Lines 5, 6, and 7 are SAP connection request/response messages from a workstation.

Line 8 is an outgoing SAP broadcast message.

Troubleshooting Using TRACK ON

If you are not able to login to the network and you want to check that your workstation is communicating to a file server:

1. Enable TRACK ON at the file server.
2. Load the workstation shell.

   The tracking display should show:

   GET NEAREST SERVER
   GIVE NEAREST SERVER
   ROUTE REQUEST

If this is displayed the workstation has established a connection with the server.

If only GET NEAREST SERVER is displayed, the server has received the request but did not respond. The problem could be a faulty or improperly configured NIC in the server.

If GET NEAREST SERVER and GIVE NEAREST SERVER appear but not the ROUTE REQUEST, the problem could be a faulty NIC or a configuration problem at the workstation or server.

Troubleshooting Workstation Conflicts

When installing network boards or other cards in your workstation, if you have system conflicts, your computer may not operate properly. The four types of conflicts are: IRQ, DMA, I/O address, and Base memory address:

Interrupt Requests (IRQ)

When adding devices on your computer it is important to configure them with interrupts that have not already been assigned. A common PC problem is an interrupt conflict where two devices are trying to use the same IRQ. An interrupt request is used by a hardware device to let the CPU know that a device is requesting a type of service or has completed an operation. Each device must have a unique IRQ assigned. Newer computers have 16 IRQs available.

When dealing with IRQs, another important concept to remember is "cascading". As mentioned before, new PCs have 16 IRQs. They use two banks and each bank has eight IRQs. IRQ 2 (on the first bank) links the first bank to the second. If IRQ 2 is used for this purpose, it cannot be used by devices. Because some devices can use IRQs only from the first bank, it is not a good idea to lose an IRQ from the first bank as a gateway to the second bank. That is why IRQ 9 is addressed as IRQ 2. This relationship is called cascading. IRQ 9 cannot be used by devices if IRQ 2 is used.

The following is a list of IRQ numbers and their uses:

IRQ 0 - System Timer

1. Keyboard

2. Used in AT-type PCs as a gateway to IRQ 8 to 15. Some EGA/VGA video and ARCnet cards use this IRQ.

3. COM2: This is a good choice for a NIC card if COM2 is not used. Ethernet NICs use this by default.

4. COM1

5. LPT2: This is a good choice for a NIC if LPT2 is not used.

6. Floppy drive

7. LPT1

8. System Clock

9. Redirected as IRQ 2

10. Available

11. Available

12. Available

13. Math Coprocessor

14. Hard Drive Controller

15. Available: Generally used for a second hard drive controller.

Direct Memory Access (DMA)

Some devices can write data into the PC memory directly, without CPU intervention. This is called Direct Memory Access (DMA). The DMA gives increased performance.

The old XT-type computers had four DMA channels (0-3) while the AT type computers have eight channels (0-7). Some of these channels are used by standard PC components (hard disk, floppy disk controllers). The rest can be used by other devices. DMA channels can be shared by devices that do not need to use them simultaneously.

Channels

0. Dynamic memory refresh.
1. Hard disk controller.
2. Floppy disk controller.
3. Available.
4 -7. Available on AT and PS/2 computers.

I/O Address (Input/Output Address)

Each device needs a unique I/O address (also called Base I/O or I/O Port) to communicate (read/write) with the CPU. An I/O address is a reserved address in memory. I/O addresses are like post office boxes. If a device has data for the CPU, it puts the data in an I/O address (analogous to a post office box). When the CPU wants to read data from that device, it looks in the I/O address (post office box). CPUs know devices through their I/O addresses. The communication between the CPU and the device is actually communication between the CPU and the I/O address of that device.

The following is a list of the commonly used I/O address ranges:

000 - 00F - Reserved for the system.

1F0 - 1F8 - Hard disk controller.

200 - 207 - Game port.

278 - 27F - LPT2.

2F8 - 2FF - COM2.

378 - 37F - LPT1.

3F0 - 3F7 - Floppy disk controller.

3F8 - 3FF - COM1.

Base Memory Addresses

Some controller cards and LAN boards need a reserved area of PC memory for loading on-board ROM instructions. Some LAN boards may also have a little RAM on-board to buffer incoming or outgoing packets. This on-board RAM also needs a reserved area of PC memory. This reserved area of PC memory is called base memory address. Each card that requires base memory address must use a unique address for proper operation. If two cards are looking for their ROM at the same memory location, neither will work. Some programs may overwrite the card's base memory and cause the workstation to hang indefinitely. You can use the Exclude parameter with EMM386 to protect a card's base memory.

Some cards allow moving the starting addresses of ROM to avoid conflicts, but a card's ROM addresses should not be changed because many software modules rely on a card's standard addresses.

The following base memory addresses are commonly used:

00000 - 9FFFF - System memory

A0000 - B7FFF - Monochrome

B8000 - BFFFF - Super VGA

C0000 - C7FFF - CGA or Super VGA (available for ROM if not used)

D0000 - D7FFF - System memory (available for ROM if not used)

E0000 - EFFFF - AT computers

F0000 - FFFFF - System BIOS

You can see from the above discussion that computer devices can have conflicts and may not work properly. It is important to know which PC resources are already used and which are available when installing new cards in the PC. Check✓It Pro is one of the utilities that can give you this information about your PC. Check✓It Pro, unlike many other utilities, does not just check the BIOS information but actually checks the computer components.

Workstation Setup

CMOS Setup

Most computer systems store system configuration information in a separate configuration memory called the CMOS (Complementary Metal Oxide Semiconductor) chip. The system configuration parameters include the numbers and types of disk drives installed, the amount of system memory, and the date and time. To keep configuration information from being lost when power is removed (by shutting off the system), a battery on the system board provides power for the CMOS configuration chip. During the boot sequence the computer performs a hardware check and compares what it finds against the information stored in CMOS. If the information compares, then normal booting proceeds. If the information is not the same, the system will display a "setup configuration" error. A special BIOS setup routine can be used to configure the CMOS. This routine is usually activated by pressing the <Del> key during the boot process.

Automatic Setup Routine

To simplify installation and avoid an accidental hardware conflict, MCA and EISA boards are designed to be configured automatically through a software setup routine and setup diskette. The software configuration program selects non-conflicting values for the boards and devices installed in the system, and writes the configuration information to the diskette and to memory. This simplifies the process of installing new devices in the system.

Most new network boards do not use DIP switches or jumper to configure IRQ or I/O port, etc. They come with a setup program that is used to configure the board for the desired settings and to save the configuration information in the on board PROM.

IBM Reference Diskette

PS/2 computers come with a reference diskette that contains system programs. When the computer is booted using this diskette, configuration automatically takes place. There are Adapter Definition Files (ADFs) that the reference programs use to accommodate network interface cards. The ADFs that come with the NIC must be copied to the reference diskette. If a configuration conflict exists, the programs eliminate the conflict by assigning different values.

EISA Configuration Program

This is a menu-driven setup program that automatically configures EISA boards and resolves board conflicts. EISA configuration program reads the .CFG file that comes with the board to allocate system resources.

PC - Modes of Operation

The following are the two modes of operation supported by PCs.

Real Mode

This is a PC's basic mode of operation and uses the original design of Intel's 8086 and 8088 microprocessors. Using real mode the CPU is limited to direct addressing of 1MB of memory. When running DOS only 640K of memory is available. The memory above 640K is reserved for various driver interfaces and system functions. In the newer processors, 80286 and above, real mode is emulated to provide backward compatibility with older programs that are single task and can only run in real mode.

Protected Mode

This is the normal mode of operation for 80286 and above microprocessors. Protected mode means that when running more than one application at a time (multitasking), the memory used by the application is protected from being overwritten by another application. 80286 PCs can address up to 16 MB of memory, 80386 and above PCs can address up to 4GB (gigabytes) of memory.

Memory Types

Conventional Memory

DOS was designed to directly use 640 KB of RAM. This is called conventional memory. All DOS programs basically run in 640 KB of memory. Other operating systems like OS/2, Windows NT, and NetWare do not have this limitation. Microsoft Windows and some other programs can also use memory above 640 KB.

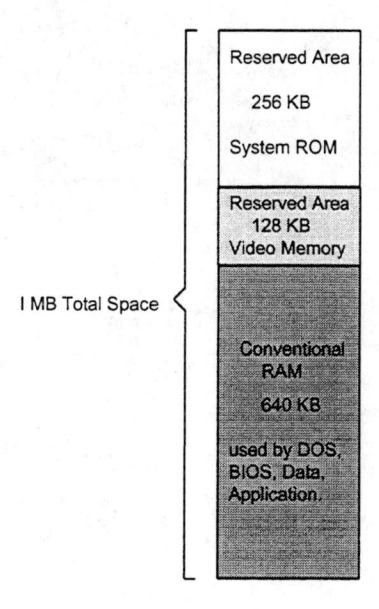

```
                    ┌─ Reserved Area
                    │   256 KB
                    │   System ROM
                    │
                    │   Reserved Area
                    │   128 KB
                    │   Video Memory
1 MB Total Space  ──┤
                    │   Conventional
                    │   RAM
                    │   640 KB
                    │   used by DOS,
                    │   BIOS, Data,
                    │   Application.
                    └─
```

Figure 5-4 Conventional Memory

Extended Memory

Any memory in the computer beyond the 1 MB that the CPU can address is called Extended memory. It is the memory on 286 computers between 1 and 16 MB (a 286 processor can address up to 16 MB of memory), and on a 386 computer it can be up to 4 GB (gigabytes). 8086 and 8088 computers do not have extended memory because these processors can only address up to 1 MB of memory.

As we have seen 80286 and other processors can support a lot more than 1 MB of memory, but DOS is still limited to 640 KB of RAM (initial design problem). Programs like MS Windows can use extended memory.

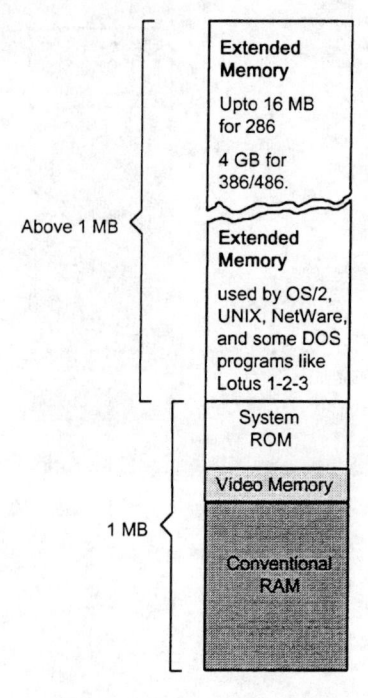

Figure 5-5 Extended Memory

Expanded Memory

Expanded memory (also known as Paged memory) is any computer memory that is not addressable by the CPU or cannot be used directly by DOS. This memory can be used by the help of a special program called EMS (Expanded Memory Specification). The latest EMS software, LIM EMS 4.0 (developed by Lotus, Intel, and Microsoft) uses a technique called **page switching** to swap different pages, usually 16 KB in size, of expanded memory in and out of the 256 KB of reserved area. We have discussed before that the 256 KB of system ROM reserved area is part of 1 MB RAM and it is directly addressable by the CPU. Expanded memory is limited to 32 MB in any system. Expanded memory can be used in 8086/8088, 80286, 80386, and above computers.

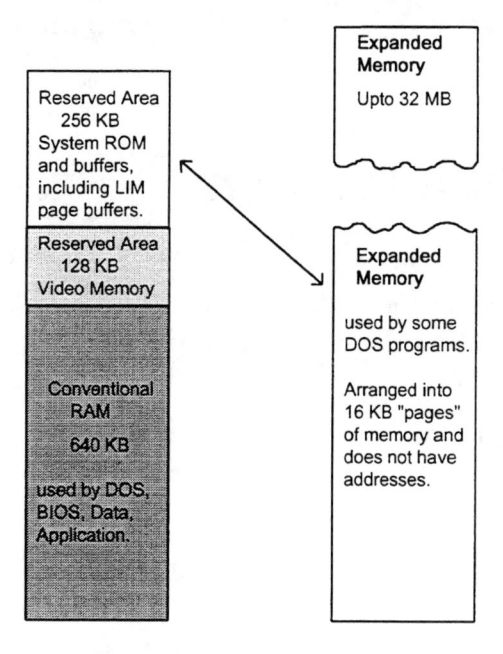

Figure 5-6 Expanded Memory

Some portions of PC memory are also referred to as Upper memory and High memory:

Upper Memory

This is the 384 KB of memory between 640 KB and the real mode boundary of 1 MB. This area is used for special purposes such as ROM BIOS, serial ports, adapter cards, and video. When using Microsoft DOS the HIMEM.SYS device driver works in conjunction with EMM386.SYS, expanded memory manager, to provide UMB (Upper Memory Blocks), which can be used for device drivers and memory resident programs.

High Memory

High memory is the first 64 KB of memory located just above the 1MB real mode boundary (1024 KB to 1088 KB). This memory can be used by DOS when using an extended memory manager (HIMEM.SYS) without having to change to protected mode.

Memory Optimization

After loading NetWare workstation files you usually do not have enough conventional memory to run some DOS applications. One solution is to move NetWare files, device drivers, and TSRs to upper memory. It will give you more than 600 KB of conventional memory for DOS applications.

Here is a sample CONFIG.SYS to get about 614 KB of conventional memory after loading NetWare.

```
DEVICE=C:\DOS\EMM386.EXE /NOEMS
BUFFERS=40
FILES=50
DOS=HIGH, UMB
DEVICEHIGH=C:\DOS\SETVER.EXE
```

Chapter 5: Troubleshooting the Workstation

DEVICEHIGH=C:\DOS\ANSI.SYS

Load NetWare workstation files as follows:

```
LH LSL
LH NE2000        (or any other MLID)
LH IPXODI
LH NETx          (or  LH VLM)
```

Note: VLMs are loaded in extended memory by default and you do not have to load them high. The executable file VLM.EXE can be loaded high, if desired.

Review Questions

Q.1. How many commands do you need to enter to unload a LAN driver if you have ODI drivers and VLM loaded.

    a. 5   b. 4
    c. 3   d. 2

Q.2. Which one of the following is a correct way to unload a LAN driver?

    a. LSL U, NE2000 U
    b. VLM U, IPXODI U, NE2000 U
    c. NE2000 U
    d. VLM U, IPXODI U, LSLU, NE2000 U

Q.3. Which is not a reason to implement ODI?

    a. the LAN will be able to communicate with both existing equipment and the new technologies.
    b. the LAN will be able to deal with many media types and protocols
    c. the server will be able to support different clients
    d. the server will be able to support diskless workstations

Q.4. Which is not an advantage of ODI drivers over IPX.COM

a. ODI Supports multiple protocols on a single network
b. ODI supports LANalyzer for Windows
c. ODI supports faster and more reliable file transfer
d. ODI files can be unloaded in reverse order

Q.5. What is wrong in the following NET.CFG file if your workstation is using Ethernet_802.3 frame?

>   LINK DRIVER NE2000
>   FRAME Ethernet_802.2
>   FRAME Ethernet_802.3

a. section heading is wrong
b. line 2 should be after line 3
c. line 2 and 3 should not be indented
d. there is nothing wrong

Q.6. Which one of the following is related to multiple boot image files?

a. DOSGEN   b. NET$DOS.SYS
c. BOOTCONF.SYS   d. BOOTROM.SYS

Q.7. DR/Novell DOS is reported to NetWare as a DOS version of 3.31. To avoid mapping to the same COMSPEC, What should you do?

   a. add LONG MACHINE TYPE to your NET.CFG
   b. add LONG MACHINE TYPE to your CONFIG.SYS
   c. Use COMSPEC in login script
   d. add DRDOS=3.31 in NET.CFG

Q.8. DMA means _____.

   a. writing data to memory without CPU intervention
   b. Data Memory Active
   c. Digital Memory Active
   d. Digital Asynchronous Mode

Q.9. If your CONFIG.SYS has DEVICE=C:\DOS\EMM386.EXE /FRAME=NONE /X=CC000-DFFF, which of the following address should you use for a Token Ring card?

   a. B8000   b. CCBBB
   c. E8000   d. FCC00

Q10. Consider the following files and determine what is the correct order of loading NetWare DOS Requester?

  1. VLM   2. LSL   3. IPX
  4. ODI   5. NETX   6. IPXODI
  7. NE2000

  a. 1,2,7,6   b. 3,5
  c. 2,7,6,1   d. 2,7,4,1
  e. 2,7,6,5

Q.11. Consider the following files and determine what is the correct order of loading the old NetWare Shell with non-ODI drivers?

  1. VLM   2. LSL   3. IPX
  4. ODI   5. NETX   6. IPXODI
  7. NE2000

  a. 1,2,7,6   b. 3,5
  c. 2,7,6,1   d. 2,7,4,1
  e. 2,7,6,5

Q12. Consider the following files and determine what is the correct order of loading the old NetWare Shell with ODI drivers?

1. VLM   2. LSL   3. IPX
4. ODI   5. NETX   6. IPXODI
7. NE2000

a. 1,2,7,6   b. 3,5
c. 2,7,6,1   d. 2,7,4,1
e. 2,7,6,5

Chapter 6 Troubleshooting and Optimizing the Server

The NetWare Advanced Administration course covers server optimizing techniques using the MONITOR.NLM and SET utilities. MONITOR.NLM is used to view the server's resource usage. SET is used to change parameters to optimize server performance. In this chapter we will discuss the following topics on network optimization and troubleshooting:

- Server Abends and Lockups
- Using the Latest Patches, NLMs, and Utilities
- General Optimization Points
- Optimizing using Hubs, Bridges, and Routers
- Using a Protocol Analyzer (LANalyzer for Windows)

Server Abends and Lockups

Server Abends

The NetWare operating system stops execution with an abend (ABnormal END) message whenever it detects a condition that corrupts its internal data. The abend condition is detected by the CPU (CPU-detected errors) or consistency check process (code-detected errors). Whenever the server's CPU detects an error, it stops program execution by issuing a nonmaskable interrupt (NMI) or processor-detected exception. NMIs are generated when there are hardware problems. Exceptions are generated because of errors in instructions (programs).

NetWare performs consistency checks to validate critical processes running on the server and to ensure integrity of internal data.

Consistency check errors are generated because of a corrupted operating system file, corrupted or outdated NLMs, including hardware drivers, bad packets sent by clients, or hardware failure. Defective memory chips, faulty power supplies, or line power problems can also cause consistency check errors.

An abend message displayed on the server's screen includes date and time at which the system was halted, the abend message itself (CPU-detected error or Code-detected error), operating system version, and the name of process running at the time of abend.

The abend message displayed also shows the 30 hexadecimal bytes that represent part of the CPU's stack for the current running process at the time of abend. This stack dump may be helpful for Novell Technical Support people to diagnose the cause of the abend.

Server Lockups

Like server abends, another serious problem is server lockups. Server lockups are caused by corrupted operating system file, corrupted or outdated NLMs including hardware drivers, or hardware failure. In a server lockup, either the CPU or other server resources are not released by a process.

In a full server lockup, no processes can run and the server is not accessible for anything. A partial lockup may allow users to log in and may clear itself up. It may lead to a full server lockup.

To help diagnose the cause of a server lockup, you may generate a memory image file. A memory image file or core dump is a snapshot of the server's RAM at the time the server abended or locked.

Troubleshooting Server Abends and Lockups

Following steps may be taken to troubleshoot server abends and lockups:

- Gather and analyze all error messages including message on the server screen, system error log file, and volume error log file.

    You also need to gather information about server configuration including NCF files and CONFIG.SYS and a listing of current NLMs loaded.

    Novell provides CONFIG.NLM to gather above information about your server. When you run CONFIG.NLM it saves the above information about your server in the CONFIG.TXT file in SYS:SYSTEM directory. CONFIG.TXT file contains server's AUTOEXEC.BAT, CONFIG.SYS, AUTOEXEC.NCF, STARTUP.NCF, and directory listing of SYS:SYSTEM and your local drive.

    You can download CONFIG.NLM from NetWire or NSEPro. (NSEPro (Version 95-9) contains the file

TABND1.EXE that includes CONFIG.EXE. Run CONFIG.EXE to extract CONFIG.NLM.)

- Pay special attention to recent changes made to the system. It includes any hardware and software changes. For example, memory upgrade, video adapter changes, controller changes, loading a new NLM, etc.
- Check for any unusual activities before abend or lockup such as very high workload (may be because of backup or database queries) or installation of new hardware or software.
- Make sure you are using the latest patches and fixes. Most server problems can be solved by applying the latest patches and files.
- Get help from friends, Novell user groups, CompuServe, or Internet.

After you have done all the above steps, and problem still exists, call Novell Technical Support for help. If you suspect that the problem is related to a specific hardware or software, call the vendor technical support.

The Novell Technical Support engineers may ask you to create a memory image or core dump of the server to analyze the problem.

Using the Latest Patches, NLMs, and Utilities

To avoid or troubleshoot server problems, make sure (before you do anything else) you are using the latest patches, NLMs, and other NetWare utilities. You can download latest and updated software from NetWire (library areas) or from NSEPro CD-ROM. For example, you can download 311PTD.EXE, 312PT6.EXE, and 410PT2.EXE to update 3.11, 3.12, and 4.10 operating systems respectively. Novell uses the following naming convention for these files:

First 3 digits for the operating system version, PT for Passed Test or IT for In Test, and revision number or letter.

NetWare uses two types of patches:

1. **Dynamic:** This type of patch is implemented as an .NLM file that can be loaded and unloaded when the server is up.

2. **Static:** This type of patch modifies the NetWare operating system SERVER.EXE file. The patch is DOS-executable and once applied it is a permanent change. Keep a backup of SERVER.EXE when applying this type of patch. The command **Patch-name SERVER.EXE** can be used to apply a static patch.

Dynamic patches modify SERVER.EXE in RAM and must be loaded each time the system is brought up. These types of patches can be loaded automatically by placing the LOAD <patch> command in the STARTUP.NCF file or AUTOEXEC.NCF file. Check the README file that comes with the patch kit for instructions. PATCHMAN.NLM (the Patch Manager) must be loaded before any dynamic patches can be loaded. The Patch Manager is used to manage all patches. Typing the PATCHES command at the server console shows the patches according to their type.

General Optimization Points

The MONITOR.NLM utility and the SET command are mainly used to view memory usage and to change default settings. One of the most important statistics to monitor is the Cache Buffers percentage. It should be 40% - 60% of total memory or more. The more memory you have in a file server, the better the performance.

1. You should have at least 16 MB RAM in your server even if you calculate that you need less memory. The server will use all extra RAM for file caching. Cached files are accessed as much as 100 times faster than files stored on hard disk. There are also directory cache buffers to cache Directory Entry Table (DET) and the File Allocation Table (FAT).

   Note: As directory cache buffers increase, file cache buffers decrease. Both should be balanced for optimum performance.

2. Use MONITOR.NLM to view file cache buffers and directory cache buffers and use related SET parameters to change the setting, if desired.

   a) If MONITOR.NLM screen shows a continuous growth in the number of **Dirty Cache Buffers** and **Current Disk Requests**, it indicates a disk I/O bottleneck. If the server is constantly accessing the hard disk (disk light on the server is constantly flashing), it may also indicate a disk I/O problem.

   To solve disk I/O bottlenecks, use faster disks and

Chapter 6: Troubleshooting and Optimizing the Server

controllers, use multiple smaller disks instead of one big disk. This way there will be more read/write heads working to give you better performance.

For server hard disk a Fast SCSI II (data transfer rate is 10 MB/second), or Wide SCSI II controller (data transfer rate is 20 MB/second), or controller with on-board processor is a good choice to eliminate disk I/O problems.

b) If MONITOR.NLM shows a high CPU utilization percentage, upgrade to a faster processor. Using bus master NIC and disk controller will also reduce CPU utilization since a bus master board relieves the CPU of some of the processing load.

c) If your network is slow because of using heavy database applications, graphic files, or heavy file and print services, you may have a network I/O problem.

Check MONITOR utility (LAN Information option in NetWare 3.12 or LAN/WAN Information in NetWare 4.1) for the "NO ECB available", "Send Packet too big", "Receive Packet Overflow", "Receive Packet too big", "Send Packet miscellaneous errors", and "Receive Packet miscellaneous errors" values. If these values are constantly high and growing, you may have a network I/O problem.

To avoid network (NIC) I/O problems, use an EISA or MCA server with EISA or MCA NIC, or use a bus master NIC. Also consider using a bridge or router to

Troubleshooting & Supporting Networks

isolate high-network-traffic segments.

3. Loading and Unloading NLMs frequently can fragment the memory and you may not be able to load an NLM. You cannot use DOS utilities to defragment the server's RAM. The only way to defragment the RAM is to bring down the server and load it again.

4. Each NIC has a maximum packet size it can support. You should be using the maximum size possible for better performance. NetWare's default physical receive packet size is 1514 bytes. You can change this using SET Maximum Physical Receive Packet Size parameter.

5. When using routers or telephone connections in your network, NetWare Packet Burst Protocol and Large Internet Packet (LIP) support can give you significant performance improvement.

6. Novell's Service Advertising Protocol (SAP) broadcast affects traffic performance over slow telephone lines (when using WAN). You can use the NetWare Service Advertising Restrictor (NSAR) to filter or minimize the SAP traffic. NSAR's main module, RESTRICT.NLM, is also used to hide certain servers and other resources from some segments. NSAR is bundled with the NetWare Multi-Protocol Router.

7. If using a name space for the support of non-DOS files, it is better to use a separate volume for each name space. If you have volumes with multiple name spaces, increase the

Minimum Directory Cache Buffers to speed up the mounting of volumes and to gain faster access.

Optimizing Using Hubs, Bridges, and Routers

Hubs

A hub is defined as a central point of concentration for wiring. Hubs (which operate at the OSI Physical layer) are also referred to as concentrators and multistation access units. Hubs use the Star topology that means if there is a problem with a single connection, the rest of the network continues to operate. Intelligent hubs can accept different types of wiring (Physical layer media) into a single unit.

Bridges

Bridges work at the Data-Link layer and are used to connect two segments of a single network. They are capable of reading the packet's physical source and destination addresses. Bridges are mostly used to divide a network that has an overload of traffic by selectively routing traffic based on the physical address.

There are two types of bridges — transparent and source routing. Transparent bridges have intelligence in that they store source and destination addresses in a table and use this information to determine whether to forward a packet or not.

Source Routing bridges do not have the intelligence of transparent bridges. The entire route must be transmitted by the source node along with the data packet. This type of bridge is found primarily on IBM networks.

Routers

Routers work at the Network layer and can read the logical source and destination network addresses of a packet. They use algorithms based on the network addresses to determine the best path through the internetwork. Routers are slower than bridges because there is more overhead in their processing.

Troubleshooting Tips for Hubs, Bridges, and Routers

1. Remember the 5-4-3 Ethernet rule. There can be up to 5 segments connected by up to 4 repeaters or hubs, and only 3 of the segments can be populated. The unpopulated segments are used for extending the distance.

2. Whenever the traffic on a network segment exceeds 60% to 70% of capacity, the network segment should be divided using a bridge or router.

3. As a general rule the best possible throughput when using a bridge is 60%.

4. When installing a remote bridge you should plan to allow for the increased response time of any applications that are accessed over this bridge.

5. When using an IBM Source Routing Bridge, remember to load ROUTE.NLM at the server and ROUTE.COM at the workstations.

6. Routers from different vendors may not interoperate because of the lack of standards.

7. When making the choice between a router and a bridge remember that a router can be as much as three times slower than an equivalent bridge. Another choice would be a Brouter; a device that can operate as a bridge or router.

8. When hubs are used as repeaters, the SQE (Signal Quality Error) or heartbeat on Ethernet cards should be turned off, as it is with any repeaters.

Using a Protocol Analyzer (LANalyzer)

A protocol analyzer allows you to see how efficiently your network is functioning. One way of performance tuning is to measure your network performance under current conditions, make changes, then measure the performance again to see if the changes were effective. A protocol analyzer can be software only or a combination of hardware and software. Novell's protocol analyzer is called LANalyzer for Windows (LZFW) and is a software-only protocol analyzer.

LANalyzer allows you to monitor the activity of Ethernet and Token Ring networks, establish base-line and trend information, produce reports, optimize and troubleshoot the network, and plan for future growth. Another important feature of LZFW is packet decoding. You can capture all packets or specific packets for detailed analysis. You can view each captured packet in its raw hex form to find out exactly what is inside the packet. Packet decoding can be used to troubleshoot difficult-to-find protocol errors. LZFW requires a promiscuous driver at the workstation where it is being used, meaning the NIC will accept all packets not just the packets sent (addressed) to it.

Using LZFW

This section should give you a conceptual understanding of LZFW on an Ethernet network. For proper performance, LZFW should be run on a 386 DX or above CPU and a 32 bit NIC card is recommended. Do not run with an 8 bit NIC card. LZFW does not require a dedicated-workstation. It can run in the background while other work is being performed.

Following tasks can be accomplished with LZFW:

- Monitoring Real Time Activity
- Trend Analysis
- Troubleshooting

Monitoring Real Time Activity

The LZFW main screen has three analog dashboard gauges to show packets per seconds, bandwidth utilization percentage, and errors per seconds. Underneath the dashboards are alarm indicators for networks, servers, and routers. The Station Monitor provides detailed traffic and error information for each active station on the network.

Trend Analysis

LZFW allows you to document the activity of your network over a period of time (up to 6 months). This process of getting normal data about your network is called baselining. Baselining helps you to identify and diagnose problems and plan for network growth. LZFW shows you detailed graphs for packets transmitted, kilobytes transmitted, network errors, and percentage of bandwidth utilization over a period of time. By looking at these graphs, you can identify normal and peak conditions of your network.

Detailed graphs and other reports on Station Monitor data, Ring Monitor data (Token Ring), and alarm logs can be printed. Select the Monitor option from the main menu and then Detailed Statistics to view any of the four detailed graphs. Packets/second, utilization percentage, and errors/second graphs can be viewed by double-clicking on the corresponding dashboard gauge.

Alarm Thresholds

LZFW allows you to set alarm thresholds according to your network baseline. Alarm thresholds notify you of unusual activity that might indicate a problem. Network alarms include the NetWare Expert — an artificial intelligence help utility. The NetWare Expert further analyzes the problem and provides possible solutions.

To set alarm thresholds, capture trend data for at least a month to establish a baseline. After you have a baseline, set the six alarm components as follows:

1. **Packets/second.** This threshold should be set at 10% over your normal peak activity, as established by your baseline.

2. **Utilization (%).** Utilization should be set at 5% above your normal peak activity.

3. **Broadcasts/second.** You can start with 10. Increase as the utilization increases.

4. **Fragments/second.** You can start with 15. Increase as the utilization increases.

5. **CRC Errors/second.** CRC (Cyclical Redundancy Check) Errors/second can begin at 5.

6. **Server Overloads/minute.** This can be set to 5. Increase this as you add more workstations.

Other advanced alarms, as shown in Figure 6-3, can be enabled to signal events that should never occur on the network. There are no threshold values for them. If the alarm is enabled, it will go off at the first instance of the event.

Troubleshooting & Supporting Networks

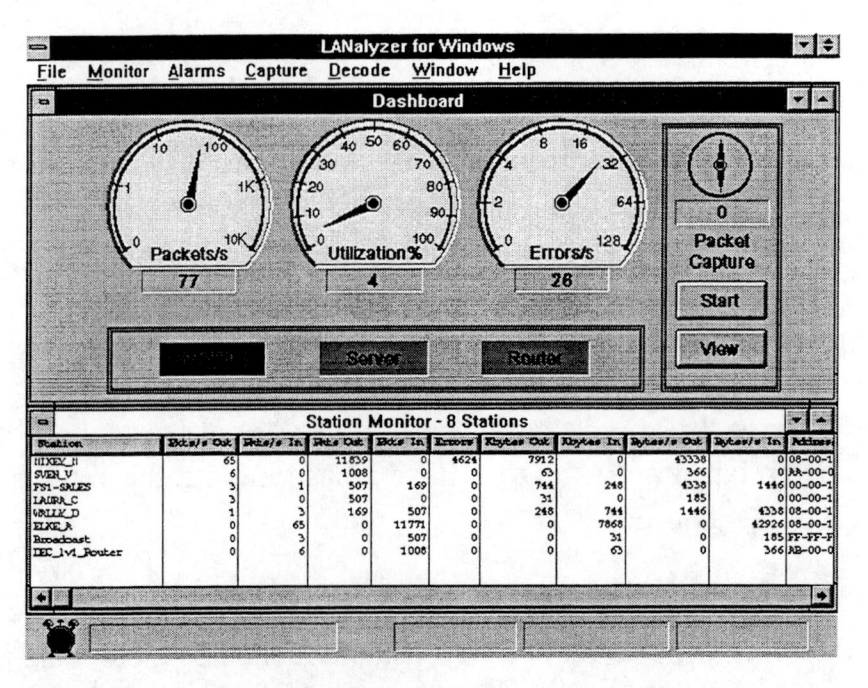

Figure 6-1. LANalyzer for Windows Dashboard

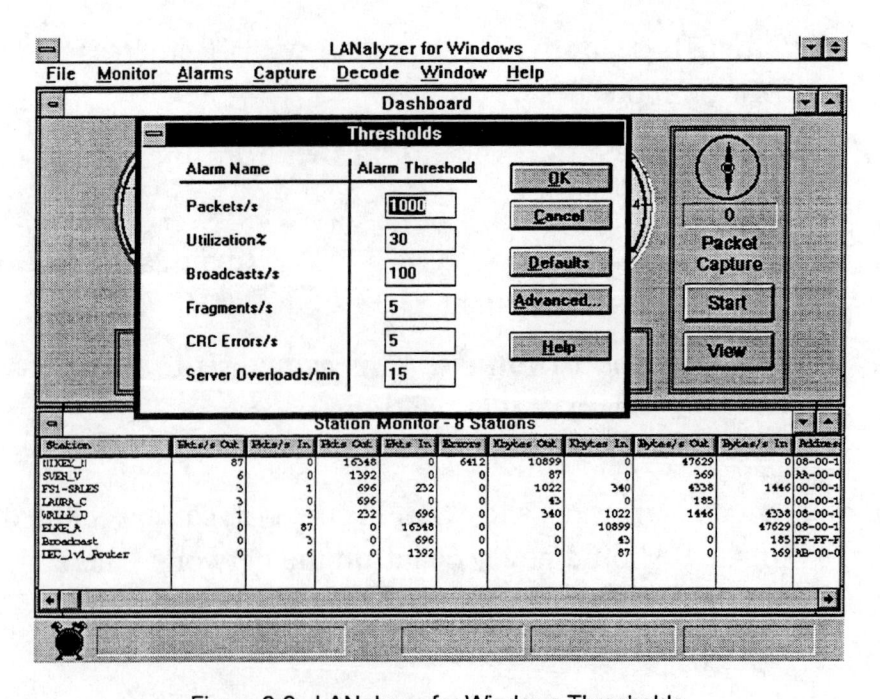

Figure 6-2. LANalyzer for Windows Thresholds

© 1993 - 96 · PC Age, Inc. All Rights Reserved · 20 Audrey Place · Fairfield, NJ 07004 · U.S.A. · Tel: 201-882-5370

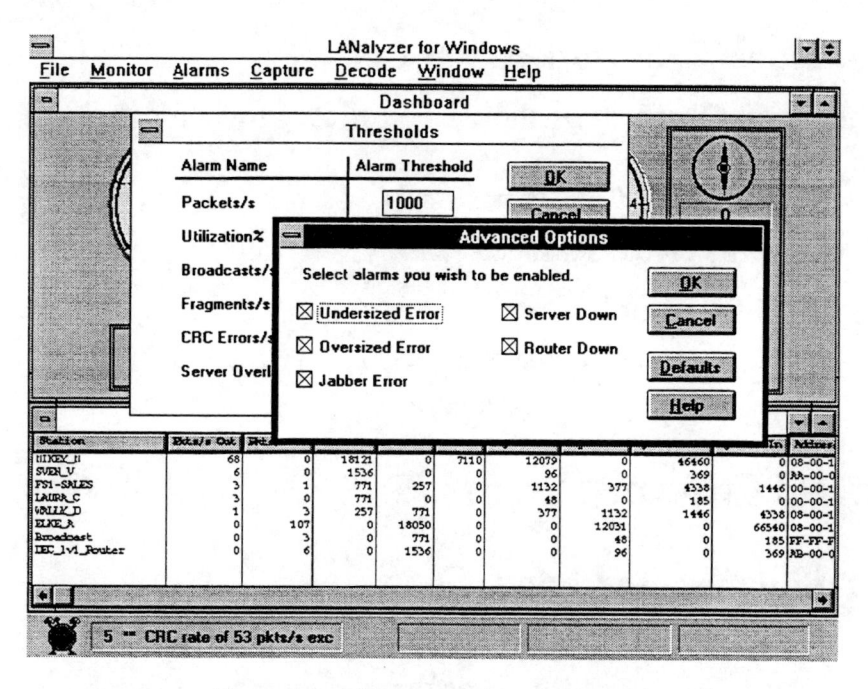

Figure 6-3. LANalyzer Advanced Options

Troubleshooting Using LZFW

LZFW can be used to troubleshoot problems that occur at different layers of the OSI model. For example, it can point to Physical layer problems like defective NICs, repeaters, transceivers, or hubs, ungrounded segment or improper segment termination, and improper taps spacing (10Base5).

Data-link layer problems include different Data-Link protocols being used between workstations and server and defective LAN drivers.

Network layer and above problems that can be diagnosed using LZFW include routing inefficiencies, logical addressing conflicts, and problems with NetWare, TCP/IP, or AppleTalk protocols.

When Does A Network Alarm Occur?

The following three steps should be followed when a network alarm occurs:

1. Read the error message.
2. View the error log.
3. Double click on the NetWare Expert icon for help.

Typical Ethernet Errors

CRC/Alignment Errors

A legal sized packet (64 to 1518 bytes) was received with a faulty Frame Check Sequence (FCS) or the packet was not evenly divisible by 8 (the number of bits in a byte). Possible causes are: a defective NIC or transceiver, a segment is not properly grounded, the 10Base5 taps are too close, there is an improper terminator, an exceeded cable length specification, crosstalk or noise interference, etc.

If multiple stations are generating CRC errors, check for cable problems. If only one station has CRC errors, check the station's NIC or transceiver.

Fragment Error

An undersized packet (less than 64 bytes) with a faulty FCS. Fragments are caused by packet collisions. A certain amount of fragmenting is normal on an Ethernet network. If you get a higher number of fragments/second, your network may be overloaded. Divide your network into segments using bridges or routers. If the network is not overloaded, you may have a faulty NIC or transceiver. Use the Station Monitor to point out the faulty NIC or transceiver.

Undersized Packets

These packets are smaller than the 64 byte minimum used by Ethernet but have a good FCS that means they have reliable data. Usually a defective LAN driver causes this problem. Find the error-causing workstation using the Station Monitor and replace the LAN driver.

Oversized Packets

These packets are larger than the 1518 bytes maximum used by Ethernet with a good FCS. Again check for a faulty LAN driver.

Jabber Errors

These errors are generated because of oversized packets with a faulty FCS. Check cable terminator or locate the faulty NIC.

Wrong Frame Types

This is a common problem with Ethernet networks. If a workstation is not using the frame type supported by the server, this station will get the error message "File Server Not Found" when attempting to log in to the server. After checking other simple things first, such as, physical connections are fine, server is up and running, other stations are connected O. K., etc.; you can use LZFW for help. Check the station that is getting errors in the Station Monitor. If this station is not getting any packets (Pkt/s In=0), it may be using the wrong frame type. Capture some packets using START button. Examine a packet (use VIEW button) sent by the station having the problem. Find out the frame type by looking at the Data-Link layer (it will be marked as 802.3, 802.2, or Ethernet). Now examine packets from the server and other stations that are connecting with the server. You may find a frame type mismatch.

Overloaded Server

When a server cannot immediately process a request from a client it responds with a "Server Overload" or "Server Busy" packet. A few server overloads per minute is normal for a very busy network.

A server overload could be caused by an increased number of devices on the network, an increase in applications usage, and large file transfer.

Symptoms of an overloaded network may include:

- Slow response when loading applications.
- Network receiving or sending errors.
- Duplicate client requests.

If the server overload is caused by a normal increase in network traffic it may be time to segment the network using a bridge or router — splitting or balancing the load across segments. LZFW can be used to verify that the load has been balanced. Other options may be upgrading the current server (more RAM, faster CPU), adding another server to the network, or upgrading the disk drives and I/O channels. Check also MONITOR.NLM before you take any action.

Typical Token Ring Errors

Beaconing Problems

As we have discussed before that if a workstation does not receive a seven-second greeting from its nearest active upstream neighbor (NAUN), it starts sending a beacon packet. A user may complain that he is timing out of the network in this situation. For an administrator, sometimes it becomes very difficult to determine a fault domain (physical locations of beaconing station, its NAUN, and every thing in between) if a proper physical layout of the network is not available. LZFW can be used to determine the fault domain. Here are the steps:

- Select the **Monitor** option on the main (top) strip menu of the Dashboard. Select **Ring Monitor** from the pull-down menu.

- Sort **Beacons Upstream** column (you may have to scroll to the right) by double-clicking the header, so that the station with the largest number of beacons goes to the top. Note the name or node address of the station.

- Double-click on the user name in the **Station** column to get user's **Station Detail** Screen. You may have to click on Ring Information to walk through the ring (to find upstream or downstream neighbor).

- You will see that the beaconing station is reporting many beaconing activities upstream. If you click on the **Upstream** button, you will see information about upstream neighbor. It will report many beaconing activities downstream. This information will help you determine the fault domain.

Congestion Problems

A user may experience long delays or momentary hang-ups when using database files due to congestion. You can use LZFW to confirm that the user has congestion (you can double-click on the red Network Alarm and check the alarm log). Access the NetWare Expert for help. The Expert suggests that if a station transmits congestion errors consistently, it means it is unable to copy the frame due to lack of buffer space. This indicates a possible misconfiguration of the Token Ring LAN driver receive buffers, or an overloaded CPU. Check the receive buffer settings in NET.CFG file. Upgrade the NIC, if desired, to one with additional on-board buffer space. Consider upgrading the CPU.

Review Questions

Q.1. When you go from repeaters to gateways, which of the following is true?

    a. Cost increases, speed increases, functionality decreases
    b. Cost increases, speed increases, functionality increases
    c. Cost increases, speed decreases, functionality increases
    d. Cost decreases, speed increases, functionality increases

Q.2. Which type of error message would it be if your server abend message has the following line:

Abend: SERVER-4.00-3128:SubAllocFreeSectors given invalid. FAT chain end that was already free.

    a. CPU-detected   b. Code-detected
    c. NLM has failed   d. consistency check

Q.3. Which type of error message would it be if your server abend message has the following line:

Abend: Page Fault Processor Exception (Error code 00000000)

    a. CPU-detected   b. Code-detected
    c. NLM has failed   d. consistency check

Q.4. To gather information about a server's configuration that is experiencing problems, which of the following files would you use?

    a. MONITOR.NLM   b. CONFIG.NLM
    c. INSTALL.NLM   d. CONFIG.EXE

Q.5. What is true about consistency check errors? (select all that are true)

    a. they are CPU-detected errors
    b. they are code-detected errors
    c. the purpose of consistency check is to ensure the stability and integrity of internal operating system data.
    d. the purpose of consistency check is to validate critical disk, memory, and communications processes

Q.6. If you are experiencing server abends or lockups, the very first thing you should do is to _____.

    a. call Novell Technical Support
    b. apply the latest patches, drivers, and NLMs
    c. use MONITOR.NLM to identify the problem
    d. create a memory image file

Chapter 6: Troubleshooting and Optimizing the Server

Q.7. If MONITOR screen shows "Send packet too big count" and "Receive packet too big count" values very high, you should _____. (select all that apply)

    a. update to faster NICs
    b. update to faster CPU
    c. divide overloaded network segments with a bridge or router
    d. use many smaller disks instead of one large disk

Q.8. If you are receiving Jabber errors on an Ethernet network, you should_____.

    a. find out fault domain
    b. check for a faulty LAN driver
    c. check cable terminator or faulty NIC
    d. check whether your server is overloaded

Q.9. All OS patches should be applied _____.

    a. through AUTOEXEC.NCF
    b. through STARTUP.NCF
    c. through CONFIG.NLM
    d. according to README file that comes with the patch kit

Q.10. Which file would you edit to correct I/O port of a disk driver that is loaded automatically on server bootup?

    a. AUTOEXEC.NCF   b. STARTUP.NCF
    c. CONFIG.NCF   d. INSTALL.NLM

Q.11. To verify that a user USER1 has frame mismatch error, what should you do using LZFW?

   a. examine packets sent by user USER1 and received by him
   b. examine packets sent by user USER1 only
   c. examine packets sent by user USER1 and other users
   d. examine packets sent by other users only

Q.12. What is the correct procedure to apply the latest patches to the OS?

   1. copy the patches to the server directory on the DOS partition
   2. load the server by typing SERVER
   3. edit the STARTUP.NCF file to load the Patch Manager and patches first
   4. enter PATCHES at the server console
   5. down the server and load it again

   a. 1,2,3,5,4   b. 2,1,3,4,5
   c. 1,5,3,4   d. 5,1,2,3,4

Chapter 7   Troubleshooting Network Printing

In this chapter we will discuss troubleshooting techniques related to network printing.

This chapter discusses only troubleshooting techniques. Setting up a network for printing is taught in the System Administration and Advanced System Administration courses. Please review the following topics from these courses:

- Setting up printing (creating queues and print server, defining printers, assigning queues to printers, and running PSERVER and RPRINTER, etc.).

- Using menu printer utilities such as PCONSOLE, PRINTDEF, and PRINTCON.

- Using command line printer utilities such as CAPTURE, ENDCAP, NPRINT, and PSC.

Printing problems can be categorized in two ways:

- Physical printer problems.
- Problems in the network printing setup (logical or software problems).

Physical Printer Problems

To prevent physical problems, you should clean the printer regularly using a good vacuum cleaner and performing regular maintenance procedures according to the manufacturer's documentation.

If the printer is not printing, make sure that the printer is on, is in good condition, cleaned on the inside, no parts are broken, there is no paper jam, and the toner cartridge is not empty. Turn the printer off, wait a few seconds, then turn it on again to re-initialize its settings. Run the printer self-test to make sure the printer is in proper working condition. You should try to print from DOS to check whether the problem is in the printer itself or in the network printing setup.

If you cannot print from DOS, the printer cable or printer port on the computer or on the printer may not be working properly. Use the following problem isolating techniques:

- Check the printer cable. Make sure pins on your printer cable match the pins on your computer's printer port. You can use a multimeter to check your pin-outs.
- Change the computer to make sure the problem is not in the computer itself.

If you can print using the Print Screen key but cannot print from an application, check the application's settings for the printer.

If you are using a device that allows you to connect two computers with one printer, make sure the sharing device is set properly. Sometimes resetting the printer sharing device will also help. Try to print without using the device to isolate the problem.

Laser Printer Tips

- When changing the toner cartridge, change the fuser bar (rectangular cotton bar) and clean the roller and corona wire carefully.

- If you are getting fuzzy laser output, check for dirty corona wire or you may be running out of toner. Horizontal lines or splotches on the output indicate dirty or damaged print drums or rollers. If output is totally black pages, you may have a broken or fouled corona wire. If output is speckled, you may have faulty primary corona grid that is part of the toner cartridge. Many of these problems can be fixed just by changing the toner cartridge.

- If output looks disproportionately long or short, the drive motor may not be moving the paper through at the correct speed. Check printer manual or manufacturer for troubleshooting procedure.

- Use envelopes and labels that are designed to be used with laser printers. Otherwise, glue may damage the printer components.

- Laser printers should be placed in rooms with adequate ventilation. They need to dissipate much heat.

- When working with an open laser printer, make sure it is unplugged. Some printers do not have shielded power supplies. Working with a plugged-in printer can be extremely dangerous.

PostScript Printer Tips

PostScript printers are used for high-quality print outs. Print jobs that are not in PostScritp format can cause problems. Use the following tips for PostScript printers.

- Make sure you have updated printer driver.
- Make sure cartridge is properly installed in the bay.
- If there is any switch to enable PostScript in your printer, make sure it is on.
- Use the No Banner (NB) and No Tabs (NT) options for all PostScript print jobs. NetWare banner page data is considered as non-PostScript data and the print job will be deleted by the PostScript printer.

  Also check that you are using Byte Stream mode (default mode) for print jobs. Byte Stream mode does not change tabs to spaces (similar to NT option). It is important for the print data that include graphics or preformatted text.

Dot Matrix Tips

- Use quality ribbons.
- Check for the proper DIP switch settings. For example, if you have single-spaced text on computer screen but printed output is double-spaced, you may need to change DIP switch settings.
- If the printer is attached with a serial port, use the DOS MODE command to configure port, speed, parity, and the start and stop bits. Try to avoid serial printing. Parallel printing is easier to setup and is faster. Usually people use serial printing if the printer is more than 10 feet away from the computer. Parallel printers support 10 feet as the standard distance, but you can sometimes go up to 150 feet using quality cable from some manufacturers.
- Some printers support bi-directional printing that is faster than unidirectional printing. Some applications may have

problems with it. Try using unidirectional printing. Make sure to set the DIP switches for unidirectional printing.

Problems in the Network Printing Setup

If a printing problem persists after verifying that there are no problems with printer and other hardware components, you should check the network printing setup.

The first thing to remember is that you should always be using the latest print utilities, IPX, and NetWare shell. Printing utilities can be found in the compressed files on NetWire. Novell uses the following naming convention for these files: PU (Print Utilities) or PS (Print Server), the operating system version, and version number or letter. For example, PU3X01.EXE, PS3X02.EXE, PS4X03.EXE, and PU4X03.EXE.

Files starting with PU have updated print utilities such as CAPTURE, NPRINT, PCONSOLE, PRINTCON, PRINTDEF, PSC. Files starting with PS have updated print server files such as PSERVER, RPRINTER, and NPRINTER.

Network printing problems can be categorized as follows:

- Problems with queues.
- Problems with print servers.
- Problems with remote printers.
- Problems with printing utilities.

Problems with Queues

In network printing, jobs are sent to queues using the CAPTURE command or using other methods such as NPRINT and PCONSOLE. If nothing is printing, check whether the print jobs are going to the queue or not. You can determine which queue is being used by using the CAPTURE command with the /SHOW option. Then use PCONSOLE to check whether the print jobs are actually going to the queue. If jobs are not going to a particular queue, then the queue may be corrupted. If jobs are in the queues but are not being printed, check the status of the print job. If the status is "Ready" then the print server is not printing the print job. The reason may be that the print server is not loaded or there is a physical problem with the printer. Check that printer is turned-on and on-line, printer cable is connected and not loose, there is no jammed paper, and whether printer needs paper, etc. Check whether the print server is loaded or not. Also check whether that queue is assigned to a printer or not. A queue is basically a directory on the server. When you create a queue using PCONSOLE, NetWare creates a directory on the server. This queue or directory holds the print job until the print server prints this job. You should have enough space available on the server to hold the print jobs. If you do not have enough space for print jobs, you will see this error message: "WARNING -- CANNOT CREATE SPOOL FILE." Use VOLINFO (NetWare 3.12), FILER (NetWare 4), or NWADMIN (NetWare 4) to verify space availability and take appropriate actions to add more space.

If print job is not arriving at the queue, arrives corrupted, arrives but print job status does not change to Ready, or print job merges with another print job at the printer, check if your application is using the most current printer driver and printing setup inside the application is correct.

Problems with Print Servers

A print server is a device that provides printing services. You create a print server account using PCONSOLE or NWADMIN (NetWare 4). The print server can then be loaded either on a file server using PSERVER.NLM or on a workstation using PSERVER.EXE (called a dedicated print server in NetWare 3.12). A NetWare print server can support up to 16 printers in NetWare 3.12 and up to 255 in NetWare 4 but the more printers supported, the slower the performance.

Loading/Unloading PSERVER.NLM

To unload or down PSERVER.NLM you can use the UNLOAD console command or use PCONSOLE. Using PCONSOLE is the preferred method because if the print server is printing a job, it may hang the file server.

Using PSERVER.EXE — Dedicated Print Server (NetWare 3.12 only)

If you are using PSERVER.EXE, make sure you have at least 512 KB of conventional memory for DOS and NetWare files (NetWare shell, etc.) and 10 KB for each printer supported.

PSERVER.EXE will have problems if you are using old versions of IPX or the NetWare shell or if there are any conflicts with the network board.

The "SPX CONNECTIONS=60" statement is required in the NET.CFG file to use PSERVER.EXE.

The utilities in the NETERR.ZIP file on NetWire can be used to automatically reboot your print server after an interruption.

Note: If you have heavy printing needs or are using plotters with CAD/CAM applications, it is recommended that you use a print server device. Many companies, including HP and Intel, offer print server devices.

Troubleshooting Tips

Sometimes slow or erratic printing problems are because of a corrupted print server. The solution may be to delete and then recreate the print server account.

You can specify a password to load the print server. If you do not specify a password but are prompted for a password when loading a print server, you may have misspelled the print server name or there may be errors in the print server configuration. Use PCONSOLE to check print server account name and its configuration.

If you change the print server definitions using PCONSOLE's "Print Server Configuration" option, be sure to unload and load the print server again.

Try to avoid using old PCs (8086, 80286, etc.) as print servers, especially when you want to connect printers directly to them.

Problems with Remote Printers

To use a remote printer (network printer connected to a workstation), you first define the printer as a remote printer using PCONSOLE then you run the RPRINTER.EXE program on the workstation. When using NetWare 4 you specify Manual Load for the remote printer and run NPRINTER.EXE on the workstation. If you see the message "Not Connected" on the print server screen, check if RPRINTER or NPRINTER is running.

RPRINTER.EXE (or NPRINTER.EXE) and other related files (check the *NetWare Print Server* manual for the list of files) can also be copied to a local drive for loading without logging in.

If you are having problems using RPRINTER.EXE or NPRINTER.EXE, the problem may stem from one or more of the following:

- You may be using old NetWare files (IPX, NetWare shell, RPRINTER, etc.). The latest RPRINTER.EXE, NPRINTER.EXE, and NPRINTER.NLM can be found on NetWire.

- You may not have enough RAM.

- Your workstation may not be truly IBM compatible.

- RPRINTER.EXE or NPRINTER.EXE, a memory resident program, may have problems with other TSRs (Terminate and Stay Resident programs). Try to use it without any other TSR program to isolate the problem.

- If using serial remote printer, make sure the printer is configured through its DIP switches and you have defined the printer in print server (using PCONSOLE) using the same configuration (data speed, data bits, stop bits, etc.).

- RPRINTER or NPRINTER can be installed without error only after print server (PSERVER) is loaded. To make sure of this, create a batch file at the workstation to run RPRINTER or NPRINTER. This batch file should include an IF statement to retry RPRINTER or NPRINTER until print server is up and running.

- The person at the workstation with the remote printer attached should not print locally without using the PSC PRIvate option, otherwise the print job will be ruined.

Make sure CAPTURE command is made active if the remote printer is in SHARed mode.

- If you reboot the workstation to reinitialize RPRINTER or NPRINTER, wait at least 30 seconds after booting before you run RPRINTER. Otherwise, you may get an error message stating that the remote printer is in use.

- If you are using RPRINTER or NPRINTER over the router, you may have to increase the "SPX ABORT TIMEOUT" and "IPX RETRY COUNT" parameters in the NET.CFG file.

Problems with Printing Utilities

PCONSOLE

PCONSOLE is the main utility for setting up and configuring network printing. PCONSOLE is used to create queues and print server accounts, and to define the printers on the network.

If a printer is dropping characters or words on a printout, increase the buffer size of the printer in PCONSOLE.

If you get very slow and erratic printing because of an interrupt conflict, do not use interrupt for the printer. You can disable interrupt for the printer using PCONSOLE.

If you are using the PCONSOLE "Print Server Status/Control" (NetWare 3.12) or "Information and Status" (NetWare 4) option, you may have problems when using routers. Try increasing the "SPX TIMEOUT" and "IPX RETRY" parameters in the NET.CFG file.

PRINTCON

The PRINTCON utility is used to create print job configurations to be used with the CAPTURE, NPRINT, or PCONSOLE utilities. Each user is limited to 37 print job configurations. Print job configurations are created for each user and saved in the PRINTCON.DAT database file that is located in the USER_ID subdirectory of the SYS:MAIL directory. One way to share a PRINTCON.DAT file is to store it in the SYS:PUBLIC directory and then change the Search Mode of the CAPTURE, NPRINT, and PCONSOLE files to "5" using the SMODE (NetWare 3.12) or FLAG (NetWare 4) command.

For example:

    SMODE CAPTURE.EXE 5

Now the CAPTURE program will look for the PRINTCON.DAT file on the default path first and then on the search drives. In this case PRINTCON.DAT file should not be in user's MAIL directory or it will be used instead of PRINTCON.DAT file in SYS:PUBLIC directory.

If you are using the TIMEOUT setting in the print job configuration file and getting a printout on multiple pages instead of just one (premature page breaks), increase the TIMEOUT seconds or disable it. It is the most common problem with graphics files.

PRINTDEF

The PRINTDEF utility is used to define forms and print devices. PRINTDEF sends control codes to the printer that change printer modes (bold, condensed, character size, font, etc.). For complex printers, and especially postscript printers, the default buffer space for control codes may not be enough.

If you have faulty printing, try increasing the buffer size using the PRINT HEADER and PRINT TAIL commands in the NET.CFG file.

CAPTURE and NPRINT

The CAPTURE command is used to redirect print jobs from a local port to a specific print queue. The NPRINT command is used to print files to the network printers (by directly sending them to a print queue).

If you do not specify a queue name with these commands, you will get an error message that no default queue is specified. To specify a default queue, use the SPOOL console command.

If you have problems printing graphics, use the No Tabs (/NT) parameter with the CAPTURE and NPRINT commands.

Include the /Keep option with the CAPTURE command to ensure that the file server keeps and prints all data it has captured from the workstation even if the workstation loses the connection with the server. If you do not use the /Keep option, and your workstation loses the connection during CAPTURE, the file server discards the data it has received.

Note: When using postscript printers, use the No Banner (/NB), No Tabs (/NT), and No Form Feed (/NFF) parameters with the CAPTURE and NPRINT commands.

Common Problems Associated With Network Printing

1. User tries to print without issuing a CAPTURE command or he/she is using CAPTURE command incorrectly.

   Make sure the user is using CAPTURE correctly by using CAPTURE /SHOW command.

2. CAPTURE command is issued through the login script, without specifying a queue name while there is no default queue specified.

   Either specify queue name with CAPTURE command or specify a default queue using SPOOL command (NetWare 3.12) at the server console.

3. Jobs are going to the queue, but not being printed.

     Check if:
   i. queue is assigned to a printer.
   ii. print server is loaded.
   iii. RPRINTER or NPRINTER is loaded on a workstation to which a remote printer is connected.

4. A supervisor cannot perform the Print Server Operator functions.

   Check if supervisor is deleted from the "Print Server Operator" list.

5. Running RPRINTER or NPRINTER without specifying a remote printer.

6. Running RPRINTER or NPRINTER before loading the print server.

7. Two printers are using the same parallel port setting. Loading the print server will cause an error message to appear on the screen.

8. After making changes in the print server account under PCONSOLE by selecting the Print Server Configuration option, remember to down (unload) the print server and reload it so that the changes may take effect.

9. When using PSERVER.EXE (dedicated print server in NetWare 3.12), the NET.CFG file, for that workstation, is missing the "SPX CONNECTIONS=60" line. Also make sure NET.CFG file is located in the same directory from where workstation files are running.

10. RPRINTER is made PRIVATE, nobody is able to access the remote printer.

    Try the "SHARE" option with the PSC utility to solve the problem.

11. A user has defined a default print job configuration file under PRINTCON that he does not want to use but he is unable to delete it.

    You cannot delete default print job from PRINTCON

utility. To delete a default print job configuration for that user, you will need to go to the directory SYS:MAIL\USER_ID and delete PRINTCON.DAT file from there.

12. Users' jobs get intermixed (part of one user's job prints, then another user's job prints before the first one is finished). Increase the Timeout. Some applications such as graphics or databases take a long time to print.

13. If you are getting odd characters mixed in the print job or problems like printing one character on one page, very slow printing, etc.

    Try the following:

    i. use /NT (No Tab) option with CAPTURE.
    ii. use polled mode instead of interrupt mode. You can change this in the printer definition using PCONSOLE.
    iii. make sure you are using the latest versions of printing utilities (PSERVER.NLM, RPRINTER.EXE, etc.) and workstation files (NETx, IPX, etc.). This is important if you are using NetWare 3.11.

Review Questions

Q.1. To get the latest version of RPRINTER, you should download _____ from NetWire.

    a. RPRINTER.ZIP   b. PS3X0x.EXE
    c. PU3X0x.EXE   d. PUTILx.EXE

Q.2. When using serial printers attached with the server, which of the following commands would you be using?

    a. MODE COM1:96,N,8,1,P
    b. MODE LPT1:=COM1:
    c. load PSERVER /SERIAL
    d. none

Q.3. To preserve the part of the job that has already been CAPTURed prior to the connection loss, which of the following commands would you use?

    a. CAPTURE /KEEP   b. CAPTURE /SAVE
    c. CAPTURE /SHOW   d. CAPTURE /NOTIFY

Q.4. When using a laser printer, which of the following need not be cleaned and changed?

    a. Toner cartridge   b. Roller
    c. Ribbons   d. Corona wire

Q.5. If the laser printer output is totally black pages, you may have a:

a. Broken ribbon
b. Broken or fouled corona wire
c. Faulty primary corona grid
d. Slow drive motor

Q.6. If the laser printer output is disproportionately long or short, the probable cause might be:

a. The drive motor is not working with correct speed
b. The corona wire needs to be cleaned
c. An old ribbon
d. Inadequate ventilation

Q.7. Which DOS command should be used if you are using a serial printer?

a. SERIAL   b. SMODE
c. PORT   d. MODE

Q.8. If you have single-spaced text on the computer screen, but the printer output is double-spaced, you may need to:

a. Change the ribbon
b. Change the DIP switch settings
c. Use the DOS MODE command
d. Change the toner cartridge

Q.9. If your client is using many serial printers and complaining about printing speed, what would you recommend?

    a. Change from serial to parallel printers
    b. Add more print servers
    c. Add more printers
    d. Add more queues

Q.10. If print jobs go to the queue and are not printed, which of the following may <u>not</u> be true?

    a. Print server is not loaded
    b. Printer cable is loose or printer is off-line
    c. CAPTURE command is not working properly
    d. Queue is not assigned to printer

Q.11. Suppose you were unable to print on the network from an application. You connected the printer directly to your PC and were able to print using Print Screen. You still cannot print from the application in local mode. What could be wrong?

    a. Print Server is not loaded
    b. CAPTURE command is not issued
    c. Application or its configuration
    d. Printer cable is bad

Q.12. If printing output appears speckled, what could be wrong?

    a. primary corona grid
    b. broken or fouled corona wire
    c. drive motor speed
    d. dirty corona wire or running out of toner

Chapter 8 Disaster Recovery

The rule for disaster recovery is to have reliable backups. A potential disaster can be avoided by ensuring that your system backups of critical data are reliable. Guidelines for establishing reliable backup are:

1. Verify your backup by restoring a selected part of the backup to a disk test area (so as not to overwrite the current data).

2. Use the verify-after-write feature if available.

3. Examine the backup logs to ensure all selected data was indeed backed up.

4. Use a tape rotation method — You should never overwrite the most current backup tapes.

VREPAIR

VREPAIR (Volume Repair) is Novell's utility for correcting minor data structure errors in volumes. VREPAIR should be used if you have a reliable backup and one of the following conditions has occurred:

- A hardware failure has caused a data read error or a volume will not mount.
- A power failure has corrupted data.
- A mirroring error occurs when the server is booted.

A volume must be dismounted to run VREPAIR. It may be necessary to run VREPAIR several times before all errors are corrected.

Note : VREPAIR does not destroy any data but it may. So you should have a reliable backup before you use VREPAIR. VREPAIR is also used to remove a name space from the volume.

To repair the NetWare Directory Services (NDS) database, use DSREPAIR.NLM. Use **LOAD DSREPAIR -U** at the console to run and then unload DSREPAIR.NLM automatically.

When faced with a critical data loss and the backups are not reliable you may consider one of the following options:

- Professional Data Recovery Services — are usually very expensive and generally require you to send your damaged drive to their location. There are companies that provide on-site service at an additional charge. You should never reinstall the NetWare operating system if you plan to use a data recovery service. Reinstalling the operating system will destroy all the data.

- Use a third-party utility such as NETUTIL3 from ONTRACK DATA RECOVERY. NETUTIL3 consists of the following three programs:

    a. NETSCAN3 — is used to examine and repair NetWare volume data structure errors. It can also examine a NetWare 3.x volume for defective sectors and redirect defective blocks to hot fix redirection area.

    b. NETFILE3 — is a file editor and file recovery utility that lets you access files in a volume. This utility allows you to save files to a DOS partition or another device. The volume can then be repaired and the files restored.

    c. NETDISK3 — is used to edit and repair sectors even if DOS and NetWare cannot access the partition on the device. You can also save track 0 (the master boot record) to the DOS partition and restore it if track 0 ever becomes corrupted.

Review Questions

Q.1. Which of the following would you use first in case of valuable data loss if valid backups are unavailable?

    a. VREPAIR
    b. NetUtils3
    c. Professional Data Recovery Services
    d. Hot Fix

Q.2. To copy Master Boot Record (Track 0) of your server, which of the following utilities would you use?

    a. NetDisk3   b. VREPAIR
    c. Check It Pro   d. Recovery Services

Q.3. Which of the following utilities would you use to remove a name space of Macintosh files?

    a. VREPAIR   b. MONITOR
    c. INSTALL   d. TRACK ON

Q.4. Your server's hard disk that has very critical data has been damaged. What should you do if you have reliable and tested backup?

a. Use VREPAIR
b. use Professional Data Recovery Services
c. restore from backup
d. use third-party tools such as Ontrack Data Recovery for NetWare

Chapter 9   Network Management

Network Management

The primary purpose of any organization to use a computerized system or a network system is to work efficiently so costs can be reduced and profits can be increased. The primary purpose of network management is to make sure the organization achieves that goal.

Network management involves day-to-day troubleshooting tasks such as solving workstation configuration and printing problems. These tasks are called **administrative** tasks. It also involves planning, implementing, and maintaining the network. These tasks are known as **management** tasks.

The following tasks may be considered as network administrative tasks. These tasks are more related to day-to-day operations in which you as a network administrator respond or react to problems.

- Directory and file management.
- Installing network applications.
- Managing users and groups.
- Managing network security.

- Managing workstation connections.
- Managing drive mappings, login scripts, and menus.
- Network printing.
- Backup.

The following tasks may be considered as network management tasks. These tasks are more related to planning, implementing, and maintaining rather than reacting to problems. These tasks are usually responsibilities of the network manager.

- Implementing a network-wide virus protection system.
- Monitoring network devices and gathering network statistics for analyzing current and future trends/problems.
- Identifying performance bottlenecks and optimizing the network.
- Assuring a smooth-operational network.
- Inventorying and documenting the existing system.
- Evaluating business needs and providing network solutions.

A network management life cycle may include the following four phases:

1. Analysis and specification
2. Design
3. Implementation
4. Maintenance

1. Analysis and Specification Phase

In this phase you analyze the business needs, specify a project, and create a team to complete the project. Describe resources needed for the project and make preliminary schedules.

In this phase you also identify business needs and management goals, gather business information for the project, and possible risks to achieve business goals.

2. Design Phase

Design phase includes identifying and evaluating alternative solutions, and selecting the best solution. Testing of hardware and software to select the best solution is also done in this phase.

3. Implementation Phase

This includes creating an implementation schedule, implementing and testing the selected solution, and training the users.

4. Maintenance Phase

Maintenance phase includes troubleshooting, monitoring the network devices and gathering network statistics, optimizing the network, etc.

Introduction to ManageWise

ManageWise is a network management tool developed jointly by Novell and Intel. ManageWise simplifies network management by allowing network administrators to perform the following tasks from a central location:

- Servers, routers, workstations, and print queues management that includes monitoring and optimizing from a remote location (administrator's workstation).

- Remote monitoring and control of computers (such as users' workstations) including configuration management, network analysis including traffic analysis and network troubleshooting (similar to LANalyzer for Windows).

- Hardware and software inventory. ManageWise tracks hardware and software components of the network, keeps an up-to-date record of all computers and notifies you of any changes. It also creates graphical maps of the network.

- Network-wide real-time virus protection.

Review Questions

Q.1. Select that which is (are) true about the Analysis Phase of a network management life cycle.

   a. describing management goals, constraints, and resource requirements
   b. gathering general information about the project
   c. evaluating alternative solutions
   d. documenting the system or solution and training the users
   e. monitoring the network system

Q.2. Select that which is (are) true about the Design Phase of a network management life cycle.

   a. describing management goals, constraints, and resource requirements
   b. gathering general information about the project
   c. evaluating alternative solutions
   d. documenting the system or solution and training the users
   e. monitoring the network system

Q.3. Which of the following tasks are management tasks rather than administrative tasks?

    a. monitoring network devices and gathering network statistics
    b. inventorying and documenting the existing system
    c. installing network applications
    d. troubleshooting printing problems
    e. managing workstation connections

Q.4. Which of the following tasks are responsibilities of the network manager? (select all that apply)

    a. remotely access, manage, and troubleshoot network devices
    b. monitoring and optimizing the network
    c. troubleshooting printing problems
    d. installing a network-wide virus protection system
    e. planning to implement NetWare 4.1 at the corporate level

Appendix A

IEEE 802.3

IEEE 802.3

Preamble	Start Frame Delimiter	Destination Address	Source Address	Length	LLC INFO. and Data	FCS
Bytes: 7	1	2 or 6	2 or 6	2	46-1500	4

Ethernet

Preamble	Destination Address	Source Address	Type	Data	FCS
Bytes: 8	2 or 6	2 or 6	2	46-1500	4

Figure A-1 IEEE 802.3 And Ethernet Frame Format

IEEE 802.3 Frame Fields

Preamble

The frame begins with a preamble, which consists of 56 bits having alternating 1 and 0 values. The preamble is used for synchronization.

Start Frame

Following the preamble is the start frame delimiter, which consists of the bit sequence 10101011. The start frame delimiter indicates the start of a frame of data.

Address Fields

The destination address field identifies the station or stations that are to receive the frame. The source address field identifies the station that sent the frame. The address field can be either 2 bytes or 6 bytes in length. Destination addresses are referred to as "unicast," "multicast," or "broadcast" addresses. IEEE is responsible for assigning the first three bytes to each NIC vendor. The vendor typically assigns the last three bytes to its 802.3 or Ethernet board.

Length Count

The length count field is a 2-byte field that indicates the length of the data field that follows. This field is used to determine the length of the information field when a pad field is included in the frame.

Data Field

The data field contains the protocol data unit that was passed from the logical link control sublayer. This data may contain user data and upper layer protocol headers. If the total length of data and headers is less than 46 bytes, data will be padded to equal 46 bytes.

Pad Field

To detect collisions properly, the frame that is transmitted must contain a certain minimum number of bytes (64 bytes — 46 bytes for data, 12 bytes for source and destination addresses, 2 bytes for length field, and 4 bytes for the FCS (Frame Check Sequence)) field. If a frame being assembled for transmission does not meet this minimum length, a pad field is added to bring it up to that length.

Frame Check Sequence

The sender calculates a CRC and puts the value into the FCS field. If the receiver's CRC does not match the sender's CRC value, the frame is discarded.

Note that the main difference between the IEEE 802.3 frame and the Ethernet II frame is that the Ethernet II frame contains a type field instead of a length field. The type field is used to identify the protocol used, such as TCP/IP or IPX/SPX.

Token Ring Frame Format

Data/Command Frame

Starting Delimiter	Access Control	Frame Control	Destination Address	Source Address	Data	FCS	Ending Delimiter	Frame Status
Bytes 1	1	1	2 or 6	2 or 6	>= 0	4	1	1

Token

Starting Delimiter	Access Control	Ending Delimiter
Bytes 1	1	1

Abort

Starting Delimiter	Ending Delimiter
Bytes 1	1

Figure A-2 IEEE 802.5 Frame Format

IEEE 802.5 defines three kinds of frames. An information (data/command) frame can contain either a protocol data unit passed from the LLC or control information generated by the MAC. A token frame is three bytes long. It contains only an access control field and the starting and ending delimiters. Another format is called the abort sequence and it is used to terminate the transmission of a frame prematurely.

Descriptions of Fields

Starting Delimiter

The starting delimiter is a unique pattern that identifies the start of a frame. Token Ring uses Differential Manchester encoding that allows for signal values that do not correspond to either 1 or 0 bit. These non-data values are used as part of the starting and ending delimiters. This ensures that no data sequence will be mistaken for a delimiter.

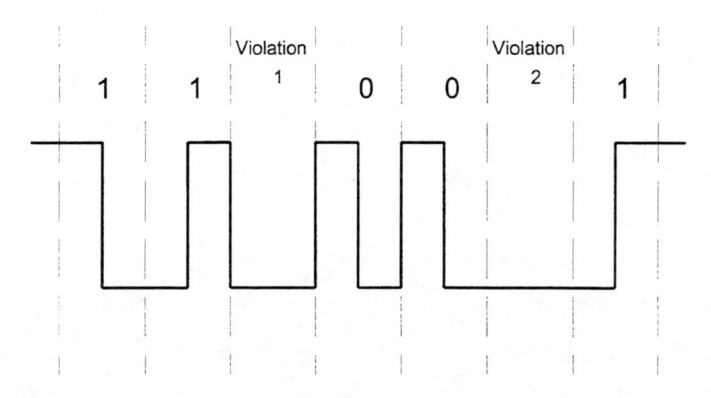

Figure A-3 Code Violations

Access Control Field

The access control field identifies whether the frame is a data/command frame (Token bit = 1) or a token frame (Token bit = 0). It also contains three priority bits and three reservation bits. These six bits implement the Token-Ring priority mechanism. Only stations that have a priority equal to or higher than the priority designated in the token can seize the token and transmit. The station can use the reservation bits to reverse the next token at the station's higher priority. The next token is generated with the reserved priority. The station that raises the token priority is responsible for eventually restoring the token priority to the original lower value.

The monitor bit in the access control field is used by the active monitor to identify endlessly repeated frames. When frames are generated for the first time, the bit is "0". The active monitor changes it to "1". When it is "1", the active monitor removes the frame from the ring because this is the repeated frame and the transmitter did not remove it from the ring.

3 Priority Bits	Token Bit	Monitor Bit	3 Reservation Bits
Bits 1 2 3	4	5	6 7 8

Figure A-4 Access Control Field (Bytes)

Frame Control Field

This field identifies the type of frame (data or control information) and, for certain control frames, the particular function to be performed.

Examples of control frames are Claim Token (used by a station to become an active monitor), Duplicate Address Test, Active Monitor Present (to announce active monitor presence), Purge (to reinitialize the ring), and Beacon .

Addresses

Addresses can be either 2 or 6 bytes in length, depending on whether they are locally administered or universal. The length used must be consistent throughout a given network. The source address is an individual address. The destination address can be an individual, group, or a broadcast address.

Information Field

The information field can contain either data passed from the LLC or control information supplied by the MAC sublayer.

Frame Check Sequence (FCS)

This field stores the CRC value. The sending station performs a CRC calculation on the Frame control, Destination address, Source address, and Information fields. If the receiving station's CRC differs from the senders CRC, an error is assumed.

Ending Delimiter

The ending delimiter identifies the end of the frame. Like the starting delimiter, it also contains non-data values. In addition, it contains bits, that are used to identify whether or not this is the last frame in a multiframe transmission and whether an error has already been detected by some other station.

Frame Status Field

This field contains the address-recognized and frame-copied bits that are used to indicate whether or not a frame has been successfully received by a destination station.

The source sets address-recognized and frame-copied bits to 0. If the destination finds the frame acceptable, it sets these bits to 1 before retransmitting the frame. It is a kind of acknowledgment to the source that the frame was received correctly. If the destination finds the frame unacceptable, it sets address-recognized bits to 1 but does not change frame-copied bits. When the source receives these bits, it knows that the frame was received by the destination but was not acceptable. It now has the option to retransmit the frame.

When the source receives the frame and all bits are unchanged, it assumes that the destination is not currently on the ring.

FDDI Frame Fields

Preamble

The preamble is used to synchronize each station's clock with the transmission. It consists of 16 idle symbols.

Starting Delimiter

This field contains a unique signal pattern that identifies the start of the frame.

Frame Control

This field identifies the frame's type and indicates whether the frame is synchronous or asynchronous, whether 16-bit or 48-bit addresses are used, whether the frame is a data or command frame, and it provides control information for command frames.

Addresses

The destination address can be an individual, group, or broadcast address. The source address must identify an individual station.

Information field

This field contains data or control information.

Frame Check Sequence

This field contains a CRC value computed on the control, address, and information fields.

Ending Delimiter

This delimiter consists of either one or two non-data terminate (T) symbols. The ending delimiter for a token uses two symbols, while other frames use one symbol.

Frame Status Field

This field contains information about the status of a frame, including whether an error was detected, if the address was recognized, and if the frame was copied. Three separate symbols are used to indicate the above conditions.

4-Bit Data	5-bit Symbol
0000	11110
0001	01001
0010	10100
0011	10101
0100	01010
0101	01011
0110	01110
0111	01111
1000	10010
1001	10011
1010	10110
1011	10111
1100	11010
1101	11011
1110	11100
1111	11101
Control Symbols	
Quiet	00000
Idle	11111
Halt	00100
Starting Delimiter-J	11000
Starting Delimiter-K	10001
Ending Delimiter-T	01101
Control Reset (logical zero)	00111
Control Set (logical one)	11001

Figure A-5 FDDI 4B/5B Code

FDDI Encoding

FDDI uses a 4-bit of 5-bit (4B/5B) encoding scheme. In this scheme, each 4-bits of data is replaced by a 5-bit symbol. The 5-bit symbol is then represented using Nonreturn to Zero Inverted (NRZI) encoding.

With NRZI, a 1 bit is represented by a transition at the beginning of the bit interval and a 0 bit by no transition.

The 5-bit symbols are chosen so that there will never be more than three 0 bits in a row and thus no more than three bit times without a transition.

Only 16 of the 32 possible 5-bit symbols are used to represent data. The remaining symbols are either invalid or used as control symbols.

FDDI encoding scheme is very different from other schemes as Manchester used in Ethernet and Differential Manchester used in Token Ring. This 4B/5B scheme was chosen to get better efficiency than other methods.

In Manchester and Differential Manchester, there are two transitions per bit time (mid-bit transition is to maintain synchronization (clocking)). It means, to transmit at 10 Mbps we need a 20 MHz signal and to get 16 Mbps speeds we require a 32 MHz signal. This translates to a 50% efficiency that was not good enough to get FDDI speed of 100 Mbps.

In 4B/5B method, we replace 4-bits of data with a 5-bit symbol. This is a 25% overhead. We then transmit this 5-bit symbol using the NRZI scheme that does not have a mid-bit transition, so to get a 100 Mbps speed we need only a 125 MHz signal that translates to an 80% efficiency (100/125 X 100%=80%). We do not need mid-bit transition for FDDI to maintain synchronization because we are transmitting a 5-bit symbol from a predefined set and error detection is easier.

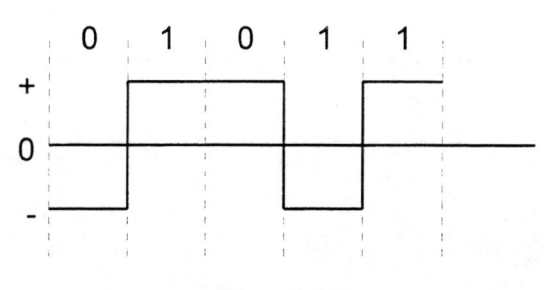

Figure 3-14

This figure shows the NRZI scheme representing 4-bit data "0101" by a 5-bit value "01011".

FDDI Bandwidth Allocation

FDDI supports the real-time allocation of network's bandwidth. To do so, FDDI specifies two types of bandwidths: synchronous and asynchronous.

Synchronous

Synchronous bandwidth is allocated for continuous transmission, like voice and video transmission.

Asynchronous

After the synchronous bandwidth is allocated, all remaining bandwidth is allocated for asynchronous transmission . Asynchronous transmission uses eight levels of priorities.

Synchronous stations can have an extended dialogue with other stations by temporarily taking control of all of the asynchronous bandwidth. It is done by issuing a restricted token so that only stations with the synchronous bandwidth may transmit.

FDDI Frame Format

Data/Command Frame

Preamble	Start Delimiter	Frame Control	Destination Address	Source Address	Data	FCS	End Delimiter	Frame Status
Bytes: 16	2	2	4 or 12	4 or 12	>=0	8	1	3

All lengths are in 5-bit symbols

Token Frame

Preamble	Start Delimiter	Frame Control	End Delimiter
16	2	2	2

All lengths are in 5-bit symbols

Figure 3-15: FDDI Frame Format

FDDI defines two basic types of frames: Token and Data/Command frames. Command frames carry ring maintenance commands and data frames carry data.

Appendix B

The NetWire Message Forums

Forum Name	Description	Sections
The NetWare 2.X Forum *(NETW2X)*	This forum deals with NetWare 2.2 and 2.15.	Printing NetWare Utilities Disk Drives/Controllers LAN Cards/Drivers 2.1x and below OS Operating System
The NetWare 3.X Forum *(NETW3X)*	This forum deals with NetWare 3.x.	Printing NetWare Utilities Disk Drives/CDs/Controllers LAN Cards/Drivers Upgrade/Migration SFT III NLM/OS/Console Utilities
The NetWare 4.X Forum *(NETW4X)*	This forum deals with NetWare 4.	Printing NetWare Utilities isk Drives/CDs/Controllers LAN Cards/Drivers Upgrade/Migration ElectroText/Documentation Directory Services NLM/OS/Console Utilities
The Novell Client Forum *(NOVCLIENT)*	This forum deals with various interfaces between client and NetWare.	IPX/ODI Issues NETX Issues VLM Issues ODINSUP Issues NetBIOS Issues NetWare and MS Windows

(continued...)

The Novell Connectivity Forum *(NCONNECT)*	This forum deals with products that are used to connect multiple platforms, such as connection between mainframes and NetWare networks.	Access Services NW Connect/NACS NW for SAA AS/400 Connectivity Host Printing SNA Links LAN/LAN Links NetWare Macintosh NetWare for LAT Portable NetWare NW NFS-TCP/IP Email/MHS/FAX LAN Workplace/Group
The Novell Desktop Forum *(NOVDESKTOP)*	This forum deals with products maintained by the Novell Desktop Systems Group.	DRDOS/Applications DRDOS/Disk DRDOS/Memory DRDOS/Utilities Customer Service Programming Questions DataClub NetWare Lite NetWare NT Client
The Developer Product Info. Forum *(NDEVINFO)*	This forum deals with pre-sales questions on Novell's Software Development Kits.	General Business Btrieve NetWare SQL NetWare Client SDK NetWare Server SDK Macintosh SDK Personal NetWare SDK AppWare Foundation SDK LAN WorkPlace SDK Telephony SDK Visual AppBuilder

(continued...)

Appendix B

The Developer Support Forum *(NDEVSUPP)*	This forum deals with post-sales questions on Novell's Software Development Kits.	General Business Btrieve NetWare SQL NetWare Client SDK NetWare Server SDK Macintosh SDK Communication SDKs Personal NetWare SDK AppWare Foundation SDK LAN WorkPlace SDK
The Novell Information Forum *(NGENERAL)*	This forum deals with questions about Novell programs.	Product Information Suggestion Box Applications/Utilities User Groups/Training CNEs CNEPA NSEPro AppNotes National Authorized Service Centers Other Information The Lighter Side
The Novell Networking Hardware Forum *(NOVHW)*	This forum deals with hardware topologies and other hardware problems.	Power Monitoring Token Ring Ethernet ARCnet Backups Cabling
The Novell Network Management Forum *(NOVMAN)*	This forum deals with questions about Novell's diagnostic and management tools.	Network Management NetWare Management System LANtern System Manager LANalyzer for Windows NW for SAA Management
The Novell OS/2 Forum *(NOVOS2)*	This forum deals with OS2 and related products.	OS/2 Printing Client/Server OS/2 Requester NSM (OS/2) NW 4.x for OS/2 GUI Tools WINOS2/DOS

(continued...)

The Novell UnixWare Forum *(UNIXWARE)*	This forum deals with bringing the UNIX OS to desktop computers, which permits the effective integration of desktop computer into client-server networks.	General Info Product Info Developers DOS Merge Installation XWindows Networking Device Drivers Printing Communications Applications Bug Watchers Updates
The Novell Users Forum *(NOVUSER)*	This forum deals with questions about files that have been uploaded to the Novell Users Library. This forum also handles Classifieds and Help Wanted.	NOVUSER Library Q&A Job Postings Classified
The Novell Vendors A Forum *(NVENA)*	This forum is used for communication with vendors who work with Novell.	Folio BindView Computer Tyme Infinite Tech. Dell Computer AST Research Blue Lance Best Power Knowzall Notework RoseWare Multi-User DOS TriCord Synoptics
The Novell Vendors B Forum *(NVENB)*	This forum is used for communication with additional vendors who work with Novell.	Ontrack Data NetWorth

Appendix B

Note: T go to any forum, you will use "GO" command. For example, to use the NetWare 3.X forum, type GO NETW3X. To go to a new public forum that services the Novell Professional Developers Program, type GO NDEVREL.

Answers to Review Questions

Chapter 1

(1). c (2). b (3). b (4). a (5). b

(6). b,c (7). a (8). d (9). d (10). b

(11). b (12). d

Chapter 2

(1). b (2). b (3). a (4). b (5). c

(6). b (7). d (8). a (9). a,c,e (10). a

(11). b,c

Chapter 3

(1). b (2). b (3). a (4). a (5). b

© 1993 - 96 · PC Age, Inc. All Rights Reserved · 20 Audrey Place · Fairfield, NJ 07004 · U.S.A. · Tel: 201-882-5370

(6). e   (7). a   (8). c   (9). b   (10). c

(11). b   (12). d

Chapter 4

(1). c   (2). a   (3). c   (4). a   (5). b

(6). c   (7). c   (8). d   (9). b   (10). a

(11). a,b,c   (12). b

Chapter 5

(1). c   (2). b   (3). d   (4). c   (5). b

(6). c   (7). a   (8). a   (9). b   (10). c

(11). b   (12). e

Chapter 6

(1). c   (2). b,d   (3). a   (4). b   (5). b,c,d

(6). b   (7). a,c   (8). c   (9). d   (10). b

(11). c   (12). a

Chapter 7

(1). b   (2). d   (3). a   (4). c   (5). b

(6). a   (7). d   (8). b   (9). a   (10). c

(11). c   (12). a

Chapter 8

(1). c   (2). a   (3). a   (4). c

Chapter 9

(1). a,b   (2). c   (3). a,b   (4). a,b,d,e

Answers to the Exercises

Answer to Exercise 3-1

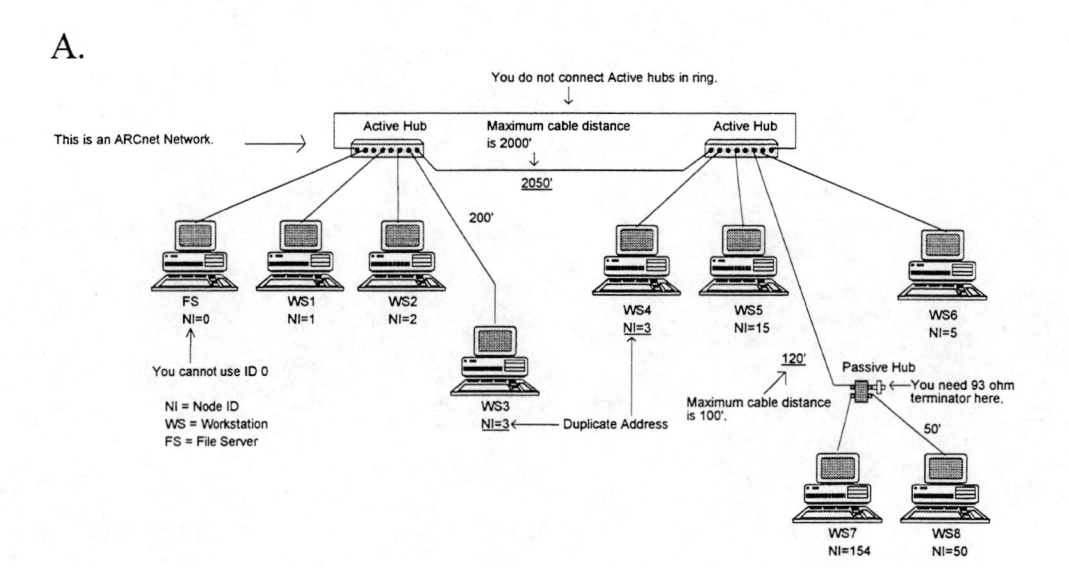

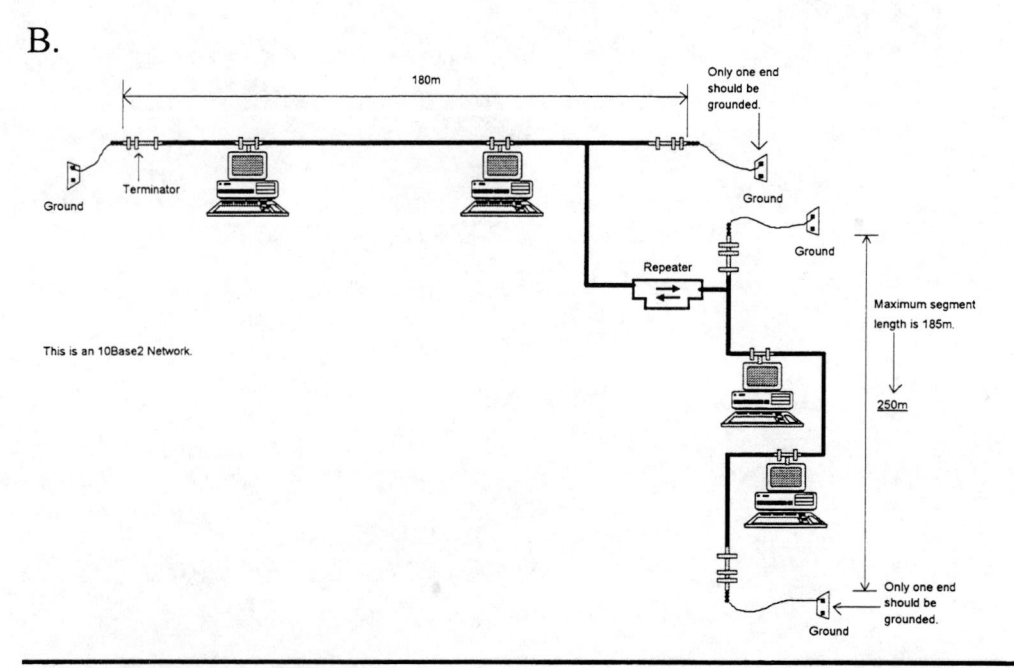

A.

This is an ARCnet Network.

You do not connect Active hubs in ring.

Active Hub — Maximum cable distance is 2000' — Active Hub

2050'

200'

FS NI=0 — You cannot use ID 0

WS1 NI=1

WS2 NI=2

WS3 NI=3 ← Duplicate Address

WS4 NI=3

WS5 NI=15

WS6 NI=5

120' — Maximum cable distance is 100'.

Passive Hub — You need 93 ohm terminator here.

50'

WS7 NI=154

WS8 NI=50

NI = Node ID
WS = Workstation
FS = File Server

B.

This is an 10Base2 Network.

180m

Only one end should be grounded.

Ground — Terminator

Ground

Repeater

Ground

Maximum segment length is 185m.

250m

Only one end should be grounded.

Ground

Answers

C.

Minimum distance between tranceivers is 2.5 m.

Maximum standard distance of a segment is 500 m.

$\frac{600m}{5m}$

2m

Terminator

Terminator

Ground

40m

20m

5m

100m
Maximum cable length is 50 m.

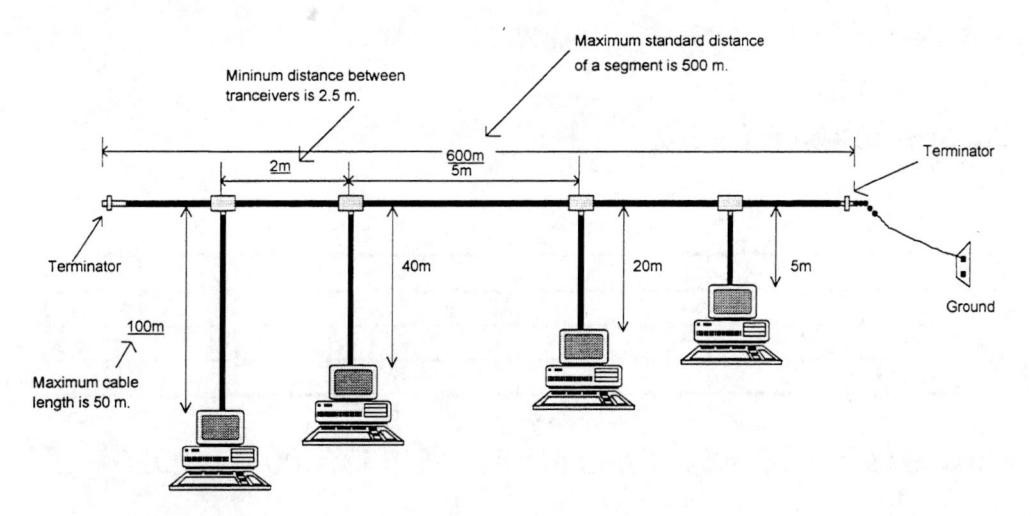

This is a 10Base5 network.

D.

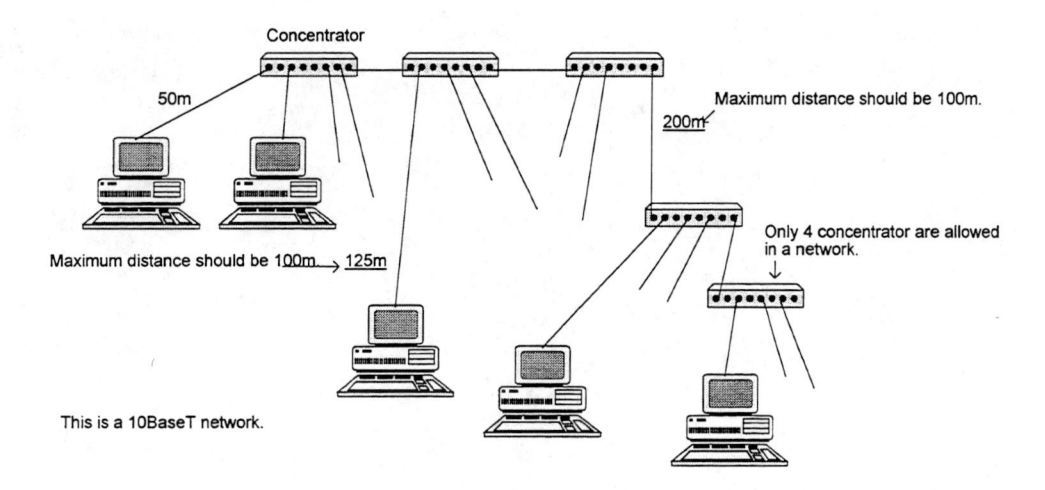

Concentrator

50m

Maximum distance should be 100m.

200m

Maximum distance should be 100m. → 125m

Only 4 concentrator are allowed in a network.

This is a 10BaseT network.

© 1993 - 96 · PC Age, Inc. All Rights Reserved · 20 Audrey Place · Fairfield, NJ 07004 · U.S.A. · Tel: 201-882-5370

Q.2. Answer II and III are correct. All others are wrong.

Answer to Exercise 3-2

Switches	1	2	3	4	5	6	7	8
Off/Open	-	-	-	1	1	1	-	-
On/Closed	0	0	0	-	-	-	0	0
Decimal Value	1	2	4	8	16	32	64	128

Answer: Node ID = 56 decimal = 8 + 16 + 32 = 00011100.

Multiple-Choice Practice Questions

Note: Select the best answer. You may not find direct answers to some of the questions in this manual. Consider these questions a learning tool.

Q.1. If you do not have proper number of twists when using twisted pair cable, which problem will you most probably get?

    a. transient   b. noise
    c. crosstalk   d. ESD

Q.2. You must use terminators with _____.

    a. Unused active hub ports
    b. Unused passive hub ports
    c. Both unused active hub and passive hub ports
    d. Termination is not necessary with unused ports

Q.3. If you are installing an IDE drive and you do not find your drive type in the CMOS setup, which type would you usually select?

    a. Type 0   b. Not Installed
    c. Type 47   d. Type 1

© 1993 - 96 · PC Age, Inc. All Rights Reserved · 20 Audrey Place · Fairfield, NJ 07004 · U.S.A. · Tel: 201-882-5370

Troubleshooting & Supporting Networks

Q.4. When installing a SCSI drive which drive type you would select in the CMOS setup?

    a. Type 0 or "Not Installed"   b. Type 47
    c. Type 1   d. Type 48

Q.5. When installing an ESDI drive which drive type you would select in the CMOS setup?

    a. Type 0 or "Not Installed"   b. Type 47
    c. Type 1   d. Type 48

Q.6. Vampire tap is used with a(n) _____ network.

    a. 10Base2   b. 10Base5
    c. 10BaseT   d. ARCnet

Q.7. For which kind of hard disk do you have a master/slave relationship?

    a. IDE   b. SCSI
    c. ESDI   d. Master Disk

Q.8. When you go from repeaters to gateways, which of the following is true?

    a. Cost increases, speed increases, functionality decreases
    b. Cost increases, speed increases, functionality increases
    c. Cost increases, speed decreases, functionality increases

d. Cost decreases, speed increases, functionality increases

Q.9. To get the latest version of RPRINTER, you should download _____ from NetWire.

    a. RPRINTER.ZIP   b. PS3X0x.EXE
    c. PU3X0x.EXE   d. PUTILx.EXE

Q.10. When using serial printers attached with the server, which of the following commands would you be using?

    a. MODE COM1:96,N,8,1,P
    b. MODE LPT1:=COM1:
    c. load PSERVER /SERIAL
    d. none

Q.11. How would you recognize if a card is 8-bit or 16-bit?

    a. A 16-bit card has one large edge and one small edge
    b. An 8-bit card has one large edge and one small edge
    c. A 16-bit card has only one edge
    d. A 16-bit card is 4.8 inches tall

Q.12. How can you recognize that a card is a NIC?

    a. A NIC has a socket for the remote boot PROM
    b. Every NIC has "network board" written on it
    c. Every NIC has DIP switches to set up the node address
    d. Every NIC has one large edge and one small edge

Q.13. You can install an ISA card in an MCA computer?

    a. Never
    b. Only if you use the IBM setup disk
    c. Always
    d. Only if the ISA card is 32-bit

Q.14. For hard disks that have master/slave relationship, you use:

    a. A 40-pin cable
    b. A 50-pin cable
    c. A 25-pin cable which can connect to two disks
    d. A 34-pin cable which can connect to one disk only

Q.15. For an RLL disk you use:

    a. A 50-pin control cable   b. A 40-pin control cable
    c. A 34-pin control cable   d. A 50-pin data cable

Q.16. If the drive type is lost from the CMOS setup, a probable cause is:

    a. The computer power supply is not working
    b. The controller electronics has failed
    c. The battery that supports CMOS has failed

Q.17. To protect your system from viruses, you shouldn't:

    a. Control the use of BBS
    b. Download BBS files to hard disks
    c. Control the installation of new applications
    d. Use virus scan software every day

Q.18. To preserve the part of the job that has already been CAPTURed prior to the connection loss, which of the following commands would you use?

    a. CAPTURE /KEEP   b. CAPTURE /SAVE
    c. CAPTURE /SHOW   d. CAPTURE /NOTIFY

Q.19. If your client wants to install a network for graphic applications and they want good throughput, which network would you suggest?

    a. ARCnet   b. FDDI
    c. Token Ring   d. Ethernet

Q.20. For four circuits with one closed and three open you can have:

    a. 8-pins with one pair closed with a jumper
    b. 4-pins with one pin closed with a jumper
    c. 8-pins with two pairs closed with a jumper
    d. 8-pins with one pair closed with a jumper and one pin with a jumper
    e. Both a and d are true

Troubleshooting & Supporting Networks

Q.21. Which utility can be used to set up the interleave ratio of a disk without destroying the data?

    a. NSEPro
    b. MTL
    c. Check It Pro
    d. None of the above

Q.22. Which tool would you use to download the very latest version of a file?

    a. NSEPro
    b. NetWire
    c. MTL
    d. Check It Pro

Q.23. Which tool would you use to find the I/O address settings of a NIC?

    a. NSEPro
    b. MTL
    c. NetWire
    d. Check It Pro

Q.24. Which tool would you use to download a file inexpensively?

    a. NSEPro
    b. NetWire
    c. MTL
    d. Check It Pro

Q.25. Which tool would you use to find out the model number of an HP I/O card?

    a. NSEPro
    b. MTL
    c. NetWire
    d. Check It Pro

Q.26. Which tool would you use to make a copy of your CMOS setup?

    a. MTL
    b. COMCHECK
    c. Check It Pro
    d. NSEPro

Q.27. Which tool would you use for low-level formatting for a variety of hard disks?

    a. MTL
    b. Check It Pro
    c. NSEPro
    d. DISKCHECK

Q.28. If your modem uses IRQ 3, and you want to use an Ethernet card, what would you do?

    a. Change the IRQ on the NIC and in the NET.CFG file
    b. Change the IRQ on the NIC
    c. Change the IRQ in the NET.CFG file
    d. No change is necessary

Q.29. If your modem uses IRQ 3, and you want to use the ARCnet card, what would you do?

    a. Change the IRQ on the NIC and in the NET.CFG file
    b. Change the IRQ on the NIC
    c. No change is necessary
    d. Change the IRQ in the NET.CFG file

Q.30. When using a laser printer, which of the following need not be cleaned and changed?

    a. Toner cartridge   b. Roller
    c. Ribbons   d. Corona wire

Q.31. If the laser printer output is totally black pages, you may have a:

    a. Broken ribbon
    b. Broken or fouled corona wire
    c. Faulty primary corona grid
    d. Slow drive motor

Q.32. If the laser printer output is disproportionately long or short, the probable cause might be:

    a. The drive motor is not working with correct speed
    b. The corona wire needs to be cleaned
    c. An old ribbon
    d. Inadequate ventilation

Q.33. Which DOS command should be used if you are using a serial printer?

    a. SERIAL   b. SMODE
    c. PORT   d. MODE

Multiple-Choice Practice Questions

Q.34. If you have single-spaced text on the computer screen, but the printer output is double-spaced, you may need to:

    a. Change the ribbon
    b. Change the DIP switch settings
    c. Use the DOS MODE command
    d. Change the toner cartridge

Q.35. If you have corrupted data because of using caching controller, you should:

    a. Disable NetWare caching   b. Turn off controller caching
    c. Flush buffers by hand   d. Add more RAM

Q.36. 10Base2 and 10BaseT segments can be connected by using:

    a. Special NICs   b. Special transceivers
    c. Special cabling   d. They cannot be connected

Q.37. AppNotes are available on:

    a. Hard copy only
    b. NSEPro only
    c. Hard copy and NSEPro
    d. Hard copy, NSEPro, and NetWire

Troubleshooting & Supporting Networks

Q.38. How many nodes can you have on a 10BaseT network?

    a. 512 using 4 repeaters
    b. 1024 using 5 repeaters
    c. 1024 using 4 repeaters
    d. Unlimited using repeaters

Q.39. You should replace your hard disk _____

    a. when the Hot Fix redirection area is unable to accept data
    b. when the hard disk is almost full
    c. when the SCSI controller is not working properly
    d. when the NetWare SYS volume is almost full

Q.40. How would you set a node address of 182 if switch 1 serves as the least significant bit (LSB)?

a.	OFF	OFF	OFF	ON	OFF	OFF	ON	OFF
b.	ON	OFF	OFF	ON	OFF	OFF	ON	OFF
c.	OFF	OFF	OFF	ON	OFF	OFF	ON	ON
d.	ON	ON	OFF	ON	OFF	OFF	ON	ON

Q.41. If your client is using many serial printers and complaining about printing speed, what would you recommend?

    a. Change from serial to parallel printers
    b. Add more print servers
    c. Add more printers
    d. Add more queues

Q.42. Which of the following networks does not support fiber optic cable?

    a. Ethernet
    b. ARCnet
    c. Token Ring
    d. All of them support fiber optic cable

Q.43. External transceivers can be used with _____ network(s).

    a. 10Base2   b. 10Base5
    c. 10BaseT   d. all of the above

Q.44. External transceiver must be used with _____ network(s).

    a. 10Base2   b. 10Base5
    c. 10BaseT   d. all of the above

Q.45. If you have a network with coax and fiber optic cables, which tool would you not use to troubleshoot the cable problems?

    a. TDR   b. OTDR
    c. Optical power meter   d. Spare NIC

Troubleshooting & Supporting Networks

Q.46. If print jobs go to the queue and are not printed, which of the following may not be true?

    a. Print server is not loaded
    b. Printer cable is loose or printer is off-line
    c. CAPTURE command is not working properly
    d. Queue is not assigned to printer

Q.47. The minimum distance between two transceivers in a 10Base5 network is _____.

    a. 50 m   b. 2.5 m
    c. 0.5 m   d. 100 m

Q.48. How many commands do you need to enter to unload a LAN driver if you have ODI drivers and VLM loaded.

    a. 5   b. 4
    c. 3   d. 2

Q.49. If lightning is common in your area, what should you consider using?

    a. power monitor
    b. transient suppressor
    c. high quality cable
    d. proper FCC rating equipment

Q.50. If you have devices that draw a lot of power, on the same circuit with computers, which problem will you most probably get?

    a. transient   b. noise
    c. crosstalk   d. ESD

Q.51. If you are running cables close to fluorescent lights, which problem will you most probably get?

    a. transient   b. noise
    c. crosstalk   d. ESD

Q.52. Shielding can protect from _____ .

    a. transient   b. noise
    c. crosstalk   d. ESD

Q.53. You should use shielded twisted pair or fiber optic cable to _____ .

    a. avoid crosstalk
    b. get speed more than 10 Mbps
    c. avoid transient
    d. avoid ESD

Q.54. To feel an ESD, the charge should be equal to _____ volts, but computer components may be destroyed or degraded by discharges as low as _____ volts.

    a. 1000, 20 or 30   b. 3000, 30 or 40
    c. 5000, 10 or 20   d. 3000, 20 or 30

Q.55. It is difficult to trace intermittent problems caused by _____ .

    a. transient   b. noise
    c. crosstalk   d. ESD

Q.56. To prevent static you should _____ . (select the one that is not true)

    a. use a proper wrist strap and mat before working on printed circuits
    b. use a proper wrist strap before working on monitors.
    c. never touch computer components and ICs by their electrical leads
    d. not let any one touch you when working on ICs
    e. transport and store computer boards and ICs in static shielding bags

Q.57. To prevent static you should _____ . (select the one that is not true)

a. transport and store computer boards and ICs in static shielding bags
b. keep humidity low
c. keep nonconductors, such as plastic and styrofoam away from components
d. never place components on any conductive surface

Q.58. To ensure EDP (Electronic Data Processing) environmental security, you should _____ . (select the one that is not true)

a. restrict access to computer facilities on a "need-to-be-there" basis
b. put proper security on dial-up phone lines
c. change phone number frequently
d. not touch computer components and ICs by their electrical leads

Q.59. To ensure EDP (Electronic Data Processing) environmental security, you _____ . (select the one that is not true)

a. use software applications that use encryption schemes
b. transport and store computer boards and ICs in static shielding bags
c. monitor and control system access by vendor maintenance staff
d. use UPSs

Q.60. To ensure EDP (Electronic Data Processing) environmental security, you should _____ . (select the one that is not true)

   a. enforce password length and periodic password change
   b. arrange off-site backup of data
   c. use a hardware transient suppressor
   d. monitor for tapping devices

Q.61. To ensure EDP (Electronic Data Processing) environmental security, you should _____ . (select the one that is not true)

   a. have plans to get vital services in case of fire or flood
   b. duplex your hard disks in the servers
   c. make sure your hardware error detection capabilities are working
   d. use shielded twisted pair or fiber optic cable

Q.62. To protect your system from viruses, you should not _____ .

   a. flag .EXE and .COM files as Read-Only if files do not store configuration information internally.
   b. grant Read, File Scan, and Write rights to all users in PUBLIC directory
   c. download files from BBs to floppies
   d. use virus protection program on every workstation

Q.63. To protect your system from viruses, you should not
_____ .

   a. check new software applications for viruses
   b. run virus protection programs through login scripts
   c. flag a .EXE file Read-Only if the file stores configuration information internally
   d. make backups daily

Q.64. To troubleshoot a system, you should not _____ .

   a. turn every thing off and turn it back on
   b. eliminate user error by watching him performing the task he thinks is giving the errors
   c. remove TSRs
   d. replace a NIC if user is able to login but unable to run an application

Q.65. To troubleshoot a system, you should not _____ .

   a. boot the computer without CONFIG.SYS and AUTOEXEC.BAT
   b. backup data if problem involves disks
   c. make sure all spare parts are present and connected
   d. create a rescue disk to recover from the loss of CMOS setup files

Q.66. If you are working as a consultant for a company which is located in an area known for violent thunderstorms, the next door neighbor uses very high power equipment, and which has a heating plant, which of the following suggestion would you not give?

a. smart UPSs (which down the server automatically) for all servers
b. high-grade electrical conditioning
c. duplex drives on all servers
d. LANalyzer for every workstation.

Q.67. If a company is using a server in a heating plant which uses an outlet shared by other devices like coffee-pot, which of the following suggestion does not sound right?

a. a separate power line for the server
b. air conditioning for the server
c. a high quality cable tester for the server
d. UPS for the server

Q.68. If a company uses temporaries around Christmas, where employees use polyester ties, and whose 5 server 80 workstation system is runing a little slow lately, which of the following suggestion would you not give as a consultant?

a. get an on-site CNE
b. no polyester ties on premises
c. use LANalyzer on the network segment that is getting slow
d. buy a faster server right away
e. set expiration date for temporaries' accounts

Q.69. Which one of the following is not a valid EDP environmental security suggestion?

    a. keep an up-to-date physical layout of the network
    b. change locks on server's room as needed
    c. enforce minimum password length and periodic password changes.
    d. educating users about viruses

Q.70. Which of the following network uses 2 terminators and one ground?

    a. 10Base5   b. 10BaseT
    c. Token Ring   d. FDDI

Q.71. To troubleshoot a Token Ring network, you should have _____ .

    a. a NAUN
    b. physical layout of the network
    c. a beaconing station
    d. a MAU (or MSAU)

Q.72. Which of the following may not be a reason to use a token Ring network?

    a. it has fault tolerance features
    b. it offers excellent throughput under heavy loads
    c. easy to connect with IBM mainframe and mini computers

d. it needs minimum user intervention because of "beaconing" and "autoreconfiguration" features

Q.73. Which of the following device is not an active device?

    a. Multistation Access Unit   b. Active hub
    c. Controlled Access Unit   d. Concentrator

Q.74. Which is not true about Token Ring?

    a. it is relatively expensive
    b. it is easy to manage because of "beaconing" and "autoreconfiguration" features.
    c. its token-passing method gives excellent throughput under heavy loads
    d. it can be installed using unshielded twisted pair

Q.75. Early token release means _____.

    a. token is released after transmitting the last bit of the last frame
    b. token is released after receiving the last bit of a frame
    c. there may be more than one tokens at the same time
    d. active monitor releases the token whenever necessary

Q.76. What is not true about Token Ring?

    a. you cannot mix 4 Mbps and 16 Mbps cards in the same ring
    b. you connect Ring In (RI) and Ring Out (RO) ports even if one MSAU is used
    c. a network's physical layout is important to isolate Token Ring Problems
    d. reinitializing all parts and reconnecting the drop cables is a good quick fix for Token Ring

Q.77. Which one of the following is not an advantage of Ethernet?

    a. it is an inexpensive high speed network
    b. it is an IEEE standard and supports various wiring configurations
    c. it offers excellent throughput under heavy loads
    d. it works well with a large number of LAN and micro-to-mainframe applications

Q.78. To prevent crosstalk, a 10BaseT cable should have _____.

    a. high quality copper core.
    b. proper number of twist per foot
    c. proper shielding.
    d. six twisted pairs

Q.79. Which is not true about 10BaseT?

   a. it is susceptible to EMI
   b. it supports up to five concentrators in sequence
   c. it supports up to 1,024 workstations on a network
   d. it supports only unshielded twisted pair

Q.80. Which is not true about 10BaseT?

   a. it can have 80, 90, and 120 nodes in three segments
   b. it permits a modular approach to LAN construction
   c. it is resistant to interference from fluorescent light ballasts
   d. it can be connected to 10Base5 using special transceivers

Q.81. The distance between a hub and a workstation or between two hubs must be between _____ in a 10BaseT network.

   a. 0.6 meter and 100 meters
   b. 0.5 meter and 100 meters
   c. 2.5 meters and 100 meters
   d. 2.5 meters and 500 meters

Q.82. Which is not true about 10Base2?

   a. it uses RG-58 A/U or RG-58 C/U coax cable in bus topology
   b. it supports 185 meters segment length and 925 meters entire network length
   c. devices must be at least 0.5 meter apart

d. it uses two 50-ohm terminators and both ends grounded

Q.83. Which is not true about 10Base2?

a. both ends must be terminated and only one end should be grounded
b. SQE or "heartbeat" test must be turned on when using repeaters
c. It supports maximum 5 segments using 4 repeaters
d. it is reliable and easy to manage

Q.84. Which is not true about 10Base5?

a. maximum network length is 2.5 kilometers and segment length is 500 meters
b. each transceiver must be separated by 2.5 meters
c. maximum distance between transceiver and NIC is 100 meters
d. it can be connected to 10Base2 using special adapters

Q.85. Which one of the following is the right way to bind a protocol?

a. BIND IPX to ETH net = AAA1
b. BIND IPX to ETH addr = AAA1
c. BIND IP to ETH net = 135.26.30.56
d. BIND NE2000 to IPX net=AAA1

Q.86. Which one of the following can not be used to troubleshoot an Ethernet cabling problem?

    a. Volt-Ohm-Milliameter   b. COMCHECK
    c. TDR   d. transceiver

Q.87. Which one of the following is not related to 10Base5?

    a. Vampire tap   b. T-Connector
    c. 50-ohm terminator   d. DIX connector

Q.88. Which is not related to Token Ring?

    a. Patch cable   b. Adapter cable
    c. Transceiver cable   d. 8228 unit
    e. set-up aid

Q.89. Which is not related to Token Ring?

    a. NAUN   b. CAU
    c. active monitor   d. CDDI

Q.90. Which is not related to ARCnet?

    a. Active and Passive hub   b. RG-62A/U cable
    c. 93-ohm terminators   d. DIX connector

Q.91. A common problem with ARCnet is _____ .

   a. beaconing
   b. duplicate node addresses
   c. Unused active hub ports which are not terminated
   d. Limited total network length

Q.92. Which of the following media can be used to maintain ground isolation between buildings?

   a. UTP   b. STP
   c. Fiber optic   d. thick Coax

Q.93. Which of the following networks are similar in operation?

   a. Ethernet and ARCnet   b. Token Ring and FDDI
   c. Token Ring and Ethernet d. ARCnet and FDDI

Q.94. Which is not true about FDDI?

   a. it supports beaconing and autoreconfiguration
   b. it supports very high speeds and long distances
   c. it can be a good choice for high electrical interference environments
   d. it is easy to install and maintain

Q.95. Which is not related to FDDI?

   a. OTDR
   b. Dual Counter Rotating Rings
   c. Class A stations
   d. TDR

Q.96. Which is not true about FDDI?

   a. it is an ANSI standard
   b. multimode fiber is used to cover longer distances than single-mode fiber
   c. it has no EMI
   d. concentrators can be connected to other concentrators

Q.97. Which of the following networks is a good choice for a company which uses a lot of graphic files and wants good throughput?

   a. ARCnet   b. Ethernet
   c. Token Ring   d. FDDI

Q.98. Which one of the following is a correct way to unload a LAN driver?

   a. LSL U, NE2000 U
   b. VLM U, IPXODI U, NE2000 U
   c. NE2000 U
   d. VLM U, IPXODI U, LSLU, NE2000 U

Q.99. Which of the following would you use first in case of valuable data loss if valid backups are unavailable?

    a. VREPAIR
    b. NetUtils3
    c. Professional Data Recovery Services
    d. Hot Fix

Q.100. To copy Master Boot Record (Track 0) of your server, which of the following utilities would you use?

    a. NetDisk3   b. VREPAIR
    c. Check It Pro   d. Recovery Services

Q.101. 34-pin cable is used with which of the following drives? (select all that are true)

    a. MFM   b. RLL
    c. ESDI   d. SCSI

Q.102. Floppy and hard drive cables can be interchanged.

    a. true
    b. false
    c. only on IBM AT computers
    d. only with IDE drives

Troubleshooting & Supporting Networks

Q.103. IDE drives use?

    a. 34-pin cable
    b. 40-pin cable, 17 inches long
    c. 40-pin cable, 25 inches long
    d. 25-pin cable, 18 inches long

Q.104. Select the one which is not true about SCSI cables.

    a. it may be 25 or 50-Pin
    b. it may be 34 or 40-Pin
    c. the maximum distance between connectors on a SCSI cable is 18 inches
    d. the minimum distance between connectors on a SCSI cable is 12 inches

Q.105. When using SCSI external disk subsystems, you should use _____ .

    a. 34-pin cables
    b. impedance-matched cables
    c. connectors on the cable at least 25 inches apart
    d. connectors on the cable at least 10 inches apart

Q.106. Which one of the following is not related to SCSI installation?

    a. correct IDs
    b. impedance-matched cables
    c. hardware, firmware, and software revision levels

d. correct terminating power
e. flushing the buffers on the controller

Q.107. When using NetWare's VOLINFO utility to view volumes, how would you recognize a CD-ROM volume?

    a. it says "Read-Only" next to the volume name
    b. it says "CD-ROM" next to the volume name
    c. there will be no "Free" bytes available for CD-ROM volume
    d. there will be zero "Total" bytes for CD-ROM volume

Q.108. Which one of the following is a good choice for unattended backup, archived data storage, and scanned documents?

    a. CD-ROM   b. RAID
    c. DAT   d. Magneto-Optical

Q.109. Which one of the following is a good choice when you need data reliability and improved performance with increased capacity?

    a. CD-ROM   b. DAT
    c. RAID   d. Megneto-Optical

Troubleshooting & Supporting Networks

Q.110. Which one of the following is a good choice when you need to distribute large volumes of data for read-only purposes?

    a. CD-ROM   b. DAT
    c. RAID   d. Magneto-Optical

Q.111. Which one of the following is a good choice for daily backup of data?

    a. CD-ROM
    b. DAT (Digital Audio Tape)
    c. RAID
    d. Magneto-Optical

Q.112. Which one of the following can be used to automatically load the disk driver with correct I/O address?

    a. AUTOEXEC.BAT   b. INSTALL.NLM
    c. STARTUP.NCF   d. AUTOEXEC.NCF

Q.113. Which is not a reason to implement ODI?

    a. the LAN will be able to communicate with both existing equipment and the new technologies.
    b. the LAN will be able to deal with many media types and protocols
    c. the server will be able to support different clients
    d. the server will be able to support diskless workstations

Q.114. Which is not an advantage of ODI drivers over IPX.COM

   a. ODI Supports multiple protocols on a single network
   b. ODI supports LANalyzer for Windows
   c. ODI supports faster and more reliable file transfer
   d. ODI can be unloaded in reverse order

Q.115. What is wrong in the following NET.CFG file if your workstation is using Ethernet_802.3 frame?

        LINK DRIVER NE2000
        FRAME Ethernet_802.2
        FRAME Ethernet_802.3

   a. section heading is wrong
   b. line 2 should be after line 3
   c. line 2 and 3 should not be indented
   d. there is nothing wrong

Q.116. Which one of the following is related to multiple boot image files?

   a. DOSGEN   b. NET$DOS.SYS
   c. BOOTCONF.SYS   d. BOOTROM.SYS

Q.117. To copy CMOS configuration from one PC to another, which one of the following can be used?

   a. Check It PRO   b. DOSGEN
   c. NSEPro   d. COMCHECK

Troubleshooting & Supporting Networks

Q.118. Which type of error message would it be if your server abend message has the following line:

Abend: SERVER-4.00-3128:SubAllocFreeSectores given invalid. FAT chain end that was already free.

a. CPU-detected
c. NLM has failed
b. Code-detected
d. consistency check

Q.119. Which type of error message would it be if your server abend message has the following line:

Abend: Page Fault Processor Exception (Error code 00000000)

a. CPU-detected
c. NLM has failed
b. Code-detected
d. consistency check

Q.120. DR/Novell DOS is reported to NetWare as a DOS version of 3.31. To avoid mapping to the same COMSPEC, What should you do?

a. add LONG MACHINE TYPE to your NET.CFG
b. add LONG MACHINE TYPE to your CONFIG.SYS
c. Use COMSPEC in login script
d. add DRDOS=3.31 in NET.CFG

Q.121. In which forum would you ask questions on NetWire if you are having problems with a third-party NetWare product?

    a. NVENA   b. NVEND
    c. SYNOPTICS   d. NVENDOR

Q.122. Suppose you were unable to print on the network from an application. You connected the printer directly to your PC and were able to print using Print Screen. You still cannot print from the application in local mode. What could be wrong?

    a. Print Server is not loaded
    b. CAPTURE command is not issued
    c. Application or its configuration
    d. Printer cable is bad

Q.123. If printing output appears speckled, what could be wrong?

    a. primary corona grid
    b. broken or fouled corona wire
    c. drive motor speed
    d. dirty corona wire or running out of toner

Q.124. If printing output is fuzzy, what could be wrong?

    a. primary corona grid
    b. broken or fouled corona wire
    c. drive motor speed

d. dirty corona wire or running out of toner

Q.125. If white streaks appear in printing output, _____ .

    a. shake the toner cartridge or clean the transfer corona assembly
    b. change defective fusing roller
    c. clean corona wire
    d. adjust drive motor speed

Q.126. A repetitive pattern of printing defects, such as an identical smudge every two inches, means _____ .

    a. defective or dirty fusing roller
    b. you are running out of toner
    c. broken or fouled corona wire
    d. faulty primary corona grid

Q.127. If the printer self-test is working O.K., but not printing from the computer, which of the following may not be true?

    a. DIP switches' setting is wrong
    b. application or its configuration is wrong
    c. you need to change ribbon or printer head
    d. bad or disconnected cable

Q.128. To verify that your pin-outs are correct on any suspect cable connector, you would use _____ .

    a. Multimeter
    b. TDR
    c. OTDR
    d. volt-ohm-millimeter

Q.129. If a printer sometimes goes off-line without any reason and works fine when it is reinitialized, you may have _____ .

    a. bad or disconnected cable
    b. application or its configuration problem
    c. static problem
    d. not enough ventilation

Q.130. To avoid printing problems, you would use _____ .

    a. parallel printers
    b. serial printers
    c. dot-matrix printers
    d. laser printers

Q.131. What should you do if print jobs do not go to queue sometimes?

    a. use CAPTURE /show and then monitor the Current Job Entry option in PCONSOLE
    b. assign queue to a printer
    c. load print server
    d. use PSC /status

Troubleshooting & Supporting Networks

Q.132. If you receive error message: "WARNING -- CANNOT CREATE SPOOL FILE", you should _____ .

    a. check if enough disk space is available on the server
    b. issue spool command at the server console
    c. load print server
    d. use CAPTURE /show option

Q.133. To have your print server automatically reboot (unattended print server) after an interruption, which of the following files would you need?

    a. PSERVER.EXE   b. NETERR.ZIP
    c. PSERVx.EXE   d. PUTILx.EXE

Q.134. You should set SPX CONNECTION to at least 60 when working with _____ .

    a. PCONSOLE   b. PSERVER.NLM
    c. PSERVER.EXE   d. RPRINTER

Q.135. Which of the following commands would you use when using RPRINTER over a router? (select all that are true)

    a. SPX ABORT TIMEOUT
    b. IPX RETRY COUNT
    c. PRINT HEADER
    d. PRINT TAIL

Q.136. When using PRINTCON and PRINTDEF, which of the following commands may you need to use? (select all that are true)

   a. SPX ABORT TIMEOUT
   b. IPX RETRY COUNT
   c. PRINT HEADER
   d. PRINT TAIL

Q.137. A supervisor can have a maximum of _____ print job configurations?

   a. 37
   b. 60
   c. 72
   d. supervisor does not have any limit

Q.138. Which of the following cable(s) should be used with Ethernet?

   a. RG58   b. RG58A/U
   c. UTP   d. STP

Q.139. If you receive a message similar to "Disk Controller failure" after you have installed one IDE disk, the problem probably is that _____.

   a. you have a bad IDE controller
   b. you have configured the IDE disk as a "Slave"
   c. you have an IDE bus termination problem

d. the IDE address is not setup properly

Q.140. DMA means _____.

    a. writing data to memory without CPU intervention
    b. Data Memory Active
    c. Digital Memory Active
    d. Digital Asynchronous Mode

Q.141. What is the proper order of an IDE disk setup?

1. CMOS setup
2. I/O address, base memory setup
3. configuring the disk as "Master" or "Slave"
4. attaching disk cable

    a. 3, 2, 1, 4   b. 2, 3, 4, 1
    c. 1, 2, 3, 4   d. 4, 3, 2, 1

Q.142. To gather information about a server's configuration that is experiencing problems, which of the following files would you use?

    a. MONITOR.NLM   b. CONFIG.NLM
    c. INSTALL.NLM   d. CONFIG.EXE

Q.143. What is true about consistency check errors? (select all that are true)

   a. they are CPU-detected errors
   b. they are code-detected errors
   c. the purpose of consistency check is to ensure the stability and integrity of internal operating system data.
   d. the purpose of consistency check is to validate critical disk, memory, and communications processes

Q.144. If you are experiencing server abends or lockups, the very first thing you should do is to _____.

   a. call Novell Technical Support
   b. apply the latest patches, drivers, and NLMs
   c. use MONITOR.NLM to identify the problem
   d. create a memory image file

Q.145. There can be a maximum of _____ volume segments per volume and up to _____ volume segments per disk.

   a. 8, 64   b. 16, 64
   c. 32, 8   d. 32, 64

Q.146. Which of the following utilities would you use to remove a name space of Macintosh files?

   a. VREPAIR   b. MONITOR
   c. INSTALL   d. TRACK ON

Q.147. If your CONFIG.SYS has DEVICE=C:\DOS\EMM386.EXE /FRAME=NONE /X=CC000-DFFF, which of the following address should you use for a Token Ring card?

a. B8000
b. CCBBB
c. E8000
d. FCC00

Q.148. Which of the following is Novell's WWW address?

a. http://www.novell.com
b. ftp://www.novell.com
c. gopher://www.novell.com
d. www://http.novell.com

Q.149. If your file server's hard disk has 3 partitions DOS, NetWare, and UNIX, what do you need so NetWare can mirror all partitions?

a. disks with similar types and sizes
b. two controllers
c. two volumes of the same size
d. NetWare does not mirror partitions other than NetWare partitions

Q.150. Select that which is (are) true about the Analysis Phase of a network management life cycle.

   a. describing management goals, constraints, and resource requirements
   b. gathering general information about the project
   c. evaluating alternative solutions
   d. documenting the system or solution and training the users
   e. monitoring the network system

Q.151 Select that which is (are) true about the Design Phase of a network management life cycle.

   a. describing management goals, constraints, and resource requirements
   b. gathering general information about the project
   c. evaluating alternative solutions
   d. documenting the system or solution and training the users
   e. monitoring the network system

Q.152. Which of the following tasks are management tasks rather than administrative tasks?

   a. monitoring network devices and gathering network statistics
   b. inventorying and documenting the existing system
   c. installing network applications
   d. troubleshooting printing problems
   e. managing workstation connections

Troubleshooting & Supporting Networks

Q.153. A 16-bit ISA card can be used _____.

    a. in all ISA computers
    b. only in 16-bit ISA slots
    c. in 16-bit ISA and EISA slots
    d. in 16-bit ISA, EISA, and MCA slots

Q.154. If MONITOR screen shows "Send packet too big count" and "Receive packet too big count" values very high, you should _____. (select all that apply)

    a. update to faster NICs
    b. update to faster CPU
    c. divide overloaded network segments with a bridge or router
    d. use many smaller disks instead of one large disk

Q.155. Which of the following is used when using NetWire on Internet? (select all that are true)

    a. Go NetWire
    b. hypertext links and graphic
    c. Web browser
    d. NovCIM Internet browser

Q.156. If you are receiving Jabber errors on an Ethernet network, you should_____.

    a. find out fault domain
    b. check for a faulty LAN driver

c. check cable terminator or faulty NIC
d. check whether your server is overloaded

Q.157. All OS patches should be applied _____.

a. through AUTOEXEC.NCF
b. through STARTUP.NCF
c. through CONFIG.NLM
d. according to README file that comes with the patch kit

Q.158. Which file would you edit to correct I/O port of a disk driver that is loaded automatically on server bootup?

a. AUTOEXEC.NCF   b. STARTUP.NCF
c. CONFIG.NCF   d. INSTALL.NLM

Q.159. Which of the following tasks are responsibilities of the network manager? (select all that apply)

a. remotely access, manage, and troubleshoot network devices
b. monitoring and optimizing the network
c. troubleshooting printing problems
d. installing a network-wide virus protection system
e. planning to implement NetWare 4.1 at the corporate level

Troubleshooting & Supporting Networks

Q.160. To verify that a user USER1 has frame mismatch error, what should you do using LZFW?

    a. examine packets sent by user USER1 and received by him
    b. examine packets sent by user USER1 only
    c. examine packets sent by user USER1 and other users
    d. examine packets sent by other users only

Q.161. Your server's hard disk that has very critical data has been damaged. What should you do if you have reliable and tested backup?

    a. Use VREPAIR
    b. use Professional Data Recovery Services
    c. restore from backup
      d. use third-party tools such as Ontrack Data Recovery for NetWare

Q.162. To get latest patches for NetWare 4.1, which of the following files would you download?

    a. 410PT1.EXE   b. 410PT2.EXE
    c. 410UT3.EXE   d. SERVER.EXE

Q.163. What is the correct procedure to apply the latest patches to the OS?

    1. copy the patches to the server directory on the DOS partition

2. load the server by typing SERVER
3. edit the STARTUP.NCF file to load the Patch Manager and patches first
4. enter PATCHES at the server console
5. down the server and load it again

a. 1,2,3,5,4
b. 2,1,3,4,5
c. 1,5,3,4
d. 5,1,2,3,4

Q.164. Which of the following commands are related to NSEPro? (select all that apply)

a. PATH=D:\PROGRAMS\WIN
b. LASTDRIVE=Z
c. MAP S16:=NESPRO\PROGRAMS\WIN
d. SET NESPRO= NETWORK
e. SET NSE_DOWNLOAD =D:\DOWNLOAD\

Q165. Consider the following files and determine what is the correct order of loading NetWare DOS Requester?

1. VLM   2. LSL   3. IPX
4. ODI   5. NETX   6. IPXODI
7. NE2000

a. 1,2,7,6
b. 3,5
c. 2,7,6,1
d. 2,7,4,1
e. 2,7,6,5

Q.166. Consider the following files and determine what is the correct order of loading the old NetWare Shell with non-ODI drivers?

1. VLM
2. LSL
3. IPX
4. ODI
5. NETX
6. IPXODI
7. NE2000

a. 1,2,7,6
b. 3,5
c. 2,7,6,1
d. 2,7,4,1
e. 2,7,6,5

Q167. Consider the following files and determine what is the correct order of loading the old NetWare Shell with ODI drivers?

1. VLM
2. LSL
3. IPX
4. ODI
5. NETX
6. IPXODI
7. NE2000

a. 1,2,7,6
b. 3,5
c. 2,7,6,1
d. 2,7,4,1
e. 2,7,6,5

Q.168. Your company is using NetWare 3.11 and is planning to buy a piece of equipment to integrate with the network. You are not sure which communication protocol the new equipment will be using. What would you suggest that your company do at this point?

    a. switch to TCP/IP Protocol
    b. switch to ODI drivers
    c. switch to the NetWare DOS Requester
    d. upgrade to NetWare 4.1

Q.169. Which of the following limitations will you come across when using IDE with NetWare?

    a. a NetWare volume can not have more than 528 MB
    b. you may need to use IDE.DSK instead of ISADISK.DSK
    c. mirroring may not be adequate, because a failure in the primary IDE disk causes failure in the second disk.
    d. NetWare must use non-standard drivers to access IDE disk larger than 528 MB

Q.170. Which of the following must you have to access Novell WWW? (select all that apply)

    a. a connection to the Internet
    b. IPX protocol at your workstation
    c. TCP/IP protocol at your workstation
    d. an Internet browser
    e. NSEPro for the Internet

Q.171. Which of the following tasks can you perform using NetWire on CompuServe?

    a. find Novell Technical Conference or trade shows in your area
    b. search for a specific topic in Novell product manuals
    c. find out jumper settings to set I/O port address of a NIC
    d. download a LAN driver which is absolutely latest
    e. ask a technical question about NetWare 4.1
    f. find out specifications about a system board

Answers

(1). c   (2). b   (3). c   (4). a   (5). c

(6). b   (7). a   (8). c   (9). b   (10). d

(11). a   (12). a   (13). a   (14). b   (15). c

(16). c   (17). b   (18). a   (19). b   (20). e

(21). d   (22). b   (23). b   (24). a   (25). b

(26). c   (27). b   (28). a   (29). c   (30). c

(31). b   (32). a   (33). d   (34). b   (35). b

(36). b   (37). d   (38). c   (39). a   (40). b

(41). a   (42). d   (43). d   (44). b   (45). d

(46). c   (47). b   (48). c   (49). b   (50). a

(51). b   (52). b, c   (53). a   (54). d   (55). d

(56). b   (57). b   (58). d   (59). b   (60). c

(61). d   (62). b   (63). c   (64). d   (65). d

(66). d   (67). c   (68). d   (69). a   (70). a

(71). b   (72). d   (73). a   (74). b   (75). a

(76). b   (77). c   (78). b   (79). b   (80). c

(81). a   (82). d   (83). b   (84). c   (85). a

Troubleshooting & Supporting Networks

(86). d   (87). b   (88). c   (89). d   (90). d

(91). b   (92). c   (93). b   (94). d   (95). d

(96). b   (97). d   (98). b   (99). c   (100). a

(101). a,b,c   (102). b   (103). b   (104). b   (105). b

(106). e   (107). c   (108). d   (109). c   (110). a

(111). b   (112). c   (113). d   (114). c   (115). b

(116). c   (117). a   (118). b,d   (119). a   (120). a

(121). a   (122). c   (123). a   (124). d   (125). a

(126). a   (127). c   (128). a   (129). c   (130). a

(131). a   (132). a   (133). b   (134). c   (135). a, b

(136). c, d   (137). a   (138). b, c   (139). b   (140). a

(141). b   (142). b   (143). b,c,d   (144). b   (145). c

(146). a   (147). b   (148). a   (149). d   (150). a, b

(151). c   (152). a,b   (153). c   (154). a, c   (155). b,c

(156). c   (157). d   (158). b   (159). a,b,d,e (160). c

(161). c   (162). b   (163). a   (164). a,c,e   (165). c

(166). b   (167). e   (168). b   (169). b,c   (170). a,c,d

(171). a,d,e

Explanations

Q.160.
You need to examine both frame type of packets sent by USER1 and sent by other users who are not having problems.

Q.161.
You can use VREPAIR only if having problems with the volume, not when disk is damaged. Option B is used only when reliable backup is not available and your data is irreplaceable. In this case you should not even try to use VREPAIR or ODR for NetWare. Because disk is damaged and you can not access it, option C is the best choice.

Usually if you have data loss because of volume corruption and you have reliable and tested backups available, to repair the volume, your first option may be to use VREPAIR, second option may be to use ODR for NetWare.

If both of above procedures are unsuccessful, you may reformat your hard disk or install a new one, re-install the operating system, and restore the data.

Q.168.
ODI drivers support multiple communication protocols on the same NIC. All other choices are irrelevant at this point.

Q.169.
Choice A is wrong because 528 MB limitation is for standard IDE, not for NetWare volume. Choice D is wrong because to use larger than 528 MB disk, you need special non-standard BIOS, not non-standard disk driver.

Troubleshooting & Supporting Networks

Q. Match the following descriptions with the picture numbers.

(I)	T-Connector	_____
(ii)	Terminator	_____
(iii)	V.35 Connector	_____
(iv)	Transceiver	_____
(v)	Active hub	_____
(vi)	Passive hub	_____
(vii)	IBM Data Connector	_____
(viii)	Unshielded Twisted Pair Cable	_____
(ix)	Shielded twisted Pair	_____
(x)	Coax Cable	_____
(xi)	Fiber Optic Connection	_____
(xii)	Twisted Pair Connection	_____
(xiii)	Thin Coax Connection	_____
(xiv)	Thick Coax Connection	_____
(xv)	Hubs Connecting Computers	_____
(xvi)	Multistation Access Unit (MAU)	_____
(xvii)	DB9 Connector	_____
(xviii)	DB15 Connector	_____
(xix)	RJ-11 Connector	_____
(xx)	RJ-45 Connector	_____

1

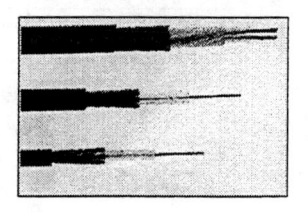

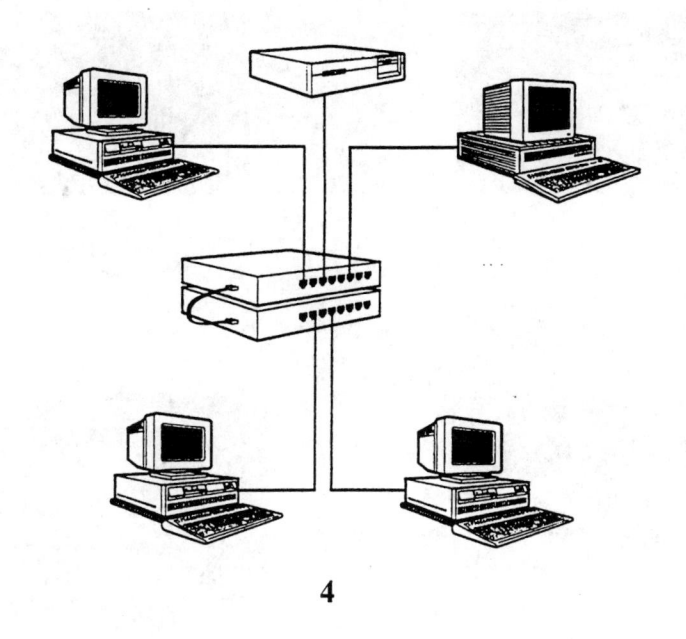

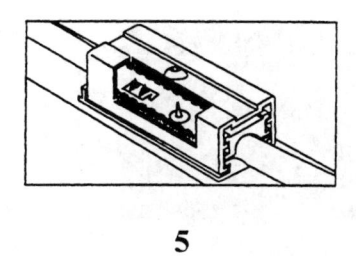

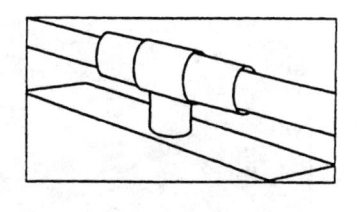

2

3

4

5

6

7

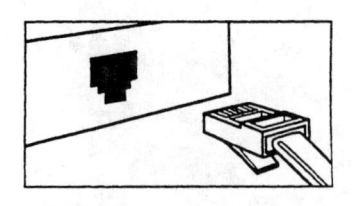

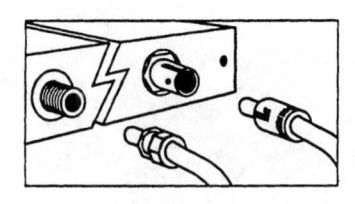

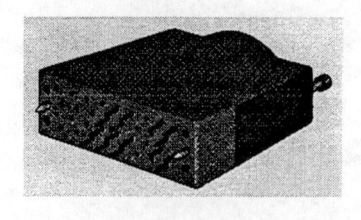

8

9

10

11

12

13

Q-54

14

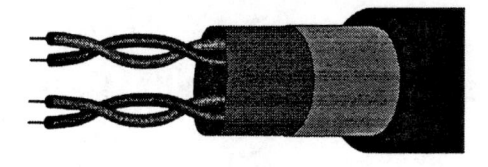

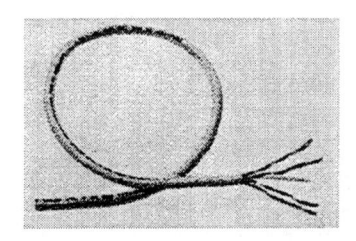

15

16   **17**   **18**

19   **20**   **21**

ANSWERS

(i)   1   (ii) 2   (iii) 11 & 18   (iv) 12

(v)   9   (vi) 10   (vii) 15   (viii) 21

(ix) 14   (x)   3   (xi) 8   (xii) 7

(xiii) 6   (xiv) 5   (xv) 4   (xvi) 13

(xvii) 16   (xviii) 17   (xix) 20   (xx) 19

Test Objectives

Test: 050-602 and 50-802 Service and Support Revision 1/02

No.	Objective	Ch. #
1.	List and describe tasks related to providing service and support on a NetWare network.	1-9
2.	Describe the troubleshooting model used in this course.	1
3.	Describe good service and support techniques, such as static protection and record keeping, and describe how to use diagnostic tools.	1
4.	Use NSEPro to find solutions to service and support problems.	2
5.	Use NetWire on CompuServe to find solutions to service and support problems.	2
6.	Use NetWire on the Internet to find solutions to service and support problems.	2
7.	Use the Micro House Technical Library (MTL) to find information about system boards, hard disks, and network interface boards.	2
8.	Choose which of the four tools is most likely to provide a solution to a specific type of problem.	2
9.	Configure, install, and troubleshoot Ethernet network boards, cables, and related hardware.	3
10.	Configure, install, and troubleshoot Token Ring network boards, cables, and related hardware.	3
11.	Configure, install, and troubleshoot ARCnet network boards, cables, and related hardware.	3

© 1993 - 96 · PC Age, Inc. All Rights Reserved · 20 Audrey Place · Fairfield, NJ 07004 · U.S.A. · Tel: 201-882-5370

Troubleshooting & Supporting Networks

No.	Objective	Ch. #
12.	Describe FDDI and ATM.	3
13.	Demonstrate skills prerequisite to installing network boards, such as identifying the appropriate board type; setting the IRQs, memory addresses, and port addresses; setting jumpers and DIP switches; and ensuring network board and slot compatibility.	3
14.	Describe basic hard disk principles, including the purpose of hard disks and the various interface types used by these devices.	4
15.	configure, install, prepare, and troubleshoot SCSI and IDE disk on a workstation and a NetWare server.	4
16.	Establish NetWare file storage by creating NetWare partitions and volumes, spanning hard disks, and mirroring hard disks.	4
17.	Install and configure a CD-ROM as a NetWare volume.	4
18.	Troubleshoot malfunctioning installations of IPX and ODI based DOS workstations.	5
19.	Install and troubleshoot a remote boot workstation.	5
20.	Diagnose and repair workstation conflicts based on resources such as memory, IRQ, and DMA.	5
21.	Locate and install the most current software for a NetWare 3.12 or NetWare 4.1 server, including patches and NLMs.	6
22.	Diagnose and troubleshoot server-related abends and lockups.	6

No.	Objective	Ch. #
23.	Diagnose and troubleshoot server-related performance problems.	6
24.	Use a protocol analyzer to diagnose performance problems and help alleviate over loaded networks or servers.	6
25.	Create a data repair and recovery plan that uses NetWare and third-party utilities to recover form hardware failure.	8
26.	Diagnose and resolve NetWare printing problems related to physical connections, print queues, print servers, remote printing, configuration, print utilities, and PostScript files.	7
27.	Prevent, diagnose, and resolve common problems with printers.	7
28.	Describe the role of network management.	9
29.	Explain the network management life cycle described in this section.	9
30.	Describe the major features of ManageWise.	9

Note: According to Novell, you will be tested on your ability to use MTL and NSEPro, NetWare and DOS. You will not be tested on your ability to use WINCheckIt, WinCIM, NOVCIM, LANalyzer for Windows, Ontrack Data Recovery for NetWare, or ManageWise presented in this course. However, you will be tested on the types of tasks, such as diagnostics, protocol analysis, or finding information on NetWire, for which they can be used.

INDEX

10BASE2 (THIN-ETHERNET)	3-7
10BASE2 CABLING	3-7
10BASET (TWISTED PAIR ETHERNET)	3-9
10BASET CABLING	3-10

A

A SAMPLE NET.CFG FILE	5-16
ADVANTAGES OF FDDI	3-39
ARCNET	3-26
ARCNET BUS WITH UTP	3-31
ARCNET CABLING (COAX CABLE)	3-30
ARCNET FRAME TYPES	3-28
ARCNET NETWORK FEATURES	3-27
ARCNET PLUS	3-35
ATM	3-41
AUTOMATIC SETUP ROUTINE	5-34

B

BASE MEMORY ADDRESSES	5-32
BEACONING	3-23
BRIDGES	6-10

C

CAPTURE AND NPRINT	7-12
CD-ROM (COMPACT DISK-READ ONLY MEMORY)	4-22
CD-ROM TIPS	4-22
CD-ROM TROUBLESHOOTING TIPS:	4-26
CHECK ERROR LOG	1-9
CHECK✓IT PRO	2-1
CMOS SETUP	5-34
COMMON PROBLEMS ASSOCIATED WITH NETWORK PRINTING	7-13
COMPLETE PRE-SITE PLANNING	1-9
COMPUTER BUS	3-46

ARCHITECTURE AND CARD COMPATIBILITY	
CONFIGURING ELEMENTS	3-1
CONFIGURING THE DRIVE	4-4
CONNECTING WORKSTATIONS	5-1
CONTENTS OF SERVICE & SUPPORT VOLUME	2-8
CONVENTIONAL MEMORY	5-37
CONVENTIONS	5-14

D

DIFFERENT TYPES OF ETHERNET	3-4
DIP SWITCHES	3-1
DIRECT MEMORY ACCESS (DMA)	5-30
DISADVANTAGES	3-27
DISADVANTAGES OF FDDI	3-39
DIVIDE COMPONENT INTO SUBUNITS	1-11
DOCUMENTING THE NETWORK	1-13
DOS REQUESTER INSTALLATION	5-10
DOT MATRIX TIPS	7-4

E

EISA CONFIGURATION PROGRAM	5-35
ESDI - ENHANCED SMALL DRIVE INTERFACE	4-2
ETHERNET	3-3
ETHERNET FRAME TYPES	3-12
EXERCISE 3-1	3-46
EXERCISE 3-2	3-49
EXERCISE: MIRRORING AND SPANNING	4-29
EXPANDED MEMORY	5-39
EXTENDED MEMORY	5-38

© 1993 - 96 · PC Age, Inc. All Rights Reserved · 20 Audrey Place · Fairfield, NJ 07004 · U.S.A. · Tel: 201-882-5370

F

FDDI	3-36
FDDI CHARACTERISTICS	3-37
FDDI TOKEN-PASSING PROCESS	3-39
FIBER OPTIC ARCNET	3-31
FILE TRANSFER PROTOCOL (FTP)	2-18

G

GENERAL OPTIMIZATION POINTS	6-6
GENERAL TROUBLESHOOTING TIPS	5-17
GOPHER	2-19

H

HANDS-ON EXERCISES	2-23
HARD DRIVE CABLING	4-9
HARD DRIVES	4-1
HARD DRIVES TIPS	4-15
HIGH MEMORY	5-40
HOW IPX AND NETX WORK	5-3
HOW TO USE NSEPRO (WINDOWS VERSION)	2-23
HOW TO USE THE MICRO HOUSE TECHNICAL LIBRARY (MTL)	2-42
HUBS	6-10

I

I/O ADDRESS (INPUT/OUTPUT ADDRESS)	5-31
IBM REFERENCE DISKETTE	5-35
IDE - INTEGRATED DRIVE ELECTRONICS	4-2
INSTALLING NSEPRO	2-4
INTERRUPT REQUESTS (IRQ)	5-28
INTRODUCTION TO MANAGEWISE	9-4
IPX.COM (INTERNETWORK PACKET EXCHANGE)	5-2
ISOLATE THE PROBLEM	1-10

J

JUMPERS	3-1

K

L

LASER PRINTER TIPS	7-3
LINK DRIVER SECTION	5-14
LINK SUPPORT SECTION	5-15

M

MAGNETO-OPTICAL (M-O) DRIVES	4-28
MANAGEMENT FEATURES	3-40
MEMORY OPTIMIZATION	5-40
MEMORY TYPES	5-37
MIRRORING AND DUPLEXING	4-15
MIRRORING AND DUPLEXING TROUBLESHOOTING TIPS	4-16
MOST POPULAR NETWORK BOARDS	3-3

N

NAVIGATING NOVELL INTERNET SERVICES	2-18
NET.CFG FILE	5-14
NETWARE 3.12 WORKSTATION SOFTWARE INSTALLATION	5-10
NETWARE 4.1 WORKSTATION SOFTWARE INSTALLATION	5-12
NETWARE CD-ROM SUPPORT	4-24
NETWARE DOS REQUESTER	5-7
NETWARE DOS REQUESTER SECTION	5-15
NETWIRE	2-10
NETWIRE FORUMS	2-10
NETWORK MANAGEMENT	9-1
NETWORK SYSTEMS SUPPORT	2-7
NETX	5-2
NOVELL ON INTERNET	2-17
NSEPRO	2-4
NSEPRO (WINDOWS VERSION)	2-5
NSEPRO EXERCISE 1	2-35
NSEPRO EXERCISE 2	2-36
NSEPRO EXERCISE 3	2-37
NSEPRO EXERCISE 4	2-38
NSEPRO EXERCISE 5	2-39
NSEPRO EXERCISE 6	2-40

Index

O

OBTAIN PHYSICAL LAYOUT	1-10
OFF	2-42
OFF	2-42
ON	2-42
OPEN DATA-LINK INTERFACE	5-4
OPTIMIZING USING HUBS, BRIDGES, AND ROUTERS	6-10
OTHER NETWORK STORAGE DEVICES	4-18

P

PC - MODES OF OPERATION	5-36
PCONSOLE	7-10
PHYSICAL ENVIRONMENT FOR COMPUTERS	1-2
PHYSICAL INSTALLATION	4-6
PHYSICAL PRINTER PROBLEMS	7-2
POSTSCRIPT PRINTER TIPS	7-3
PREPARING THE DISK FOR USE: FORMATTING AND PARTITIONING	4-11
PREVENTION TECHNIQUES	1-1
PRINTCON	7-11
PRINTDEF	7-11
PROBLEMS IN THE NETWORK PRINTING SETUP	7-5
PROBLEMS WITH PRINT SERVERS	7-7
PROBLEMS WITH PRINTING UTILITIES	7-10
PROBLEMS WITH QUEUES	7-6
PROBLEMS WITH REMOTE PRINTERS	7-8
PROCEDURE:	4-29
PROTOCOL SECTION	5-15

Q

R

RAID	4-18
ROUTERS	6-11

S

SCSI - SMALL COMPUTER SYSTEMS INTERFACE	4-2
SCSI II	4-2
SEARCHING THE MTL	2-22
SERVER ABENDS	6-1
SERVER ABENDS AND LOCKUPS	6-1
SERVER LOCKUPS	6-2
SETTING ARCNET BOARDS	3-32
SETTING ETHERNET BOARDS	3-10
SETTING THE DRIVE TYPE IN CMOS	4-10
SETTING UP A V3.12 SERVER FOR MULTIPLE FRAME TYPES	3-13
SETTING UP HARD DRIVES	4-4
ST-506	4-1
STEPS TO USE DOSGEN UTILITY	5-22
SYSINFO	2-1

T

TAKE CORRECTIVE ACTION	1-11
TEST & TOOLS	2-2
TEST EACH SUBUNIT	1-11
THE MICRO HOUSE TECHNICAL LIBRARY	2-20
THE NETWIRE LIBRARIES	2-11
THICK-ETHERNET CABLING	3-5
THOMAS CONRAD NETWORK SYSTEM (TCNS)	3-35
TOKEN RING	3-16
TOKEN RING ADVANTAGES	3-18
TOKEN RING CABLE TYPES	3-22
TOKEN RING DISADVANTAGES	3-19
TOKEN RING OPERATION	3-19
TOKEN RING OVER UNSHIELDED TWISTED PAIR	3-21
TRACK ON COMMAND	5-25
TROUBLESHOOTING AN ETHERNET NETWORK	3-14
TROUBLESHOOTING EXERCISES	3-50
TROUBLESHOOTING PROCEDURES	1-8
TROUBLESHOOTING SERVER ABENDS AND LOCKUPS	6-3
TROUBLESHOOTING TIPS	3-25
TROUBLESHOOTING TIPS	3-34
TROUBLESHOOTING TIPS	3-40

© 1993 - 96 · PC Age, Inc. All Rights Reserved · 20 Audrey Place · Fairfield, NJ 07004 · U.S.A. · Tel: 201-882-5370

TROUBLESHOOTING TIPS FOR HUBS, BRIDGES, AND ROUTERS	6-11
TROUBLESHOOTING TIPS WHEN USING IPX/NETX	5-19
TROUBLESHOOTING TIPS WHEN USING ODI FILES/VLM	5-20
TROUBLESHOOTING USING LZFW	6-17
TROUBLESHOOTING WORKSTATION CONFLICTS	5-28
TYPICAL ETHERNET ERRORS	6-18
TYPICAL TOKEN RING ERRORS	6-21

X

Y

Z

U

UPPER MEMORY	5-40
USING A PROTOCOL ANALYZER (LANALYZER)	6-13
USING LZFW	6-13
USING NETWIRE	2-13
USING NETWIRE	2-46
USING NOVCIM	2-16
USING THE LATEST PATCHES, NLMS, AND UTILITIES	6-4
USING THE MTL ENCYCLOPEDIA OF MAIN BOARDS	2-43
USING THE MTL NETWARE INTERFACE TECHNICAL GUIDE	2-44
USING WINCIM	2-13

V

VREPAIR	8-1

W

WINCHECKIT	2-3
WORKING WITH DISKLESS WORKSTATION	5-21
WORKING WITH IPX AND NETX	5-1
WORKSTATION SETUP	5-34
WORKSTATION TROUBLESHOOTING TECHNIQUES	5-17
WORLD WIDE WEB (WWW)	2-18

Now You Can Prepare for All 7 Tests to Become a Novell CNE Right on Your PC

CNE CBT™
(Computer Based Training)
for Win/Win95/NT

- Complete course material for all 7 tests
- CNE TestMaster includes hundreds of multiple choice practice questions
- NetWare Interactive Simulator teaches you NetWare by hands-on exercises
- NSEPro and MTL hands-on exercises
- Novell Networking Glossary contains over 1100 terms and commands of NetWare
- Complete material for your home-study needs for Novell CNE

If you want to become a Certified Novell Engineer (CNE) and need complete material for the preparation with convenience and flexibility, you need CNE CBT (Computer Based Training). This one CD-ROM provides you with all the material you need to become a Novell CNE. You can easily carry it with you to practice either at home or at the office.

CNE CBT contains all test preparation material from our CNE Training Manuals on CD-ROM in CBT format. There are exercises at the end of chapters allowing you to check your knowledge and understanding. Furthermore, there are hundreds of multiple choice practice questions as covered in CNE TestMaster to practice for the actual Novell tests. In addition, there are over 50 hands-on exercises for either 3.1x or 4.11 track from NetWare Interactive Simulator. You can learn through real hands-on experience with NetWare even if you don't have NetWare available.

Novell Networking Glossary helps you in searching for terms and commands used in NetWare and gives you a brief description of each. In short, CNE CBT is the complete solution for your CNE home-study needs.

System Requirements: 486+ PC, Windows 3.1+, 8 MB RAM, 4x CD-ROM Drive, 10 MB hard disk space.

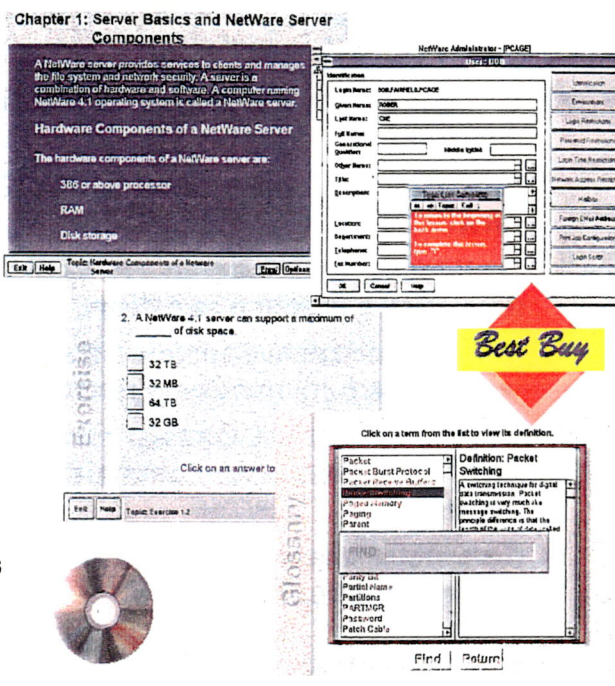

Best Buy

This is Absolutely, Positively, the ONLY thing you need to become a Novell CNE!

3.1x Track Covers the Following Novell Tests
Course 508, Administration 3.12
Course 518, Advanced Administration 3.12
Course 802, Installation & Configuration Workshop 3.12
Course 526, NetWare 3.1x to 4.11 Update
Course 801, Service & Support
Course 200, Networking Technologies
Course 605, NetWare TCP/IP Transport (elective)

4.11 Track Covers the Following Novell Tests
Course 520, Administration 4.11
Course 525, Advanced Administration 4.11
Course 804, Installation & Configuration Workshop 4.11
Course 532, Design and Implementation 4.11
Course 540, Building Intranets with IntranetWare 4.11
Course 801, Service & Support
Course 200, Networking Technologies

CNE CBT 3.1x Track Item No. CBT312-797 ....$995
CNE CBT 4.11 Track Item No. CBT411-797 ....$995
CNE CBT both 3.1x & 4.11 Tracks (one CD) $1195
Item No. CBT31411-797
5 User Version $2995. 10 User Version $4995. 25+ User, Call. (shipped in CD-ROM only)

Ask for Special Upgrade Prices

Order Today!!! 1-800-PCAGE-60 (1-800-722-4360)
PC Age, Inc.: 20 Audrey Place, Fairfield, NJ 07004. U.S.A. International: (01) 732-287-3622, Fax: (01) 732-287-4511
Visit us on the WEB at: http://www.pcage.com or E-Mail: sales@pcage.com

Effective 07/21/97

This is Absolutely, Positively, the ONLY thing you need to become a Novell CNA!

CNA CBT (Computer Based Training) for Win/Win95/NT

- Complete course material for the CNA tests
- One CD-ROM covers both CNA 3 & CNA 4
- TestMaster includes hundreds of multiple choice practice questions
- NetWare Interactive Simulator teaches you NetWare by hands-on exercises
- Novell Networking Glossary contains over 1100 terms and commands of NetWare
- Complete material for your home-study needs for Novell CNA

If you want to become a Certified Novell Administrator (CNA) and need complete material for the preparation with convenience and flexibility, you need CNA CBT (Computer Based Training). This one CD-ROM provides you with all the material you need to become a Novell CNA. You can easily carry it with you to practice either at home or at the office.

CNA Computer Based Training contains all test preparation material from our Training Manuals. There are exercises at the end of each chapter allowing you to check your knowledge and understanding. Furthermore, there are hundreds of multiple choice practice questions as covered in TestMaster to practice for the actual Novell tests. In addition, there are hands-on exercises from NetWare Interactive Simulator. You can learn through real hands-on experience with NetWare even if you don't have NetWare available.

Novell Networking Glossary helps you in searching for terms and commands used in NetWare and gives you a brief description of each. In short, CNA Computer Based Training is the complete solution for your CNA home-study needs.

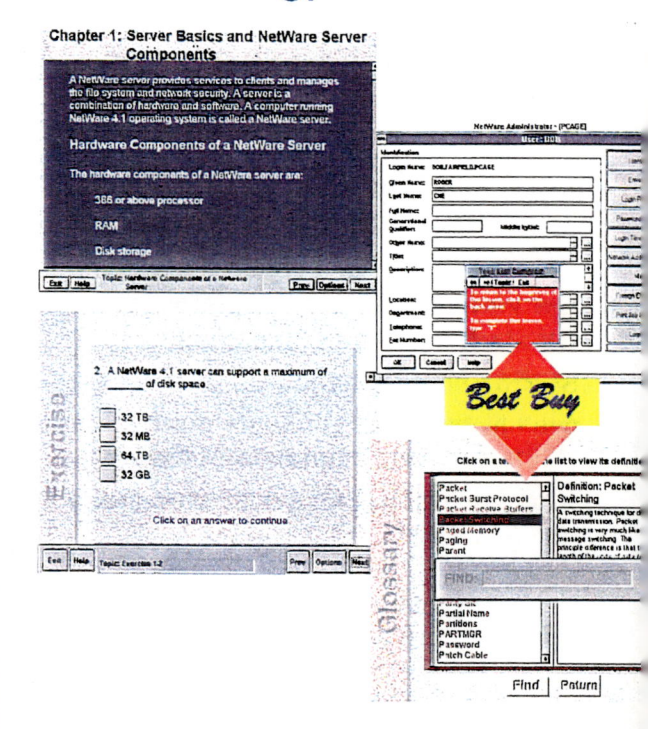

Now You Can Prepare to Become a Novell CNA Right on Your PC

CNA CBT Covers the Following Novell Tests
Novell course 508, Administration 3.1x, Certified Novell Administrator CNA/CNE test #50-130.

Novell course 520, Administration 4.11, Certified Novell Administrator CNA/CNE test #50-613.

CNA CBT for <u>both</u> 3.1x & 4.11 Tracks (one CD) Item No. CNACBT34-797	......$39
5 User Version Item No. 5CNACBT34-797	.....$119
10 User Version Item No. 10CNACBT34-797 (shipped in CD-ROM only)	....$199

Ask for Special Upgrade Pri

System Requirements: 486+ PC, Windows 3.1+, MB RAM, 4x CD-ROM Drive, 10 MB Hard Disk spac

Order Today!!! 1-800-PCAGE-60 (1-800-722-4360)

PC Age, Inc.: 20 Audrey Place, Fairfield, NJ 07004. U.S.A. International: (01) 732-287-3622, Fax: (01) 732-287-451
Visit us on the WEB at: http://www.pcage.com or E-Mail: sales@pcage.com

Effective 08/01

Conquer Your CNE Exams With These Comprehensive Training Manuals

CNE Training Manuals

- Concise, to-the-point, up-to-date, and easy to understand
- Covers all 7 CNE tests for either 3.1x or 4.11
- Used in training institutes all over the world including colleges and universities
- Great as reference manuals for NetWare LAN administration tasks
- Rated "excellent" by hundreds of students

Rated Excellent

These Training Manuals are not designed only for test preparation, they are teaching manuals and being used in training centers all over the world.

To study at home to become a Certified Novell Engineer (CNE) you need these CNE Training Manuals. They cover what you need to know to pass the exams required to become a CNE. In addition, these manuals are great as a reference for NetWare LAN Administration tasks. Choose either NetWare 3.12 or NetWare 4.11 manuals, or both, depending on the certification you want.

4.11 Track Covers the Following Novell Tests

"System Administration v4.11" for Novell course 520, Administration v4.11, CNE/CNA test #50-613.
Item No. SA411-613 ..... $100

"Advanced System Administration v4.11" for Novell course 525, Advanced Administration v4.11, test #50-614. **Item No. ASA411-614** $100

"Installing & Configuring NetWare v4.11" for Novell course 804, NetWare v4.11 Installation & Configuration Workshop, test #50-617. **Item No. IC411-617** $100

"Designing NetWare v4.11" for Novell course 532, NetWare v4.11 Design & Implementation, test #50-601.
Item No. DI41-601 ..... $100

For Novell course 540, Building Intranets with IntranetWare test #50-627.
Item No. BII411-627 ..... $100

"Data Communication & Networking Concepts" for Novell course 200, Networking Technologies, test #50-147.
Item No. NT-147 ..... $100

"Troubleshooting & Supporting Networks" for Novell course 801, NetWare Service & Support, test #50-602.
Item No. SS-602 ..... $100

All Seven Training Manuals for 4.11 Track
Item No. CSG411-797 ~~$700~~ **$495**

3.1x Track Covers the Following Novell Tests

"System Administration v3.12" for Novell course 508, Administration v3.1x, CNE/CNA test #50-130.
Item No. SA312-130 .... $75

"Advanced System Administration v3.12" for Novell course 518, Advanced Administration v3.1x, test #50-131. **Item No. ASA312-131** $75

"Installing & Configuring NetWare v3.1x" for Novell course 802, NetWare v3.1x Installation & Configuration Workshop, test #50-132. **Item No. IC312-132** $75

"NetWare v3.1x to NetWare v4.11 Update" for Novell course 526, NetWare 3.1x to 4.11 Update, test #50-615.
Item No. UD3141-615 ..... $100

"Data Communication & Networking Concepts" for Novell course 200, Networking Technologies, test #50-147.
Item No. NT-147 ..... $100

"Troubleshooting & Supporting Networks" for Novell course 801, NetWare Service & Support, test #50-602.
Item No. SS-602 ..... $100

"NetWare TCP/IP Support" for Novell course 605, NetWare TCP/IP Transport, test #50-145 (elective).
Item No. TCPIP-145 ..... $100

All Seven Training Manuals for 3.1x Track
Item No. CSG312-797 ~~$625~~ **$450**

"I just wanted to let you know that I did not miss a single question on the exam. I want to thank you and everyone else that works at PC Age for the incredible customer service, and for the great test preparation material."

Order Today!!! 1-800-PCAGE-60 (1-800-722-4360)

PC Age, Inc.: 20 Audrey Place, Fairfield, NJ 07004. U.S.A. International: (01) 732-287-3622, Fax: (01) 732-287-4511
Visit us on the WEB at: http://www.pcage.com or E-Mail: sales@pcage.com

Effective 07/21/97

Learn NetWare with Hands-On Training Without Installing NetWare!

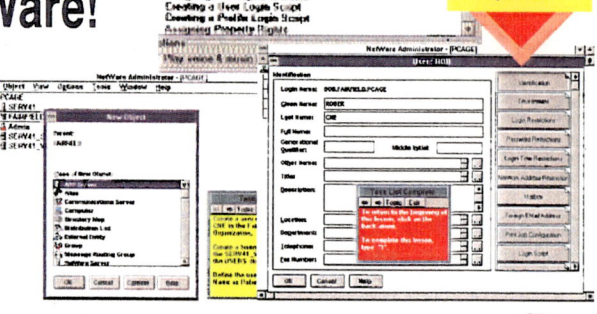

NetWare *Interactive* Simulator

for Win/Win95/NT

- Learn NetWare with step-by-step interactive training
- Practice NetWare utilities without installing NetWare
- Contains over 100 useful exercises and 60+ help screens for Server and Workstation
- NSEPro and MTL hands-on exercises
- Covers both NetWare 3.1x and IntranetWare 4.11

Do you need to study NetWare but don't want to jeopardize your current installation or don't have an installation at all? Whether you are studying for CNE exams or brushing up on your understanding of NetWare 3.1x or 4.11, the NetWare Interactive Simulator gives you hands-on experience with NetWare.

The NetWare Interactive Simulator contains over 100 NetWare 3.1x and 4.11 exercises; Its unique hands-on approach is useful for those complex Novell utilities that you just can't understand with books and study guides. With the NetWare Interactive Simulator, you learn NetWare by doing without harming your current NetWare installation or needing to be on a network at all!

No need for a File Server, Network Interface Cards (NICs), or NetWare

NetWare Interactive Simulator Item # NIS34-797 ...$295
5 user version Item # 5NIS34-797 ......$995
10 user version Item # 10NIS34-797 ......$1895
25+ user version, Call.
(shipped in CD-ROM only)

System Requirements: 486+ PC, Windows 3.1+, 8 MB RAM, 2x CD-ROM Drive, 1-2 MB hard disk space (as it runs from the CD-ROM).

Practice Taking the CNE Exams Right on Your PC

CNE TestMaster for Win/Win95/NT

- Interactive software that simulates actual Novell tests
- More than 3000 multiple-choice practice questions
- Prepared by highly qualified and experienced instructors
- Covers both NetWare 3.1x and IntranetWare 4.11

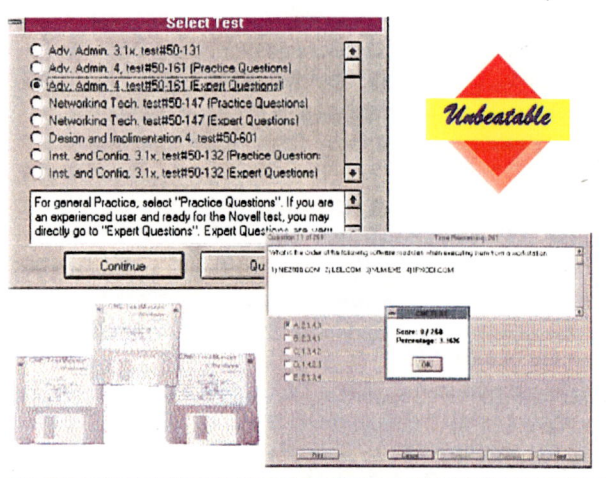

You want to be a Certified Novell Engineer (CNE), but you are not sure whether you know the right NetWare details to pass the CNE exams. Now you can quiz yourself and find out, right on your PC to determine your skills level before you take the exams.

CNE TestMaster Covers the Following Novell Tests:
Course 520, Administration 4.11
Course 525, Advanced Administration 4.11
Course 804, Installation & Configuration Workshop 4.11
Course 532, Design and Implementation 4.11
Course 540, Building Intranets with IntranetWare 4.11
Course 508, Administration 3.12
Course 518, Advanced Administration 3.12
Course 802, Installation & Configuration Workshop 3.12
Course 526, NetWare 3.1x to 4.11 Update
Course 801, Service & Support
Course 200, Networking Technologies
Course 605, NetWare TCP/IP Transport (elective)

CNE TestMaster, Item # CNETM34-797 ......$149
5 user version, Item # 5CNETM34-797 ......$595
10 user version Item # 10CNETM34-797 ......$995
25+ user version, Call.
(shipped in 3.5 inch disks only)

Note: Single test can be sold separately.

System Requirements: 386+ PC, Windows 3.1+, 4 MB RAM, 10 MB Hard Disk Space.

Order Today!!! 1-800-PCAGE-60 (1-800-722-4360)

PC Age, Inc.: 20 Audrey Place, Fairfield, NJ 07004. U.S.A. International: (01) 732-287-3622, Fax: (01) 732-287-4511
Visit us on the WEB at: http://www.pcage.com or E-Mail: sales@pcage.com

Effective 07/21/97

Now You Can Practice Taking the MCSE Tests Right on Your PC

MCSE TestMaster™

for Win/Win95/NT

- Interactive software that simulates actual Microsoft tests
- Hundreds of multiple-choice practice questions and answers
- Checks your knowledge and highlights your areas of weakness
- Prepared by highly qualified and experienced instructors

You want to be a Microsoft Certified System Engineer (MCSE) or Microsoft Certified Product Specialist (MCPS), but you are not sure whether you know the right Windows NT details to pass MCSE or MCPS exam(s). Now you can quiz yourself and find out, determining your skills level right on your PC to before you take the test(s).

MCSE TestMaster helps you determine your skills level before you take the exam(s). It can save you the time, expense, aggravation, and embarrassment of failing an exam and having to study more to retake it.

MCSE TestMaster Any Single Test	.....$139
MCSE TestMaster Core Pack (four tests)	.....$495
MCSE TestMaster All Six Tests	.....$695
For multi user version prices, call.	(Shipped in 3.5 inch disks only)

System Requirements: 386+ PC, Windows 3.1+, 4 MB RAM, 10 MB of free Hard Disk space.

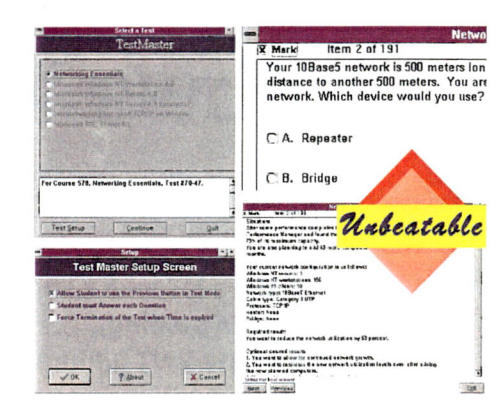

MCSE TestMaster Covers the Following Microsoft Tests

Core

Course 578, Networking Essentials, test #70-58

Course 687, Implementing and Supporting Microsoft Windows NT Workstation 4.0, test # 70-73

Course 687, Implementing and Supporting Microsoft Windows NT Server 4.0, test #70-67

Course 689, Implementing and Supporting Microsoft Windows NT Server 4.0 Enterprise Technologies, test #70-68

Electives

Course 688, Internetworking Microsoft TCP/IP on Windows NT, test #70-59

Course 867, System Administration for Microsoft SQL Server 6.5 for Windows NT, test #70-26

Guarantee to Pass Microsoft Tests:

PC Age offers you* a 90-Day 100% Money Back Guarantee. If you do not pass the Microsoft test(s) on two attempts within ninety (90) days of the purchase, call us and we will issue you a 100% credit for the MCSE TestMaster price. You do not need to return the TestMaster to us. It is yours to keep.

* This offer is good for the actual buyer only. Credit will be issued for the failed test(s) only (excluding shipping & handling). Proof of purchase may be required.

Order Today!!! 1-800-PCAGE-60 (1-800-722-4360)

PC Age, Inc.: 20 Audrey Place, Fairfield, NJ 07004. U.S.A. International: (01) 732-287-3622, Fax: (01) 732-287-4511
Visit us on the WEB at: http://www.pcage.com or E-Mail: sales@pcage.com

Effective 07/28/97

Learn Windows NT Administration with Hands-On Interactive Exercises Without Having NT!

LearnByDoing™ Windows NT®

for Win/Win95/NT

- Learn Windows NT with hands-on step-by-step interactive training
- Practice Windows NT administration without having to install NT or risk training on a running network
- Prepared by highly qualified and experienced instructors
- Helps you passing Microsoft MCSE/MCPS tests
- Compatible with all versions of Windows

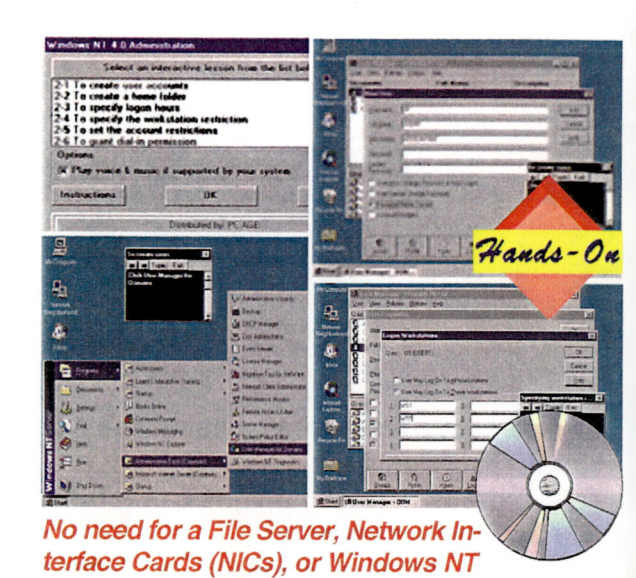

No need for a File Server, Network Interface Cards (NICs), or Windows NT

Do you want to learn Windows NT Administration but don't want to jeopardize your current installation or don't have a Windows NT installation at all? Whether you are studying for Microsoft Certified Professional exams or brushing up on your understanding of Windows NT 4.0, the LearnByDoing Windows NT gives you hands-on experience with Windows NT.

LearnByDoing Windows NT Interactive Training contains hands-on interactive exercises to teach you administration of single user and single domain networks. Its unique hands-on approach is useful for those complex Windows NT utilities that you just can't understand with books and study guides. With the LearnByDoing Windows NT, you learn through actual practice without harming your current Windows NT installation or needing to be on a network at all!

Here is a listing of some of the hands-on interactive exercises covered in LearnByDoing Windows NT®

- Creating user accounts
- Creating a home folder
- Specifying logon hours
- Specifying the workstation restriction
- Setting the account restrictions
- Granting dial-in permission
- Renaming a user account
- Deleting a user account
- Creating a template user profile
- Copying template user profile to a network server
- Specifying users who are permitted to use the profile
- Deleting the template profile user profile
- Creating a global group
- Adding members to a global group
- Determining the type of profile assigned to a user
- And many many more ...

LearnByDoing Windows NT 1 User Item No. LBDNT-797 ....$295
LearnByDoing Windows NT 5 User Item No. LBDNT5-797 ....$995
LearnByDoing Windows NT 10 User Item No. LBDNT10-797 ....$1895
25+ User, Call. (Shipped in CD-ROM only)

System Requirements: 486+ PC, Windows 3.1+, 8 MB-RAM, 2x CD-ROM Drive, 1-2 MB of free Hard Disk space.

Order Today!!! 1-800-PCAGE-60 (1-800-722-4360)

PC Age, Inc.: 20 Audrey Place, Fairfield, NJ 07004. U.S.A. International: (01) 732-287-3622, Fax: (01) 732-287-4511
Visit us on the WEB at: http://www.pcage.com or E-Mail: sales@pcage.com

Effective 07/10/97